FROM D'Aubigny
of NORMANDY, FRANCE *to*
Robert Durbin
of ENGLAND *and*
Thomas Christoper Durbin
of BALTIMORE, MARYLAND

1015 *to* 2016

Compiled by

Betty Jewell Durbin Carson

DAR Member #832584

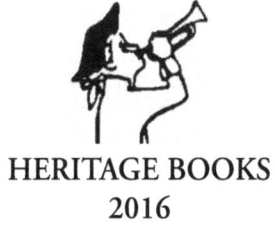

HERITAGE BOOKS
2016

HERITAGE BOOKS
AN IMPRINT OF HERITAGE BOOKS, INC.

Books, CDs, and more—Worldwide

For our listing of thousands of titles see our website
at
www.HeritageBooks.com

Published 2016 by
HERITAGE BOOKS, INC.
Publishing Division
5810 Ruatan Street
Berwyn Heights, Md. 20740

Copyright © 2016 Betty Jewell Durbin Carson

All rights reserved. No part of this book may be reproduced or transmitted in any form or by any means, electronic or mechanical, including photocopying, recording or by any information storage and retrieval system without written permission from the author, except for the inclusion of brief quotations in a review.

International Standard Book Numbers
Paperbound: 978-0-7884-5719-7
Clothbound: 978-0-7884-6448-5

Foreword

From: David Langton
Sent: Monday, February 10, 2014 3:11 PM
To: Betty Carson
Subject: RE: Durbin DNA

The Durbin DNA is very rare, there are less than 100 tested positive worldwide. So there is no doubt your brother, Jack Calvin, is a Durbin. I think there were no j2a4d in England before William the Conqueror in 1066. There were 3 or 4 j2a4d people in his army. Langton, Richards closely related to Langton, possibly Waring (De Warre) and D'Aubigny (Durbin). The most prominent of those was D'Aubigny who had the rank of Earl. I can't absolutely prove Durbin is Daubigny/Daubny but I think that is the case.

I think at various times the D'Aubignys were Earls of Lincoln Arundel and Bridgewater. Look at the text of Magna Carta 1215 and the witnesses at the end of it, these D'Aubignys were supporting the king or pretending to. However, another D'Aubigny was one of the 25 barons opposing the king. The big D'Aubigny story however is the Seige of Rochester Castle. Stephen Langton handed over the castle to William D'Aubigny and it was beseiged by King John. There is a film of this.

Dear Betty, welcome to the project, the big question is do the Durbins descend from the D'Aubigny. This question relates to almost a thousand years ago which makes it difficult to prove the matter. However, the circumstantial evidence convinces me that it is more likely than not.

1) Durbin is not a place name in England with typical forms -ham -ton -den -wick -thorpe etc.

2) Durbin is not an occupational name Cook Baker Butler Marshall Taylor.

3) It sounds non English and some non English names begin De or D' because they are French or Flemish. It is a reasonable proposition that Durbin is a name of this type and a -bin ending certainly sounds more French Flemish.

4) Not only is it 90%+ certain that the name isn't English the DNA certainly isn't English, it is Middle Eastern and so unusual that the likely explanation is traders reaching northern France/Flanders. Rich merchants do marry into local aristocracy and become land owners, it's a land for goods arrangement.

5) In the main part of England there seems to be just three j2a4d groups of names
a) Langton b) De Warre c) Durbin. As I know Langton arrived in 1066 it is reasonable to hypothesise Durbin arrived the same time.

6) Taking the negative case if Durbin are not D'Aubigny who are they, how and why did they arrive.

7) D'Aubigny is in northern France but it was an area of Flanders in 1066.

8) The name seems to be Durbin in Somerset particularly in the Bristol area and to the south of the city. Daubney is the form in Lincolnshire.

Anne Arundel County is a county located in the U.S. state of Maryland. It is named for Anne Arundell (1615–49), a member of the ancient family of Arundells in Cornwall, United Kingdom and the wife of Cæcilius Calvert, 2nd Baron Baltimore. Its county seat is Annapolis, which is also the capital of the state. As of the 2010 census, its population was 537,656, a population increase of just under 10% since 2000.

Anne Arundel County forms part of the Baltimore-Washington metropolitan area. The center of population of Maryland is located on the county line between Anne Arundel County and Howard County, in the unincorporated community of Jessup.

This fits in with the Durbins who settled in Maryland. They came over with Lord Baltimore so it is getting very interesting!

NOTE: For extended Durbin and Logsdon family genealogy, see *The Durbin and Logsdon Genealogy With Related Families, 1626-1998*. Second Revised Edition, Betty Jewell Durbin Carson, Heritage Books, Inc., 1998.

The D'Aubigny Family

INTRODUCTION

Charles III King of the West Franks granted land around Rouen to Viking raiders in [911], the territory evolving over the following century into the duchy of Normandy. The Viking leader Rollo accepted baptism with the name Robert. He and his descendants are shown in the document NORMANDY DUKES.

The earliest counties in Normandy were granted by the dukes as appanages to junior members of their family: Robert Bishop of Evreux, younger son of Richard I Duke of Normandy, was invested with the county of Evreux in the late 10th century by his father; the counties of Eu and Hiémois were granted to Robert´s illegitimate half-brothers Geoffroy and Guillaume by their other half-brother Duke Richard II; and the county of Talou was granted in the mid-11th century by Duke Guillaume II to his uncle Guillaume, who transformed the territory into the county of Arques after constructing the castle of that name on his land, although no further counts are recorded as he died childless. The Norman counties were not co-extensive with the earlier *pagi* into which the territory of the future Norman duchy had previously been divided. It is assumed that this was due to the strong central authority of the early Norman dukes who granted small landholdings to their followers, rather than creating counties, and thereby established a network of direct vassals which was a precursor to the fully fledged feudal system which Duke

Guillaume II applied in England after the conquest. Many of these minor Norman fief-holders found fortune in England after Guillaume II Duke of Normandy rewarded them with land grants. The Vicomtes d'Avranches received the earldom of Chester; the head of the Giffard family was created earl in Buckinghamshire; Guillaume FitzOsbern became earl of Hereford; Roger de Montgommery was created earl of Shrewsbury in 1074; and William de Warenne was created earl of Surrey in 1088. This process was pursued during the first half of the 12th century, with William d'Aubigny being created earl of Arundel in [1138/39] and Robert de Ferrières earl of Derby in 1138. The descendants of these families established themselves principally in England (they are hyperlinked from this document to the corresponding ENGLISH NOBILITY documents) and finally cut all ties with their Norman properties when the duchy of Normandy was acquired by the Capetian kings in the early 13th century.

The D'Aubigny family came from the Norman village of Saint Martin d'Aubigny, 14 km. north of Coutances and 36 km. north west of Montbray. In medieval naming conventions, the surnames beginning with "DE" or "D'" are Latin for "OF." (Many surnames were derived from localities, with the DE being dropped as time went on. The most common form of this name today is "Albini.")

The D'Aubigny family has a proud heritage to kings, queens, and even United States presidents like Thomas Jefferson, Abraham Lincoln, and Franklin Delano Roosevelt (who cherished his ancestry to this family).

The surname "D'Aubigny" was first found in Lincolnshire, where they were seated from very early times, and were granted lands by Duke William of Normandy, their liege Lord, for their distinguished assistance at the Battle of Hastings in 1066 A.D. They could have fought in the battle, or, more disappointingly, been butlers to William:

"I believe that it was the William, then Pincerna, and probably also Roger, his son, who were companions of the Conqueror in his expedition; Roger's eldest brother William being in disgrace in Normandy at the time, and not restored to favour, or allowed to enter England before the reign of Rufus, or it may have been Henry I."*

But it looks like they, fought, as well: Two D'Aubignys are included on the "Battle Abbey Rolls," which list the Norman combatants: GUILLAUME (WILLIAM) D'AUBIGNY and LE SIRE D'AUBIGNY (his son, ROGER). They list the commanders who accompanied William the Bastard of Falaise [later William I of England] at the Battle of Hastings. There are 375 commanders shown on the list, from a total force of about 5000 men. Subsequently, for their services, each commander was granted lordships of large areas of English countryside, albeit each being widely separated from another. To the victors went the spoils. (Various "copies" of these roll with considerable additions and thus differences exist.)

Our genealogy traces back to this butler named William (1015 - 1066), from whom the ancient Earls of Arundel descended. William married a woman named NN DE PLESSIS (b: 1024), "a sister of Grimoult du Plessis, the traitor of Valognes and Val-ès-Dunes, who died in his dungeon in 1047 (vol. i., pp. 25 and 31), and Wace may after all be right in styling him 'Le Botellier,'as it is probable that he held that office in the household of the Duke of Normandy)*

They had two sons (There may have been daughters, too, but in feudal times women, unless they were heiresses, were of small account; and often not recorded.) Anyway, William's two sons were:

CHILDREN OF WILLIAM D'AUBIGNY AND NN DE PLESSIS

☐ NELE d'AUBIGNY, aka: NIGEL de ALBINI. Nigel's grants were in Buckinghamshire, Bedfordshire, Warwickshire and Leicestershire. He was bow-bearer to the king in the reign of William II (Rufus) and was knighted by Henry I, who gave him the manor of Egmanton with parks in Sherwood Forest.

Mowbray

☐ ROGER D'AUBIGNY (1040-1138), AKA: ROGER de ALBINI, married AMICE MOWBRAY or MONTBRAY (1055 - 1084). Children listed below.

Roger married a woman named AMICE MOWBRAY or MONTBRAY (1055 - 1084) She was also known as Amicie de Coutances, sister of Geoffrey, Bishop of Coutances (according to Orderic Vital, he was "one of the bishops with attendant clerks and monks, whose duty it was to aid the war with their prayers and councils"). Amicia also had another brother, Roger de Montbray (Mowbray).

They were the children of ROGER MOWBRAY. The surname Mowbray stems from the small village of Montbray in Normandy. This lies about 10 km. north-east of the town of Villedieu-les-Poeles, which itself is 22 km northeast of Avranches on the bay of Mont Saint Michel. From this village came Geoffrey de Montbray who came to be Bishop of Coutances and accompanied Duke William of Normandy, their liege Lord, at the Conquest of England, after the Battle of Hastings in 1066. The Family Motto, translated: "Virtue stands by its own strength."

"By his wife, the sister of Grimoult (I have not yet lighted on her name), he had a son, the Roger d'Aubigny aforesaid, who married Amicia, or Avitia, sister of Geoffrey, Bishop of Coutances, and of Roger de Montbrai, and is supposed by M. Le Prévost to have been with his brothers-in-law in the battle."

Roger d'Aubigny, or De Albini, had issue by his wife Avitia de Montbrai, five sons:

CHILDREN OF ROGER D' AUBIGNY AND AMICE MOWBRAY
☐ William, known as William de Albini "Pincerna" (i.e., Butler), ancestor of the Earls of Sussex, who married Maud, daughter of Roger le Bigod, and died 1139.
☐ Richard, Abbot of St. Albans
☐ Nigel, the third son, was heir of Robert de Montbrai, or Mowbray, his first cousin, whose wife he married during the lifetime of her husband by licence of Pope Paschal, and for some time treated her with respect out of regard for her noble parents; but on the death of her brother Gilbert de l'Aigle, having no issue by her, he craftily sought for a divorce on the ground of that very kinship which he exerted so much influence to induce the Pope to overlook, and then married Gundred, daughter of Gerrard de Gournay, by whom he had Roger, who assumed the name of Mowbray, and transmitted it to his descendants, Dukes of Norfolk

and Earls Marshal of England; and Henri, ancestor of the line of Albini of Cainho."

☐ Humphrey.

☐ Ruafon, or Ralph.

Bigod

The D'Aubignys were granted lands by Duke William of Normandy, their liege Lord, for Roger's distinguished assistance at the Battle of Hastings in 1066 AD.

Roger's children, maternally from the house of Mowbray, came with the Conqueror and obtained large possessions of land. One of his sons was named WILLIAM D' AUBIGNY (1070 - 1139), born in Aubigny, Calvados, Normandy, France. He was a 'Pincerna', a butler to King William.

William D'Aubigni married MAUD BIGOD (b. 1080), daughter of ROGER BIGOD and ADELIZA DE GRENTMESNIL.

Here are their children:

CHILDREN OF WILLIAM D' AUBIGNY AND MAUD BIGOD
☐ WILLIAM D'AUBIGNY "THE STRONGHAND," 1st Earl of Arundel (1102 - 3.10.1176) He married ADELAIDE DE LOUVAIN. Children listed below.
☐ NIGEL D' AUBIGNY
☐ OLIVER D' AUBIGNY.
☐ OLIVIA D' AUBIGNY, born @ 1100, who married Ralphe de Haya.

Our ancestor was their son, EARL WILLIAM D' AUBIGNY "THE STRONGHAND," who was the Earl of Sussex, Earl of Lincoln, 1st Earl of Arundel, and the Lord of Stackhorn.
William the Stronghand was born @ 1102, in Buckenham, Nomandie, England. In 1136, he married the "Fair Maid of Brabant," ADELAIDE DE LOUVAIN (1102 - 1151), daughter of GRAF GOTTFRIED V (I) VON NIEDERLOTHRINGEN 'DER BÄRTIGE' (AKA: Godfrey Barbutus, the Bearded of Louvaine, Duke of Louvaine & Brabant +

De Louvain

Namur, Ida of Brabant. Godfrey, Duke of Lorraine; Godfried I Count of Leuven and Brabant; Duke of Low Lotharingen; Marquise of Antwerp. BRABANT) and IDA DE CHINEY, in 1138.

Also known as Adeliza de Brabant, she was born in 1102-1103 in Louvain, Belgium. Adeliza was queen consort of England from 1121 to 1135, the second wife of King Henry I of England.
She married Henry I 'Beauclerc', King of England, son of William I 'the Conqueror', King of England, and Matilda de Flandre, on the 29th of January, 1121, at Windsor Castle, Windsor, Berkshire, England. She is thought to have been aged somewhere between fifteen and eighteen; he was fifty three. It is believed that Henry's only reason for marrying again was his desire for a male heir. (Despite holding the record for the largest number of illegitimate children of any British monarch, Henry's only legitimate male heir had died in 1120.)
Adeliza was reputably quite pretty, and Louvain and England had a mutual enemy in Flanders; these were the likely reasons she was chosen. However, no children were born during the almost 15 years of the marriage. As of 30 January 1121, her married name was Queen Consort Adeliza of England.

Henry died on the 11th of December, 1135, in Gisors, St. denis, Seine-St. denis, France, and was buried on the 4th of January, 1136, in Reading Abbey, Reading, Berks, England. The cause of death was his bowels exploding -- either from food poisoning or from over-eating Lampreys.

After Henry died, Adeliza lived as a nun at Wilton, near Salisbury. As she was still young she came out of mourning some time before 1139, the third year of her widowhood, and married William, who had been one of Henry's chief advisors. (That's a tough union for a second husband to live up to! No matter what he gave her or did for her, how do you top THE KING???) She brought with her a queen's dowry, including the great castle of Arundel, and King Stephen created d'Aubigny Earl of Arundel. In feudal times, women were often bartered as wives. If they were heiresses they were married while still of tender years, and when their husbands died were often remarried three or even four times. After the way Henry died, William probably didn't eat much of her cooking. He was created 1st Earl of Arundel [England] circa 1138. In 1139 he gave shelter to the Empress Maud at Arundel Castle, but ever after adhered to King Stephen. He held the office of Lord of the Manor of Buckenham, Norfolk in 1139.

Seven of their children were to survive. Among the descendants of this marriage came two girls destined to become tragic queens; Anne Boleyn and Catherine Howard.

The union lasted about a dozen years. But then: "His wife, the Queen Dowager, retired in 1150 to a nunnery in Afflighem in South Brabant. Adeliza spent her final years in Flanders in the convent. She died on the 23rd of April, 1151, at Affligem Abbey, Afflingham, Flandre, Belgium, and was buried there.

A romantic story has been invented to account for the lion rampant subsequently borne by William's descendants in the family coat of arms: "Having captivated the heart of the Queen Dowager of France by his gallant conduct in a tournament at Paris, she offered to marry him, an honour which he respectfully declined, having already given his word and faith to a lady in England, another Queen Dowager, no less a personage than

Adeliza, widow of King Henry 1 of England. His refusal so angered the French Queen, that she laid a plot with her attendants to destroy him by inducing him to enter a cave in her garden, where a lion had been placed for that purpose; but the undaunted Earl, rolling his mantle round his arm, thrust his hand into the lion's mouth, tore out its tongue, and sent it to the Queen by one of her maids. 'In token of which noble and valiant act,' says Brooke, in his *Catalogue of Nobility*, 'this William assumed to bear for his arms a lion gold in a field gules, which his successors ever since continued.'"*

In 1153, William the Stronghand was influential in arranging the treaty where King Stephen retained the crown for life, but with Henry II as heir. In 1163/64, he was one of the embassy to Rome. In 1168, he was one of the embassy to Saxony. He was commander of the Royal army in Normandy, against the King's rebellious sons, where he distinguished himself with "swiftness and velocity" in August 1173. He fought in the battle near Bury St. Edmunds on 29 September 1173, where he assisted in the defeat of the Earl of Leicester who had, with his Flemings, invaded Suffolk.

The "Stronghand" died on the 12th of October, 1176, in Waverly Abbey, Surry, England, and is buried at Priory, Wymondham, Norfolk, England. His children:

KIDS OF WILLIAM D'AUBIGNY AND ADELAIDE DE LOUVAIN
☐ RALPH (Reyner) AUBIGNY
☐ *WILLIAM d' AUBIGNY 2nd Earl of Arundel.*
☐ HENRY AUBIGNY
☐ GEOFFREY AUBIGNY
☐ ALICE d' AUBIGNY
☐ AGATHA AUBIGNY
☐ AGNES AUBIGNY of Arundel

Their son, EARL WILLIAM IV D' AUBIGNY "LE BRETON," (1139 - 24/25 Dec 1193), 2nd Earl of Arundel, was born in Arundel, Sussex, England. He married MAUD DE ST. HILARY, daughter of JAMES DE ST. HILARY and AVELINE (de St. Hillary), in 1174. (Maud de St. Hilary was born in 1132-1137 in of Burkenham, Field Dalling, Norfolk and died on 24 Dec 1195 in Norfolk, England.) The lion in the family crest was more probably first borne by him, in token of his descent from Adeliza, widow of Henry l, in whose reign we have the earliest evidence of golden lions being adopted as a personal decoration, if not strictly an heraldic bearing.

KIDS OF WILLIAM D' AUBIGNY AND MAUD DE ST. HILARY
☐ *William de Albini, 4th Earl of Arundel (dsp 1224 or 1233) - m. Mabel (dau of Hugh 'Keveliok' de Meschines, 3rd Earl of Chester)*
☐ Hugh de Albini, 5th Earl of Arundel (dsp 1243) - m. Isabel de Warren (dau of William (Plantagenet) de Warren, Earl of Warren and Surrey)
☐ Mabel de Albini (a 1223) - m. Sir Robert de Tateshall
☐ Isabel de Albini m. John FitzAlan, lord of Oswestry, Sheriff of Shropshire (b c1164, d 1239)
☐ Nicola de Albini - m. Roger de Somerie, lord of Dudley

☐ Cecilia de Albini - m. Roger de Montalt

Their son, EARL WILLIAM V D'AUBIGNY, 3rd Earl of Arundel, and Earl of Sussex, was born in 1165 in of Belvoir Castle, Leicestershire, and died before the 30th of March, 1221, in Cainell, near Rome, Italy. William d'Aubigny was earl of Sussex (1193-1221). "...the title of earl was most known by Arundel and Chichester, at which places his chief residence used to be, yet it was of the county of Sussex that he was really earl..."** William married MATILDA (MABEL) LE MESCHINES of Chester, daughter of EARL HUGH DE KEVELIOCK, 3rd Earl of Chester, and BERTRADE D'EVREUX, after 1207. (Matilda was born in 1171 and died in 1233.) During the signing of the Magna Charta, William was on way home from 5th Crusade, but his name was appended on the document, and later assembled with the other barons at Runnemede as guarantors or counselors of King John. His children:

KIDS OF WILLIAM D' AUBIGNY AND MATILDA LE MESCHINES
☐ WILLIAM AUBIGNY
☐ HUGH d' AUBIGNY
☐ ISABEL d' AUBIGNY of Arundel
☐ *NICOLA d' AUBIGNY*

De Somery

☐ MATILDA d' AUBIGNY

They had two daughters: Matilda d' Aubigny and our ancestor, NICHOLE D'AUBIGNY. In 1225, Nichole married ROGER DE SOMERY BARON DUDLEY (b: 1208 in Dinas Powis, Wales; Death: 26 Aug 1273 in Staffordshire, England, son of Ralph de Somery and Margaret Marshal.) Nicole died in 1254, at Dudley Castle, Strafford, England, and Roger remarried, to AMABILIA de CHAUCOMBE, in 1254, and had another son: Roger de Somery. Nichole's children:

- *JOAN de SOMERY*
- MABEL de SOMERY
- MAUD de SOMERY
- MARGERY de SOMERY
- MARGARET (Margery) de SOMERY

Le Strange

JOAN DE SOMERY was born circa 1233, in Camden, Gloucestershire, England. She married JOHN LE STRANGE, IV, (Birth: 1203 in Knokyn, Salop, England; Death: 26 Feb 1276 in Knockin, Warwick, England). They had a son named JOHN LE STRANGE, V, who became the 1st Baron Strange of Knokyn (ancestor of the Barons Strange, of Knockyn, and the Le Stranges, of Hunstanton, Norfolk). He was born circa 1253 in Ellesmere, Shropshire, England. He married MAUD DE MONTIBUS, daughter of Ebulo de Montibus, Lord of Ketton. He became Baron Strange of Knockyn in 1299. He died in 1310.

JOHN LE STRANGE, the 2nd Baron Strange of Knockyn, was born on the 18th of May, 1282, in Ellesmere, Shropshire, England. He married ISOLDA (or MAUD) DE WALTON, daughter of John de Walton of Walton D'Eiville. John died on the 6th of February, 1311/12, at the age of 29 years, 8 months and 19 days.

They had a daughter, ELIZABETH LE STRANGE. She married

GRUFFUDD O'R RHUDDALLT AP MADOG FYCHAN AP MADOG. They had a son, GRUFFUDD FYCHAN AP GRUFFUDD O'R RHUDDALLT. (In Welsh conventions of patronymics, AB denotes "son of," and FERCH denotes "daughter of.")

Gruffud married ELEN FERCH THOMAS. She was the daughter of THOMAS AP LLEWELLYN and ELEANOR GOCH, and the great-aunt to Sir Owen Tudor, founder of the Tudor Dynasty in England (he was related to Katherine of France, the widow of Henry the Fifth, King of England).

They had two children:

CHILDREN OF GRUFFUDD FYCHAN AP GRUFFUDD O'R RHUDDALLT AND ELEN FERCH THOMAS
☐ *Lowri ferch Gruffyd Fychan. She married Robert Puleston. He was born Cir 1358, and died 1399*
☐ Owen Glendower, The Welsh Rebel hero.
☐ Tudor (Twdr) ap Gruffyd Fychan. He married Maud, daughter of Ienaf ap Adda.

LOWRI FERCH GRUFFUDD FYCHAN married ROBERT PULESTON, and you'd think things would start to improve with that name. They had a daughter, ANGARAHAD PULESTON. She completely lost her head over one EDWART (IORWERTH) TREVOR AP DAFYDD AB EDNYFED GA. But sanity finally reigned, and they named their daughter ROSE TREVOR. She married SIR OTEWELL WORSLEY. They had a daughter, MARGARET WORSLEY. She married ADRIAN WHETEHILL, and they had a son, SIR RICHARD WHETEHILL. He married ELIZABETH MUSTON and they had a daughter, MARGERY WHETEHILL.

Puleston

Isaac

Margery married EDWARD ISAAC. The Isaac family was first found in Devon, where they were seated from very ancient times, some say well before the Norman Conquest and the arrival of Duke William at Hastings in 1066 A.D.

Margery and Edward had a daughter, MARY ISAAC (1552 in Well Court, Ickham,Kent,Eng). Mary married THOMAS APPLETON (1538 - 1603), in 1572, in Suffolk Co., England, and they had a daughter, JOHANNA APPLETON, who was born at the dawn of the 1600's in England. She married RICHARD GILDERSLEEVE (1601 - 1681) of

Suffolk, England. They had a daughter named ELIZABETH GILDERSLEEVE (b. @1620), who married JEREMIAH WOOD (b. 1620) in Yorkshire. Jeremiah was a Puritan, and they were part of the Puritan emigration to the American Colonies.

KIDS OF RICHARD GILDERSLEEVE AND JOHANNA APPLETON
☐ ELIZABETH GILDERSLEEVE, b: ABT 1620. Married JEREMIAH WOOD between 1642 - 1644.
☐ RICHARD GILDERSLEEVE, JR., b: 1626, married a woman named DORCAS. He died in 1691.

GENEALOGY

WILLIAM D' AUBIGNY (1015 - 1066) married NN DE PLESSIS (b: 1024), and they begat...

ROGER D' AUBIGNY (1040-1138), who married AMICE and begat...

WILLIAM D' AUBIGNY (1070 - 1139), who married MAUD BIGOD (b. 1080) and begat...

EARL WILLIAM D' AUBIGNY "THE STRONGHAND" (d. 1176), who married ADELAIDE DE LOUVAIN (1102 - 1151) and begat...

EARL WILLIAM IV D' AUBIGNY "LE BRETON" (1139 - 1193), who married MAUD DE ST. HILARY (1137 - 1195) and begat...

EARL WILLIAM V D'AUBIGNY (b. 1165), who married MATILDA (MABEL) LE MESCHINES (1171 - 1233) and begat...

NICHOLE D'AUBIGNY, who married ROGER DE SOMERY BARON DUDLEY (1208 - 1273) and begat...

JOAN DE SOMERY (1233 - 1282), who married JOHN LE STRANGE, IV, (1203 - 1276) and begat...

JOHN LE STRANGE (1253 - 1310), who married MAUD DE MONTIBUS and begat...

JOHN LE STRANGE (1282 - 1311), who married ISOLDA DE WALTON and begat...

ELIZABETH LE STRANGE, who married GRUFFUDD O'R RHUDDALLT AP MADOG FYCHAN AP MADOG...

GRUFFUDD FYCHAN AP GRUFFUDD O'R RHUDDALLT, who married ELEN FERCH THOMAS and begat...

LOWRI FERCH GRUFFUDD FYCHAN, who married ROBERT PULESTON and begat...

ANGARAHAD PULESTON, who married EDWART (IORWERTH) TREVOR AP DAFYDD AB EDNYFED GA, and begat...

ROSE TREVOR, who married SIR OTEWELL WORSLEY and begat...

MARGARET WORSLEY, who married ADRIAN WHETEHILL and begat...

SIR RICHARD WHETEHILL, who married ELIZABETH MUSTON and begat...

MARGERY WHETEHILL, who married EDWARD ISAAC and begat...

MARY (or AMY) ISAAC, who married THOMAS APPLETON (1538 - 1601) and begat...

SAMUEL APPLETON (1586 - 1670), who married JUDITH EVERHARD and begat...

JOHANNA APPLETON (1601 - ?), who married RICHARD GILDERSLEEVE (1601 - 1681) and begat...

ELIZABETH GILDERSLEEVE (1620 - ?), who married JEREMIAH WOOD (1620 -) and begat...

JOSEPH WOOD, who married EUNICE JARVIS in 1680 and begat...

JOSEPH WOOD, JR. (1680 - ?) who married MARGRIET (MARGARET) WOOD and begat...

JONATHAN WOOD (1720 - ?) who married JOHANNA CROMPTON (1725 - ?) and begat...

MARTHA WOOD (1753 - 1822) who married WILLIAM HAUSE (1750 - 1818) and begat...

JOHN HAUSE (1773 - 1844) who married ESTHER KETCHAM (1779 - 1853) and begat...

AUGUSTUS HAUSE (1804 - 1875) who married JANE JONES (1802 - 1850) and begat...

LABAN HAUSE (1831 - 1906) who married MELISSA SANDERSON (1839 - 1921) and begat...

FRANK HAUSE (1867 - 1951) who married FLADELLA
RAYMOND (1869 - 1961) and begat...

CARLISLE HAUSE (1891 - 1972) who married MARJORIE
MARCHANT (1892 - 1939) who begat...

CARLETON MARCHANT HAUSE, SR. (1917 - 1983) who
married JEANNE BRUNNER (1918 - 2000) and begat...

CARLETON MARCHANT HAUSE, JR. (b. 1939) who married
MARTHA WENK (b. 1940) and begat...

JEFF (who married LORI ANN DOTSON), KATHY (who
married HAL LARSEN), ERIC (who married MARY
MOONSAMMY), and MICHELE HAUSE (who married JOHN
SCOTT HOUSTON).

LITERATURE ON THE D'AUBIGNI FAMILY

WILLIAM DE ALBINI, The Conqueror and His Companions, by
J.R. Planché, Somerset Herald. London: Tinsley Brothers, 1874.
"The Complete Peerage of England Scotland Ireland Great Britain
and the United Kingdom" - George Edward Cokayne (14 vol) I,
p234, (a)
"Rolls of Arms - Henry III - Aspilogia II" - London & Tremlett /
Sir Anthony WagnerRoyal Genealogies Website (ROYAL92.GED),
online tp://ftp.cac.psu.edu/gcnealogy/public_html/royal/Index.html.
Hereinafter cited as Royal Genealogies Website.

G.E. Cokayne; with Vicary Gibbs, H.A. Doubleday, Geoffrey H.
White, Duncan Warrand and Lord Howard de Walden,
editors, *The Complete Peerage of England, Scotland, Ireland, Great
Britain and the United Kingdom, Extant, Extinct or Dormant*, new
ed., 13 volumes in 14 (1910-1959; reprint in 6 volumes, Gloucester,
U.K.: Alan Sutton Publishing, 2000), volume I, page 233.
Hereinafter cited as *The Complete Peerage.*

Aubigny, Alibini, etc., Earls of Arundel. Saint-Martin d'Aubigny: Manche, arr. Coutances, cant. Periers. The early history of the family will be found in The Complete Peerage, surname Mowbray, new ed., vol. ix, pp. 366-7. The details of their benefactions to the abbey of Lessay as confirmed by a charter of **Henry II**, 1185-1188, identify St-Martin d'Aubigny with the Aubigny which was the caput of their Norman honour; thus the "*ecclesiam De Folgeriis*" is Feugeres 2 1/2 kil. SE of Aubigny, the "*feria Sancti Christofori*" mentioned in conjunction with the "*forum Albinneii*" is St-Christophe-d'Aubigny, a parish now united to that of St-Martin, and "*Marchesis*" is Marchesieux, 5 kil. NE of Aubigny. There is no trace of a feudal castle at Aubigny itself, but Gerville found nearby at Le Mesnil-Vigot the remains of a considerable castle with a well-defined motte, then known as "*le chateau De St-Clair*".

Sources: The Origins of Some Anglo-Norman Families, by Lewis C Loyd, 1999
Page: 7. Title: Burke's Peerage & Baronetage, 106th Edition, Charles Mosley
Editor-in-Chief, 1999 Page: 2026

William d'Aubigny
Birth: 1099, England
Death: Oct. 12, 1176, Surrey, England
Burial: Wymondham Abbey, Wymondham, Norfolk, England

Lord of the Manor of Buckenham, with the embassy to Saxony, commander of the Royal Army against Normandy, was proclaimed with "swiftness and velocity", and fought at the Battle of St Edmunds 1173 to defeat the Earl of Leicester.

Son of William d'Albini Pincerna, the Master Butler for the Royal Household and Maud Bigod. Grandson of Roger d' Aubigny and Adeliza Grantmesnil, Roger Bigod, 1st Earl of Norfolk and Berengeve de Bayeaux.
William was the husband of Queen Adeliza of Louvain, widow and second wife of King Henry I. They were married in 1138 and had seven children:
Reynor d'Aubigney
Henry d'Aubigney

Geoffrey d'Aubigney
Alice d'Aubigney, wife of John d'Eu
Olivia d'Aubigney, died young
Agatha d'Aubigney, died young
William d'Aubigney, 2nd Earl of Arundel

Sir William gave shelter to Empress Maud at Arundel but was loyal to King Stephen, who made him the first Earl of Lincoln and then Earl of Arundel, or rather, properly, the Earl of Sussex. William helped to arrange the truce between Stephen and Henry Plantagenet, the future Henry Curtmantle, creating the Wallingford Treaty. William built Castle Rising in Norfolk, and died at Waverly.

The legend of his name, "William with the strong Hand" came from the following story: The widowed Queen of France wanted to have a new husband and held a tournament in Paris to select one. William competed and won but refused to marry the Queen of France since he was already betrothed to Adeliza, the widowed Queen of England. The Queen of France lured William into a lion's cage but he subdued the lion by tearing out its tongue with his hand. When he returned to England he was made Earl of Arundel and the Lion was allowed on his coat of arms.

Parents:
William D'Albini (1070 - 1139)
Maud Bigod D'Aubigny

Spouse: Adeliza Louvain of Brabant (1094 - 1151)

Children:
Olivia d' Aubigny
Agatha d' Aubigny
William d'Aubigny (1136 - 1193)
Alice d'Aubigny (1136 - 1188)

William de Albini, Earl of Lincoln, 1st Earl of Sussex/Arundel, Chief Butler of England [1,2,3] M, #5940, b. 1110, d. 12 October 1176

Father
William d' Aubigny, Earl of Albemarle d. 1139

Mother
Maud Bigod b. c 1084

Charts

Some Descendants of Charlemagne

William de Albini, Earl of Lincoln, 1st Earl of Sussex/Arundel, Chief Butler of England was born in 1110 at of Buckenham, Norfolk, England. He married Adeliza de Louvain, daughter of Godfrey I 'the Bearded', Duke of Lorraine, Count of Brabant & Louvaine, Marquis of Antwerp and Ida von Chiny, on 2 December 1135; They had 4 sons (William, 2nd Earl of Arundel/Sussex; Reiner; Henry; Godfrey) & 2 daughters (Alice, wife of Jean I, Comte d'Eu, & of Alvred de St. Martin; & Olive).[4, 3] William de Albini, Earl of Lincoln, 1st Earl of Sussex/Arundel, Chief Butler of England died on 12 October 1176 at Waverly Abbey, Surrey, England; Buried at Wymondham Priory, Norfolk.[3]

Family
Adeliza de Louvain b. c 1106, d. 23 Apr 1151

Children
- Alice de Albini+[2] d. 11 Sep 1188
- W illiam III d' Aubeney, 2nd Earl of Arundel+ b. c 1139, d. 24 Dec 1193

Citations

1. [S1471] Unknown author, *The Complete Peerage, by Cokayne, Vol. I, p. 233/4; Ancestral Roots of 60 Colonists by F. L. Weis, p. 129.*
2. [S6] Douglas Richardson, *Plantagenet Ancestry: 2nd Edition*, Vol. I, p. 292.
3. [S4] Douglas Richardson, *Royal Ancestry*, Vol. I, p. 8-18.

4. [S2] Detlev Schwennicke, *Europaische Stammtafeln, New Series*, Vol. I/2, Tafel 236.

William d'Aubigny, 1st Earl of Lincoln and 1st Earl of Arundel (c. 1109 – 25 September 1176), also known as William d'Albini, was son of William d'Aubigny, 'Pincerna' (Master Butler of the Royal household) of Old Buckenham Castle in Norfolk, and Maud Bigod, daughter of Roger Bigod, 1st Earl of Norfolk.

Marriage + Issue- The younger William was an important member of Henry I of England's household. After Henry's death, William married his widow Queen Adeliza in 1138. He and Adeliza were parents to seven children: Reynor, Henry, Geoffrey, Alice (d. 11 Sep 1188), Olivia, Agatha, and William d'Aubigny, 2nd Earl of Arundel b. 1150, d. 24 Dec 1193.

Titles- He was loyal to Stephen of England, who made him first Earl of Lincoln and then Earl of Arundel (more precisely, Earl of Sussex). In 1143, as Earl of Lincoln he made two charters confirming a donation of land around Arundel in Sussex to the abbey of Affligem in Brabant (representing his wife Adeliza of Louvain), with William's brother, Olivier, present.

Mediator- He fought loyally for King Stephen, but in 1153 helped arrange the truce between Stephen and Henry Plantagenet, known as the Treaty of Wallingford, which brought an end to The Anarchy.

When the latter ascended the throne as Henry II, he confirmed William's Earldom and gave him direct possession of Arundel Castle (instead of the possession in right of his wife he had previously had). She had died in 1151. He remained loyal to the king during the 1173 revolt of Henry the Young King, and helped defeat the rebellion.

He was the builder of the castle of Castle Rising in Norfolk.

Sources-

- England, Earls Created 1138-1143

- Weis, Frederick Lewis, *Ancestral Roots of Certain American Colonists Who Came to America Before 1700*, 8th Ed., Lines 1-22, 18A-22, 139-26, 149-25, 149-26. (ISBN 0-8063-1752-3)
- Remfry, P.M., *Buckenham Castles, 1066 to 1649* (ISBN 1-899376-28-3)
- On the Earldom of Lincoln, previous creations: [Burke's Peerage, p. 1711]:
- Henry I's widow Adeliz married in 1138 William d'Aubigny, who the next year, probably as a result, was created Earl of Lincoln. William's father was a Norman immigrant to England in Henry I's reign. His son, who by this advantageous marriage came into the former Queen's dowry of Arundel Castle, together with its Honour (feudal administrative unit embodying several knight's fees), has been held thereby to have become Earl of Arundel. By 1142 he had been deprived of his Earldom of Lincoln, indeed even before, was spoken sometimes as Earl of Arundel and sometimes as Earl of Chichester or Earl of Sussex.
- ----------
- EARLDOM OF SUSSEX (I) 1141
- EARLDOM OF LINCOLN (I) circa 1139 to 1141
- EARLDOM OF ARUNDEL (IV, 1) 1138 or 1139 to 1176
- WILLIAM D'AUBIGNY) de Albiniaco or in the Anglo-Latin of Dugdale and other writers, de Albini, surnamed "the strong hand,"
- Lord of the manor of Buckenham, Norfolk, son and heir of William d'Aubigny (died 1139) Pincernal Regis, by Maud, daughter of Roger LE BIGOD, probably by his 2nd wife, Alice, sister and coheir of William de Tosny, Lord of Belvoir, daughter of Robert de Tosny of the same, was born early in the reign of Henry I. On his marriage with the Queen Dowager, he acquired with her, in 1138 or 1139, the Castle and Honour of Arundel, which had been settled on her in dower, whereby it may be considered that, according to the admission of 1433, he became EARL OF ARUNDEL. There is conclusive evidence from various charters, that at, or about the time of, and probably soon after, his said marriage, he was recognised as EARL OF LINCOLN, and he may be assumed to have been so created in the summer of 1139. In this year he gave shelter to the Empress Maud, at Arundel Castle, but ever

after adhered to Stephen. He can be shown to have very soon lost the Earldom of Lincoln, and in 1141 he attested a charter of Stephen as EARL OF SUSSEX, (being from time to time thereafter so described, as, e.g. where he witnesses a charter to the Abbey of Barking under that name) and may be assumed to have been so created by Stephen in 1141, after that King had regained his freedom. Early in 1142, the Earldom of Lincoln had already passed to another, viz. William de Roumare. In his own later charters he is styled, and in a charter, before 1150, of the Queen Dowager to the Abbey of Reading, she styles him EARL OF CHICHESTER. He was influential in arranging the treaty of 1153, whereby the Crown continued with King Stephen for life, though the inheritance thereof was secured to Henry II. To this instrument he subscribed as "Comes Cicestrie." Henry II, by a grant undated, but supposed to have been in 1155 (the year after his accession), confirms to him as "William, EARL OF ARUNDEL, the Castle of Arundel, with the whole honour of Arundel and all its appurtenances," and, by the same instrument, bestows on him the third penny of the pleas of the county of SUSSEX unde Comes est. No doubt, however, he was more generally known as "EARL OF ARUNDEL," and as such (only) he is spoken of by his son and heir (who styles himself Earl of Sussex) in a charter to the Priory of Wymondham; and as Earl of Arundel (only) he is described in the record of his death in the Annals of Waverley. He was justly held in great esteem by Henry II, and was one of the embassy to Rome in 1163/4, and to Saxony (on the espousal of the Princess to the Duke of Saxony) in 1168. He was also in command of the Royal army in August 1173, in Normandy, against the King's rebellious sons, where he distinguished himself for his "swiftness and velocity," and, on 29 September following he assisted at the defeat, near Bury St. Edmunds, of the Earl of Leicester, who, with his Flemings, had invaded Suffolk.

- He married, in 1138 (the 3rd year of her widowhood) Adeliz, QUEEN DOWAGER OF ENGLAND (widow of Henry I), 1st daughter of Godefroy à la Barbe, DUKE OF LOTHIER (i.e. Lorraine Inférieure), COUNT OF BRABANT AND LOUVAIN, by his 1st wife, Ide, daughter of Albert III,

COUNT OF NAMUR. His wife, the Queen Dowager, retired in 1150 to a nunnery at Afflighem, in South Brabant, where she died, and was buried 23 April 1151, aged about 48. He survived her 25 years, and died 12 October 1176, at Waverley Abbey, Surrey, and was buried, with his father, at Wymondham Priory, Norfolk. [Complete Peerage I:233-35, XIV:37, (transcribed by Dave Utzinger)]

- ----------
- William de Albini, surnamed "William with the strong hand," from the following circumstance, as related by Dugdale:---
- "It happened that the Queen of France, being then a widow, and a very beautify woman, became much in love with a knight of that country, who was a comely person, and in the flower of his youth: and because she thought that no man excelled him in valour, she caused a tournament to be proclaimed throughout her dominions, promising to reward those who should exercise themselves therein, according to their respective demerits; and concluding that if the person whom she so well affected could act his part better than the others in those military exercises, she might marry him without any dishonour to herself. Hereupon divers gallant men, from forrain parts hastening to Paris, amongst others came this our William de Albini, bravely accoutered, and in the tournament excelled all others, overcoming many, and wounding one mortally with his lance, which being observed by the queen, she became exceedingly enamoured of him, and forthwith invited him to a costly banquet, and afterwards bestowing certain jewels upon him, offered him marriage; but, having plighted his troth to the Queen of England, then a widow, he refused her, whereat she grew so much discontented that she consulted with her maids how she might take away his life; and in pursuance of that design, inticed him into a garden, where there was a secret cave, and in it a fierce lion, unto which she descended by divers steps, under colour of shewing him the beast; and when she told him of its fierceness, he answered, that it was a womanish and not a manly quality to be afraid thereof. But having him there, by the advantage of a folding door, thrust him in to the lion; being therefore in this danger, he rolled his mantle about his arm and, putting his hand into the mouth of the beast, pulled out

his tongue by the root; which done, he followed the queen to her palace and gave it to one of her maids to present her. Returning thereupon to England, with the fame of this glorious exploit, he was forthwith advanced to the Earldom of Arundel, and for his arms the lion given him."

- He subsequently obtained the hand of the Queen Adeliza, relict of King Henry I, and daughter of Godfrey, Duke of Lorraine, which Adeliza had the castle of Arundel in dowry from the deceased monarch, and thus her new lord became its feudal earl. The earl was one of those who solicited the Empress Maud to come to England, and received her and her brother, Robert, Earl of Gloucester, at the port of Arundel, in August, 1139, and in three years afterwards (1142), in the report made of King Stephen's taking William de Mandevil at St. Albans, it is stated -- "that before he could be laid hold on, he underwent a sharp skirmish with the king's party, wherein the Earl of Arundel, though a stout and expert soldier, was unhorsed in the midst of the water by Walkeline de Oxeai, and almost drowned." In 1150, his lordship wrote himself Earl of Chichester, but we find him styled again Earl of Arundel, upon a very memorable occasion -- namely, the reconciliation of Henry Duke of Normandy (afterwards Henry II) and King Stephen at the siege of Wallingford Castle in 1152. "It was scarce possible," says Rapin, "for the armies to part without fighting. Accordingly the two leaders were preparing for battle with equal ardour, when, by the prudent advice of the Earl of Arundel, who was on the king's side, they were prevented from coming to blows." A truce and peace followed this interference of the earl's, which led to the subsequent accession of Henry after Stephen's decease, in whose favour the Earl stood so high that he not only obtained for himself and his heirs the castle and honour of Arundel, but a confirmation of the Earldom of Sussex, of which county he was really earl, by a grant of the Tertium Denarium of the pleas of that shire. In 1164, we find the Earl of Arundel deputed with Gilbert Foliot, bishop of London, to remonstrate with Lewis, King of France, upon affording an asylum to Thomas à Becket within his dominion, and on the failure of that mission, despatched with the archbishop of York, the bishops of Winchester, London, Chichester, and Exeter, --

Wido Rufus, Richard de Invecestre, John de Oxford (priests) -- Hugh de Gundevile, Bernard de St. Valery, and Henry Fitzgerald, to lay the whole affair of Becket at the foot of the pontifical throne. Upon levying the aid for the marriage of the king's daughter, 12th of Henry II [1165-66], the knights' fees of the honour of Arundel were certified to be ninety-seven, and those in Norfolk belonging to the earl, forty-two. In 1173, we find the Earl of Arundel commanding, in conjunction with William, Earl of Essex, the king's army in Normandy, and compelling the French monarch to abandon Verneuil after a long siege, and in the next year, with Richard de Lucy, justice of England, defeating Robert Earl of Leicester, then in rebellion at St. Edmundsbury. This potent nobleman, after founding and endowing several religious houses, departed this life at Waverley, in Surrey, on the 3 October, 1176, and was buried in the abbey of Wymondham. His lordship left by Adeliza, his wife, widow of King Henry I, four sons and three daughters, the eldest of whom, Alice, m. John, Earl of Ewe. The eldest son, William de Albini, 2nd earl, had a grant from the crow, 23rd Henry II [1177-8] of the Earldom of Sussex, and in the 1st of Richard I [1189-90], had a confirmation from that prince of the castle and honour of Arundel, as also of the Tertium Denarium of the county of Sussex. [Sir Bernard Burke, Dormant, Abeyant, Forfeited, and Extinct Peerages, Burke's Peerage, Ltd., London, 1883, pp. 2-3, Albini, Earls of Arundel]
- --Copy of Burke's, posted at Rootsweb, free pages, Ancestors of Caden Michael Norquist, freepages.genealogy.rootsweb.ancestry.com.
- [**Hmm** is the appellation "Strong Hand" merely "Pincera" translated into English? see Martinrealm/Stirnet. William "Pincera", possibly aka "Strong Hand" de Albini was the one who lived from about 1070 to 1139 and married Maud le Bigod, see FMG and Wikipedia. Burke's says "we find this William (the father of the Earl of Arundel) styled in divers charters '*Pincerna Henrici Regis Anglorum'*". The c.1170 - 1139 William was the "chief butler" (rough translation) of the household of Henry I. Is Burke's incorrect in referring to the son as "Strong Hand"?]

- This family is yet another male-line branch of the Norman ducal house, descended from the family of **Rolf the Ganger**, first Duke. **Eystein Glumra**, Jarl of More, had a younger son **Haldrich** (uncle of Rolf). His son **Richard** (died c. 933) came to Normandy and was given the manor of St-Saveur; his son Niel or Nigel was the first vicomte de St-Saveur. This **Niel** was the father of **Roger**, father of **Neil II** (died c. 1045), who had at least two sons: the younger, **Ivo** vicomte de Cotentin, married **Emma**, daughter of **Geoffrey of Brittany**. He is the ancestor of the many-branched English families of Dutton and Hatton; and his son **Nigel de Aurenges** of Halton, Constable of Chester, married **Alice**, daughter of **Gilbert de Gant**; they had a daughter **Agnes** who married **Eustace FitzJohn** (our ancestors via Lacy, Clavering and other lines). **Haldrich** was also the father of **Hugo de Cavalcamp** (born c. 890), whose son **Ralph** was ancestor of the de Toesny family; **Ralph's** son **Ralph II de Toesny** had a younger son **Robert de Toesny**, whose son **Robert de Todeni**, lord of Belvoir, was ancestor of the Albini or Daubeney family of Belvoir (see below).
- **Neil II's** elder son **Neil III de St-Saveur** married **Adela**, daughter of **Godfrey, Count of Brionne and Eu** (see Normandy) and they were the parents of at least three children: a **daughter** who married **Robert le Bigod** and is our ancestor via Bigod); **Richard** (had a son **Ralph de la Haye**, seneschal of Mortain, who married his cousin **Olivia** [see below] and was the father of **Robert de la Haye**, lord of Halnac, whose son **Richard de la Haye** [c. 1125-1186] married **Maud Vernon** and was the father of **Nichole**, who is our ancestor via her husband **Gerard de Camville** - see Camville); and **Richard's** brother **William**.
- This **William's** descendants are known as **'d'Aubigny'** in Normandy and 'Albini' in England, after their manor of Saint-Martin d'Aubigny. He married a **sister** of Grimaldi **de Plessis** (otherwise unknown) and had at least one child: **Roger de Albini** or d'Aubigny (c.1048-p1084) who accompanied his cousin the Conqueror to England in 1066 and was granted lands in Sussex. He married **Amice**, sister (probably) of **Robert de Mowbray**, Earl of Northumberland; they were

the parents of three sons: Rualoc, who died young; **William d'Aubigny** or d'Albini (**'Pincerna'**, 1066-1139); and **Nigel** (see below).
- **William d'Aubigny** was a butler in the household of **Henry I**, and must have been a physically powerful man; his nickname Pincerna means "strong hand." He married his cousin **Maud le Bigod** and was the father of Nigel, Oliver, and **Olivia** (who married her first cousin **Ralph de la Haye**, above), and of his heir **William d'Albini**, 1st Earl of Arundel (died 1176). This **William** married the widow of **Henry I**, **Adeliza of Lorraine** (see Brabant), from whose dowry he received the lands where Arundel Castle (above) was soon built. Of course, this marriage propelled him into the first rank of the Anglo-Norman nobility. They had six or seven children: **William de Albini**, Earl of Sussex, 2nd Earl of Arundel (see below); **Alice** (married **Jean, Count d'Eu**, Lord of Hastings, see Normandy); **Agnes** [I have **Agnes Mrs. Mowbray** as daughter of William IV as do Fabpedigree and Tudorplace.] (Avice?) de Albini (married **William de Mowbray** of Axholme Castle); and three or four others.
- **William de Albini**, Earl of Sussex, 2nd Earl of Arundel (died 1193) married **Maud de St. Hilaire** (daughter of **James de St. Hilaire du Harcourt**, widow of Roger, Earl of Clare - see Harcourt). Their son **William de Albini**, Earl of Sussex, 3rd Earl of Arundel (died 1221) married **Mabel**, daughter of **Hugh 'de Keveliok' de Meschines**, 3rd Earl of Chester (see Kevilioc). Six children: (1) **William de Albini, Earl of Sussex, 4th Earl of Arundel** (married but no children); (2) **Hugh de Albini, 5th Earl of Arundel** (also married but no children); (3) **Maud** or **Mabel** (married **Robert de Tatteshall of Tatteshall**; (4) **Isabel** (married **John FitzAlan**, lord of Oswestry and Clun, Sheriff of Shropshire, our ancestors via Fitzalan); **Nicola** (married **Roger de Somery** of Dudley, our ancestors via Basset and other lines); and **Cecilia** (married **Roger de Mahaut** of Montalt or Mold; their daughter **Leuca** married our ancestor **Philip de Orreby**).
- **Nigel d'Aubigny** (died 1129), the younger brother of **William 'Pincerna,'** married (as his second wife) **Gundred de Gournay**, daughter of **Gerard de Gournay**, Sire de Gournay, lord of Yarmouth (died 1104 on Crusade). Their younger son

Henry is the ancestor of the Albini family of Camho in Wiltshire (descendants eventually used the name Daubeney). Their daughter **Gundred** married our ancestor **Bertram Haget**. The elder son **Roger** (died 1188) took his mother's name, Mowbray, as that family had died out. He married **Alice**, daughter of **Walter de Gant** or Gaunt by **Maud**, daughter of **Etienne I**, Count of Trequier and Lamballe (of the Breton ruling family). Their descendants are theMowbrays of Norfolk, who inherited Arundel Castle from them.

- **Daubeney of Belvoir**
- **Robert de Todeni**, lord of Belvoir (died 1088) married **Adela**, and had six children: (1) **William de Toeni or de Albini, 'Brito', lord of Belvoir**, see below; (2) Geoffrey, had descendants; (3) Agnes, married Hubert de Rye; (4) **Alice**, married **Roger Bigot** orBigod of Framlingham, Sheriff of Norfolk and Suffolk, 'Earl of East Anglia'; (5) Berenger, and (6) Roger.
- **William de Toeni or de Albini, 'Brito', lord of Belvoir** (died c. 1155) married **Maud**, daughter of **Simon de St. Liz**, Earl of Huntingdon and Northampton, and had three children: (1) **William de Albini, 'Meschines' or 'Brito', lord of Belvoir** (died c1168), see below; (2) **Ralph de Albini or d'Aubigne of Ingleby**, see farther below; and (3) Matilda, married Gilbert, 3rd Earl of Strathearn in Scotland
- **William de Albini, 'Meschines' or 'Brito', lord of Belvoir** (died c. 1168) married **Adelisa**, and was father of the Magna Carta surety **William de Albini, lord of Belvoir**(died 1236). He married **Margery**, daughter of **Odonel de Umfreville** of Prudhoe, Otterbourne, Harbottle and Riddlesdale (see Umfraville) and was the father of at least four sons: Sir Odinel, Robert, Nicholas (rector of Bottesford) and **William de Albini, lord of Belvoir**. This William married twice (Albreda of Biseth, and Isabel) and it is not clear which was the mother of **Isabel**, who married **Robert de Ros** of Hamlake, first Lord de Ros - thereafter, Belvoir belonged to the de Ros family.
- **Ralph de Albini or d'Aubigne of Ingleby** died at the siege of Acre in 1190. He married **Maud**, daughter of **William de Montsorel**, seigneur de Landal; they were the parents of (1)

Philip de Albini or d'Aubigne of Ingleby, Governor of Ludlow, then Jersey, etc, no children; and (2) **Sir Ralph de Albini or d'Aubigne of South Ingleby**, seigneur de Landal (died 1292), who married **Isabel de Mauley** and had three sons: (1) Sir Philip de Albini or d'Aubigne of South Ingleby, etc (died 1294), no children; (2) Owen de Albini; (3) **Eleanor**, married our ancestor **Reginald Hussey**; and (4) **Sir Helie or Elias de Albini** or Daubeney of South Ingleby, etc, first Lord Daubeney (died 1305), who married **Joan** and had one son: **Sir Ralph Daubeney of South Ingleby**, etc, 2nd Lord (living in 1343). He married first **Katherine**, daughter of **Marmaduke de Thweng**, 1st Lord, and had one daughter,
(1) **Elizabeth** (died 1433), wife of **William, first Lord de Botreaux**; he married second **Alice**, daughter of **Sir William de Montacute**, 2nd Lord, and had a son (2) **Sir Giles Daubeney** (died 1386), 3rd Lord, who married **Eleanor**, daughter **Henry de Wylington** or Wilington of Umberleigh by **Isabel de Whalesborough**; our ancestors via Champernowne.

- The arms are described as: Gules, four lozenges comjoined in fesse argent.
- Aubigny itself was purchased in 1180 by the French crown, and assigned several times to families which died out; the fief was sold to Sir John Stuart, lord of Darnley by Charles VII in 1427 (during the Hundred Years War, when many Scottish nobles were fighting for France). It was inherited by his younger son (the senior branch were the earls of Lennox) and a long line of French Stuarts followed. James VI of Scots made them dukes of Lennox in 1580, and that title went extinct in 1672. King Charles II was the nearest heir, and he assigned it to his illegitimate descendants by Louise de Kéroualle - the present dukes of Lennox and Richmond.
-
- -- From the now defunct Martinrealm.org

The interment place of William d'Aubigny, 1st Earl of Arundel. Waverley Abbey was the first Cistercian abbey in England, founded in 1128 by William Giffard, Bishop of Winchester. It is situated about one mile south of Farnham, Surrey, in a bend of the River Wey. During the first century of its existence, it founded six monasteries, and despite the members thus sent away, it had 70 monks and 120 lay brothers in 1187. It kept about thirty ploughs. The site was subject to regular flooding, however, and in 1203 the foundations for a new church and monastery were laid on higher ground. The new church was dedicated in 1231. King John visited Waverley in 1209, and Henry III in 1225. The abbey also produced the famous annals of Waverley, an important source for the period. By the end of the thirteenth century the abbey was becoming less important. By the time it was suppressed by Henry VIII in 1536 as part of the dissolution of the monasteries there were only thirteen monks in the community and the abbey had an annual net income of £174. Stones from the abbey when it lay in ruins were taken to build nearby houses, including the house at Loseley Park at Compton. The ruins of Waverley Abbey are managed today by English Heritage. -- visitsurrey.com

Arundel Castle was founded by Roger de Montgomery on Christmas Day 1067 and the first round of construction seems to have occurred mostly in 1068, which was during the reign of William the Conqueror. It served as a strategically vital fortification near the mouth of the River Arun, defending the surrounding land against invasion from the Continent. The original structure was a motte and double bailey castle. It was Roger de Montgomery who was declared the first Earl of Arundel when the King granted him the property as part of a much larger package of hundreds of manors. Roger was a cousin of King William and had stayed in Normandy to keep the peace there while William was invading England. He was rewarded for his loyalty with extensive lands in the Welsh Marches and across the country, together with one third of Sussex. (For other reasons, the generally accepted first creation of the title Earl of Arundel lies in the year 1138 with William d'Aubigny, confirmed in 1155). After Roger de Montgomery died, the castle reverted to the crown under Henry I. The King, in his will, left Arundel Castle and the attached land to his second wife Adeliza of Louvain. In 1138, three years after Henry's death, she married William d'Albini II (aka d'Aubigny, the first Earl of the d'Aubigny family of

Saint-Martin-d'Aubigny in Normandy). William was responsible for creating the stone shell on the motte, thus increasing the defence and status of the castle. The castle was damaged in the English Civil War and then restored in the 18th and 19th centuries. From the 11th century onward, the castle has served as a hereditary stately home and has been in the family of the Duke of Norfolk for over 800 years. It is still the principal seat of the Norfolk family. It is a Grade I listed building. -- Based on the Wikipedia article. Image is nl.wikipedia, Bestand:Arundel Castle Hill Fort.JPG

Arundel Castle in West Sussex, England is a restored medieval castle. The castle dates from the reign of Edward the Confessor (r. 1042–1066) and was completed by Roger de Montgomery, who became the first to hold the earldom of Arundel by the graces of William the Conqueror. The castle was damaged in the English Civil War and then restored in the 18th and 19th centuries.

From the 11th century onward, the castle has served as a hereditary stately home to several families (with a few and brief reversions to the Crown) and is currently the principal seat of the Duke of Norfolk and his family. It is a Grade I listed building.[1]

Construction
Intersection of the old and new walls

Arundel Castle was built in 1068 during the reign of William the Conqueror as a fortification for the River Arun and a defensive position for the surrounding land. The original structure was a Motte and Bailey castle before undergoing an extensive renovation during the reign of William the Conqueror which enlarged the motte and improved the defences. Roger de Montgomery is believed to have been declared the first Earl of Arundel as the King granted him the property as part of a much larger package of hundreds of manors. (For other reasons, the generally accepted first creation of the title Earl of Arundel lies in the year 1138 with William d'Aubigny, confirmed in 1155).

After Roger de Montgomery died, the castle reverted to the crown under Henry I. The King, in his will, left Arundel Castle and the attached land to his second wife Adeliza of Louvain. In 1138, three years after Henry's death, she married William d'Albani II (aka d'Aubigny, the first Earl, of the d'Aubigny family of Saint-Martin-d'Aubigny in Normandy). William was responsible for creating the stone shell on the motte, thus increasing the defence and status of the castle.

Changes to the castle — Medieval period
View of Arundel Castle's Norman motte with the quadrangle in the foreground.

Arundel Castle and the earldom have passed through generations almost directly since 1138, with only the occasional reversion to the crown and other nobles for a brief time. Since the Aubigny family first received the castle, changes have been made and the castle has been re-structured to meet the requirements of the nobility at the present time.

In 1132, the Empress Matilda was invited to stay at Arundel for some time during her travel to impress her claim to the English throne upon Stephen. The stone apartments constructed to accommodate the Empress and her entourage survive to this day.

In 1176, William d'Aubigny died and Arundel Castle then reverted to the crown, under Henry II, who spent a vast amount of capital re-structuring the building, mainly for domestic needs. When Henry died, the castle remained in the possession of Richard I ("the Lionheart"), who offered it to the Aubigny family line under William III comte de Sussex. The last in the Aubigny male line was Hugh, who died at a young age in 1243. When his sister Isabel wed John FitzAlan of Clun, the castle and earldom returned to him. The FitzAlan family enjoyed an uninterrupted hereditary line until 1555.

Upon the death of the seventh Earl in 1272, Arundel Castle and the earldom passed to his five-year-old son Richard. Thirteen years later, Edward I granted Richard the right to hold two fairs per year at the castle as well as the power to collect taxes. This grant provided funding for the much needed renovation of the castle, which, by this time, had fallen into disrepair. Once sufficient funds were available, FitzAlan added the well tower and re-constructed the entrance to the keep. After

Richard's death, his son Edmund was executed for his part in the rebellion against Edward II. Arundel subsequently passed to the 6th son of Edward I who was also executed. The castle and titles passed back to the FitzAlans four years later.

The tenth Earl, Richard, fought at the Crécy with Edward III and the Edward, the Black Prince. FitzAlan was also responsible for the building of the FitzAlan Chapel, built posthumously according to his will.

The eleventh Earl, Richard, was treated harshly by Richard II. At the funeral of the Queen Anne, the Earl was beaten for arriving late and asking to leave early. Richard II eventually grew tired of his treachery and executed the Earl before confiscating his property. Arundel was given by the crown to John Holland, 1st Duke of Exeter, but when he was executed by Henry IV, Arundel was returned to the FitzAlan line once again. The next earl, Thomas, married the daughter of John of Portugal. The couple eventually became the first members of the FitzAlan family to be buried in the chapel built by Richard FitzAlan, the tenth Earl.

The FitzAlan line ceased when Mary FitzAlan, daughter of the nineteenth earl, married Thomas Howard, 4th Duke of Norfolk. The crown seized Arundel upon his execution for conspiring to marry Mary I of Scotland, in 1572. However, the castle was later returned to his heirs, the successor Earls of Arundel.

Arundel town and castle in 1644.
Restoration of Castle

Although the castle remained in the hands of the Howard family over the succeeding centuries, it was not their favorite residence, and the various Dukes of Norfolk invested their time and energy into improving other ducal estates, including Norfolk House in London and Worksop.

Charles Howard, 11th Duke of Norfolk was known for his restoration work and improvements to the castle beginning in 1787 and continuing for a number of years, as he desired to live there and entertain his visitors there. Many of his improvements have since been revised and remodeled, but the library in the castle is still as he had it designed and built. He held a large party at Arundel Castle to reunite the various senior members of the Howard family shortly before his death in 1815.

Royal visit of 1846

In 1846, Queen Victoria and her husband Prince Albert visited Arundel Castle for a few days. Henry Charles Howard, 13th Duke of Norfolk had remodeled the castle in time for her visit. He was thinking of disposing of some of the 11th Duke of Norfolk's work, as there had been several complaints from the celebrities of the day that it was too cold, dark and unfriendly. The Duke devised a brand new apartment block for the new Queen and her Consort, Prince Albert to stay in, commissioning a portrait of the Queen and decorating the block with the finest of Victorian furniture and art. There was also a re-structuring of bedrooms for the court. The Duke spared no expense to make the Queen's visit enjoyable, and he succeeded.

The Queen was received on December 1, 1846 by the Duke, Mayor of Arundel Edward Howard Howard-Gibbon, and other town dignitaries, and then she retired to her private apartments in the castle. On her visit she walked in the newly designed grounds and visited areas of the county nearby, including Petworth House. Almost every part of the castle that the Queen would visit was re-furbished and exquisitely decorated to meet Royal standards. At the end of her visit, she wrote to the Duke and commented on how enjoyable her visit was, commenting on the "beautiful" castle and the friendliness of her reception. The suite of rooms in which Victoria stayed have remained virtually untouched, they are now called the 'Victoria Rooms'. Among other things on display in these rooms are the Queen's bed, the guest book bearing her and her Consort's signature and her toilet.

Changes to the castle — 1850 to the present day
The 19th-century embellishments had not been completed when this picture was published in 1880.

Soon after the Royal visit the 14th Duke began re-structuring the castle once again. The 14th Duke died before its completion, and the work was overseen by his successor, the 15th Duke. Work was completed in 1900, and the castle began to look like the amazing architecture on display today. Changes were made to the grounds and he addressed the dark Victorian gardens and made them exquisitely bright and colourful. The problem of light within the castle itself was addressed by the replacement of windows to make the interior brighter. The keep was restructured later on, but the original keep was kept until then for its antiquity and picturesque setting. Today, the castle is still the principal seat of the Dukes of Norfolk, also the Earls Marshal of England. Most of the building is open to the general public, except for the private apartments within the quadrangle.

Important events

- Marriage of the future Henry IV of England and Mary de Bohun (1380)
- Visit of Queen Victoria and Prince Albert (1846)
- Used as Windsor Castle in the *Doctor Who* episode *Silver Nemesis* (1988), in *The Madness of King George* (1994), in *Victoria & Albert* (2001 TV serial), and in *The Young Victoria* (2008).
- Used as Carcroft Castle in the *MacGyver* television movie *Trails to Doomsday*.
- http://patp.us/genealogy/conq/albini.aspx
- The Conqueror and His Companions by J.R. Planché, Somerset Herald. London: Tinsley Brothers, 1874.
- That one or more of the family of Aubigny (Latinised into De Albinio, and better known in England as De Albini) "came over with the Conqueror," and fought at Hastings, there can be no question; but Wace, who does not specify the individual, but simply calls him "li boteillier d'Aubignie," has been accused of an anachronism by Mr. Taylor, who considers the office of Pincerna, or butler, to have been first conferred upon the grandson of William by Henry I circa 1100, when for his services to that monarch he was enfeoffed of the barony of Buckenham to hold in grand-sergeantry by the butlery, an office now discharged at coronations by the Duke of Norfolk, his descendants possessing a part of the barony. The companion of the Conqueror he believes to have been

- William, the first of that name we know of, or his son Roger, father of the second William, and Nigel de Albini, of whom we have previously spoken (p.30).
- M. Le Prévost votes for Roger, who made a donation to the Abbey of L'Essai in 1084. There is no reason why he should not also have been in the battle.
- In the absence of conclusive evidence I have headed this chapter with William de Albini, the earliest known of that name, which he derived from the commune of Aubigny, near Periers, in the Cotentin, and with whom the family pedigree commences.
- This William married a sister of Grimoult du Plessis, the traitor of Valognes and Val-ès-Dunes, who died in his dungeon in 1047 (vol. i., pp. 25 and 31), and Wace may after all be right in styling him "Le Botellier," as it is probable that he held that office in the household of the Duke of Normandy. By his wife, the sister of Grimoult (I have not yet lighted on her name), he had a son, the Roger d'Aubigny aforesaid, who married Amicia, or Avitia, sister of Geoffrey, Bishop of Coutances, and of Roger de Montbrai, and is supposed by M. Le Prévost to have been with his brothers-in-law in the battle.
- Roger d'Aubigny, or De Albini, had issue by his wife Avitia de Montbrai, five sons: William, known as William de Albini "Pincerna" (i.e., Butler), ancestor of the Earls of Sussex, who married Maud, daughter of Roger le Bigod, and died 1139. Richard, Abbot of St. Albans, Nigel, Humphrey, and Ruafon, or Ralph. Nigel, the third son, was heir of Robert de Montbrai, or Mowbray, his first cousin, whose wife he married during the lifetime of her husband by licence of Pope Paschal, and for some time treated her with respect out of regard for her noble parents; but on the death of her brother Gilbert de l'Aigle, having no issue by her, he craftily sought for a divorce on the ground of that very kinship which he exerted so much influence to induce the Pope to overlook, and then married Gundred, daughter of Gerrard de Gournay, by whom he had Roger, who assumed the name of Mowbray, and transmitted it to his descendants, Dukes of Norfolk and Earls Marshal of England; and Henri, ancestor of the line of Albini of Cainho.
- To return to the first William, it is clear that his grandsons were mere infants even if born in 1066, and therefore I believe

that it was the William, then Pincerna, and probably also Roger, his son, who were companions of the Conqueror in his expedition; Roger's eldest brother William being in disgrace in Normandy at the time, and not restored to favour, or allowed to enter England before the reign of Rufus, or it may have been Henry I.

- Of William de Albini, third son and successor of William II, and Maud le Bigod, a romantic story has been invented to account for the lion rampant subsequently borne by his descendants.
- Having captivated the heart of the Queen Dowager of France by his gallant conduct in a tournament at Paris, she offered to marry him, an honour which he respectfully declined, having already given his word and faith to a lady in England, another Queen Dowager, no less a personage than Adeliza, widow of King Henry 1 of England. His refusal so angered the French Queen, that she laid a plot with her attendants to destroy him by inducing him to enter a cave in her garden, where a lion had been placed for that purpose; but the undaunted Earl, rolling his mantle round his arm, thrust his hand into the lion's mouth, tore out its tongue, and sent it to the Queen by one of her maids. "In token of which noble and valiant act," says Brooke, in his "Catalogue of Nobility," "this William assumed to bear for his arms a lion gold in a field gules, which his successors ever since continued."
- As this third William de Albini died as late as 1176, it is possible be might have assumed armorial bearings, but the lion was more probably first borne by his son, the second Earl of Arundel of the line of Aubigny, in token of his descent from Adeliza, widow of Henry l, in whose reign we have the earliest evidence of golden lions being adopted as a personal decoration, if not strictly an heraldic bearing.
- Added to this site through the courtesy of Fred L. Curry, who provided a photocopy of the section

2. Albini (Aubigny) Line (Earls of Arundel and Sussex)

" The family of Aubigny derived its name from Aubigny, near Periers, in the Contentin, and Wace, the chronicler, mentions `li boteillier

d'Aubigny.' The pedigree commences with Grimoult du Plessis, the traitor of Valognes and Val-Des-Dunes, who died in a dungeon in 1047. William d'Aubigny, first of the name, married the sister of Grimoult and had issue Roger, who married Amicia, sister of Geoffrey, Bishop of Coutances, and of Roger de Montbray (i.e., Mowbray). The latter had issue, William d'Aubigny II, pincerna to Henry I., who married Maud Bigot, daughter of Roger Bigot, and died in 1139."

" Roger de Montbray, referred to in Wace as `cil de Moubrai,' was a brother of Geoffrey de Montbray, Bishop of Coutances, whom he accompanied to the battle of Hastings. He witnessed a charter in Normandy, 1066, and was the father of Robert de Montbray or Mowbray, Earl of Northumberland, who died about 1125 and is therefore not believed to have attended the conquest of England. He joined the conspiracy against William Rufus and died in prison."

" Geoffrey (Geoffroi, Eveque de Coutances was from Montbrai (Montrai) in the canton of Percy, arrondissement of Saint-Lo. Geoffrey de Montbray, Bishop of Coutances, was at the battle of Senlac. Dugdale remarks, "This Geoffroi being of noble Norman extraction and more skillful in arms than divinity, knowing better to train up soldiers than to instruct clergy, did good service at the battle of Hastings," for which he received vast possessions in Somerset and other counties, amounting to 280 manors, and dedicated his immense wealth to the building of the cathedral of Coutances. In 1069 he marched against the insurgents of Dorset and Somerset and raised the siege of Montacute. Two years later he represented the king in a suit against Bishop Odo and Archbishop Lanfranc, and in 1074, with Bishop Odo, suppressed the rebellion of the Earls of Hereford and Norfolk, at which time he was appointed Earl of Northumberland but soon relinquished the earldom to his nephew, Robert, who became his heir. He assisted at the coronation of the Conqueror and died in 1093/94."

1. **Roger de Albini (d'Aubigny)**, married **Amicia**, sister of Geoffrey, Bishop of Coutances, according to Orderic Vital, "one of the bishops with attendant clerks and monks, whose duty it was to aid the war with their prayers and councils." Amicia also had another brother, Roger de Montbray (Mowbray) .He was succeeded by his eldest son, William.

- 2. **William de Albini (d'Aubigny) II** , surnamed Pincerna, whose posterity assumed, and attained such eminence under the name of Mowbray (see that lineage elsewhere), accompanied William the Conqueror into England, and acquired extensive territorial possessions by royal grants in Norfolk and other counties. Of these grants was the lordship of Bokenham, to be held by the service of being Butler to the Kings of England on the day of their coronation, and in consequence we find this William styled in divers charters "*Pin cerna Henrici Regis Anglorum* ." William de Albini founded the Abbey of Wymondham in Norfolk.
- William de Albini also gave to the monks of Rochester the tithes of his manor of Elham; as also one carucate of land in Achestede, with a wood called Acholte. He likewise bestowed upon the Abbey of St. Etienne at Caen, in Normandy, all his lands lying in Stavell, which grant he made in the presence of King Henry and his barons. He married **Maud Bigod** , daughter of Roger Bigod , with whom he obtained ten knight's fees in Norfolk.

      At the obsequies of Maud, William de Albini gave to the monks of Wymondham, the manor of Hapesburg, in pure alms, and made livery thereof to the said monks by a cross of silver in which (says Dugdale) was placed certain venerable reliques, viz., "part of the wood of the cross whereon our Lord was crucified; part of the sepulchre of the blessed Virgin; as also a gold ring, and a silver chalice, for retaining the holy Eucharist, admirably wrought in the form of a sphere; unto which pious donation his three sons were witnesses, with several other persons." The exact time of the decease of this great feudal lord is not certain (Crispin and Macary state that he died in 1139), but it is known that he was buried before the high altar in the Abbey of Wymondham, and that the monks were in the constant habit of praying for his soul, by the name of "William de Albini, the king's butler." He was succeeded by his eldest son, William.

      William de Albini (d'Aubigny), III , surnamed "William with the strong hand," from the following circumstance, as related by William Dugdale:

> "It happened that the Queen of France, being then a widow, and a very beautiful woman, became much in love with a knight from an other country, who was a comely person, and in the flower of his youth; and because she thought that no man excelled him in valor, she caused a tournament to be proclaimed throughout her dominions, promising to reward those who should exercise themselves therein, according to their respective abilities; and concluded that if the person whom she so well affected should act his part better than others in those military exercises, she might marry him without any dishonor to herself. Hereupon divers gallant men, from foreign parts hasting to Paris, amongst others came this our William de Albini, bravely accoutered, and in the tournament excelled all others, overcoming many, and wounding one mortally with his lance, which being observed by the queen, she became exceedingly enamored of him, and forthwith invited him to a costly banquet, and afterwards bestowing certain jewels upon him, offered him marriage; but, having plighted his troth to the Queen of England, then a widow, he refused her, whereat she grew so discontented that she consulted with her maids how she might take away his life; and in pursuance of that design, inticed him into a garden, where there was a secret cave, and in it a fierce lion, unto which she descended by divers steps, under color of showing him the beast; and when she told him of its fierceness, he answered, that it was a womanish and not a manly quality to be afraid thereof. But having him there, by the advantage of a folding door, thrust him to the lion; being therefore in this danger, he rolled his mantle about his arm, and putting his hand into the mouth of the beast, pulled out his tongue by the root; which done, he followed the queen to her palace, and gave it to one of her maids to present her. Returning thereupon to England, with the fame of this glorious exploit, he was forthwith advanced to the Earldom of Arundel, and for his arms the Lion given him."

- He subsequently married **Adeliza of Lorraine**, Queen of England, widow of King Henry I., and the daughter of Godfrey, Duke of Lorraine. See her ancestral lineage elsewhere in Volume I. Adeliza had the castle of Arundel in dowry from her deceased husband, the monarch, and thus her new lord became its feudal earl, 1st Earl of Arundel in this family. The earl was one of those who solicited the Empress Maud to come to England, and received her and her brother Robert, Earl of Gloucester, at the port of Arundel, in August 1139, and in three years afterwards (1142), in the report made of King Stephen's taking William de Mandeville at St. Albans, it is stated "that before he could be laid hold on, he underwent a sharp skirmish with the king's party, wherein the Earl of Arundel, though a stout and expert soldier, was unhorsed in the midst of the water by Walceline de Oxeai, and almost drowned." In 1150, he wrote himself Earl of Chichester, but we find him styled again Earl of Arundel, upon a very memorable occasion, namely, the reconciliation of Henry, Duke of Normandy, afterwards King Henry II., and King Stephen at the siege of Wallingford Castle in 1152. "It was scarce possible," says Rapin, "for the armies to part without fighting. Accordingly the two leaders were preparing for battle with equal ardor, when, by the prudent advice of the Earl of Arundel, who was on the king's side, they were prevent ed from coming to blows." A truce and peace followed this interference of the earl's, which led to the subsequent accession of Henry after Stephen's decease, in whose favor the earl stood so high that he not only obtained for himself and his heirs the castle and honor of Arundel, but a confirmation of the Earldom of Sussex, of which county he was really earl, by a grant of the *Tertium Denarium* of the pleas of the shire. In 1164, we find the Earl of Arundel deputed with Gilbert Foliot, Bishop of London, to remonstrate with Louis, King of France, upon according an asylum to Thomas a Becket within his dominions, and on the failure of that mission, dispatched with the archbishop of York, the Bishops of Winchester, London, Chichester, and Exeter, Wido Rufus, Richard de Invecestre, John de Oxford (priests), Hugh de Gundevile, Bernard de St. Valery, and Henry Fitzgerald, to lay the whole affair of Becket at the foot of the pontifical throne. Upon levying the aid for the marriage of the king's daughter, in the 12th year of Henry II., the knight's fees of the honor of Arundel were certified to be ninety-seven, and those in Norfolk, belonging to the earl, forty-two. In 1173, we find the Earl of Arundel commanding, in conjunction with William, Earl of Mandeville, the king's army in Normandy, and compelling the French monarch to abandon Verneuil after a long siege, and in the next year, with Richard de Lucy, Justice of England, defeating Robert, Earl of Leicester, then in rebellion at St. Edmundbury. This potent nobleman, after founding and endowing several religious houses, died at Waverley, in Surrey, on October 3, 1176, and was buried in the Abbey of Wymondham. He and his wife, Adeliza, widow of King Henry I., had four sons and three daughters.

- 4. **William de Albini**, 2nd Earl of Arundel and Sussex, had a grant from the crown, in the 23rd year of King Henry II., of the Earldom of Sussex, and in the first year of King Richard I., had a confirmation from that prince, of the castle and honor of Arundel, as also of the *Tertium Denarium* of the county of Sussex. He died in 1196, and was succeeded by his son, William.

  5. **William de Albini**, 3rd Earl of Arundel and Sussex, who, in 1218, embarked in the Crusade, and was at the celebrated siege of Damietta, but died in returning, in the year 1221. He married **Maud St. Hillary**, daughter and heiress of James de St. Hillary, and widow of Roger de Clare, Earl of Clare .

- 1. Robert de Todeni, one of the Norman barons who came into England in 1066 as a standard bearer of Duke William, was the founder of this renowned, ancient family. For his distinguished services at Hastings, the victorious monarch rewarded him with the eight lordships he possessed in twelve counties at the time of the first General Survey of England. On one of his estates in Lincolnshire, near the border of Leicestershire, he erected a castle which he named Belvoir, from its commanding position, and this became his chief seat. He died in 1088, leaving by his wife, Adela, a son, William.

  2. William de Albini, called the Briton, from having been born in England. He was a soldier of distinction, and acquired great renown in the celebrated battle of Tenercheby, in Normandy, when he commanded the cavalry, for "by a charge

of spirit, he determined at once the fate of the day." The monk Matthew Paris records "in this encounter chiefly deserveth honour the most heroic William de Albini, the Briton, who with his sword broke through the enemy and terminated the battle." When he became a supporter of the cause of Empress Maud, his castle of Belvoir, with all his great possessions, were seized by King Stephen, who presented them to Ranulphgerons de Meschines, the Earl of Chester. William-Brito de Albini died about 1155, leaving by his wife, Maud, daughter of Simon St. Liz, an eldest son, William.

3. William-Meschines de Albini, 2nd Baron of, Belvoir. He received back from Henry II., the castle of Belvoir, and the majority of the lordships confiscated by King Stephen. Dying in 1167, he was succeeded by his son, William.

- 4. William de Albini, Senior, the Surety of the Magna Charta, Lord of Belvoir Castle, 3rd baron for this family. When his father died, he was in ward to King Henry II., and, in 1194, he was in the army of Richard I., in Normandy. Already a wealthy man at the time of the accession of John to the throne, he received several additional grants of great value. In 1201, when the barons refused to attend their sovereign into France, King John demanded that their castles should be given up to him as security for their allegiance, beginning with William de Albini of whom he claimed Belvoir Castle, instead of which de Albini gave him his son, William, as hostage. He appears to have remained longer faithful to King John, as well as more moderate in his opposition to him, than most of the barons, and did not join the insurgents until he could no longer with safety either remain neutral, or adhere to the King, for so late as January 1214-15, he was one of the King's commissioners appointed for the safe-conduct of such as were traveling in his court, at Northampton. After he joined the baron's party, he entered with great spirit into their cause and was excommunicated; but, after having gained their point, he was looked upon with suspicion by the other sureties because he did not attend the grand tournament in Staine's Wood, on June 29, 1215, to celebrate the victory, and it was not until after other barons had alarmed him, that he forfeited his castle at Belvoir, and joined them at London. But the sequel proves their suspicions were not well grounded. He was placed as governor of Rochester Castle, when, though he found it so utterly destitute of provisions as almost to induce his men to abandon it, he recruited and held it until famine and weakness, and watching, obliged them to surrender to the King. The siege having lasted three months, and his army being attended with considerable loss, King John ordered that all nobles in the castle be hanged; but his chief counselors resolutely opposing the sentence, William de Albini and his son Odonel, with several other barons, were merely committed to the custody of Peter de Mauley, and sent prisoners to Corfe and Nottingham Castles. While de Albini remained at Corfe, the King marched on Christmas morning, 1216, from Nottingham to Langar, near Belvoir Castle, and sent a summons to surrender. Upon this, Nicholas de Albini, one of the baron's sons, and a clerk in orders, delivered the keys to the King, asking only that his father should be mercifully treated. The fortress was then committed to the custody of Geoffrey and Oliver de Buteville. His liberty was gained only by William de Albini's paying a fine to the king of six thousand marks (More than 4,000 pounds), the sum being raised from his own lands by his wife. After King John's death, though he submitted himself to King Henry III., William de Albini was forced to give his wife and son Nicholas as hostages for his allegiance; but in 1217 he was one of the king's commanders at the battle of Lincoln. He died at Offington, May 1, 1236, and was buried at Newstead, and "his heart under the wall, opposite the high altar," at Belvoir Castle.

- http://www.celtic-casimir.com/webtree/6/32369.htm
-
- **William "Strong Hand" D' AUBIGNY** 1st Earl of Arundel 593,4054,8829,8834,8835,8836
- Born: Abt 1103, St Sauveur, Manche, Normandie, France 748,4054
- Married: 1138, London, Middlesex, England 593,3664,4054,8833
- Died: 12 Oct 1176, Waverly Abbey, Surrey, England 3664,4054,8833
- Buried: 19 Oct 1176, Wymondham Priory, Norfolk, England

- Another name for William was William D' ALBINI.
- Ancestral File Number: V9VP-TD.

General Notes:

- On the Earldom of Lincoln, previous creations: [Burke's Peerage, p. 1711]:

- Henry I's widow Adeliz married in 1138 William d'Aubigny, who the next year, probably as a result, was created Earl of Lincoln. William's father was a Norman immigrant to England in Henry I's reign. His son, who by this advantageous marriage came into the former Queen's dowry of Arundel Castle, together with its Honour (feudal administrative unit embodying several knight's fees), has been held thereby to have become Earl of Arundel. By 1142 he had been deprived of his Earldom of Lincoln, indeed even before, was spoken sometimes as Earl of Arundel and sometimes as Earl of Chichester or Earl of Sussex.

- EARLDOM OF SUSSEX (I) 1141
- EARLDOM OF LINCOLN (I) circa 1139 to 1141
- EARLDOM OF ARUNDEL (IV, 1) 1138 or 1139 to 1176

- WILLIAM D'AUBIGNY) de Albiniaco or in the Anglo-Latin of Dugdale and other writers, DE ALBINI, surnamed "the strong hand," Lord of the manor of Buckenham, Norfolk, son and heir of William D'Aubigny (died 1139) Pincerna Regis, by Maud, daughter of Roger LE BIGOD, probably by his 2nd wife, Alice, sister and coheir of William de Tosny, Lord of Belvoir, daughter of Robert de Tosny of the same, was born early in the reign of Henry I. On his marriage with the Queen Dowager, he acquired with her , in 1138 or 1139, the Castle and Honour of Arundel, which had been settled on her in dower, whereby it may be considered that, according to the admission of 1433, he became EARL OF ARUNDEL. There is conclusive evidence from various charters, that at, or about the time of, and probably soon after, his said marriage, he was recognised as EARL OF LINCOLN, and he may be assumed to have been so created in the summer of 1139. In this year he gave shelter to the Empress Maud, at Arundel Castle, but ever after adhered to Stephen. He can be shown to have very soon lost the Earldom of Lincoln, and in 1141 he attested a charter of Stephen as EARL OF SUSSEX, (being from time to time thereafter so described, as, e.g. where he witnesses a charter to the Abbey of Barking under that name) and may be assumed to have been so created by Stephen in 1141, after that King had regained his freedom. Early in 114,2, the Earldom of Lincoln had already passed to another, viz. William de Roumare. In his own later charters he is styled, and in a charter, before 1150, of the Queen Dowager to the Abbey of Reading, she styles him EARL OF CHICHESTER. He was influential in arranging the treaty of 1153, whereby the Crown continued with King Stephen for life, though the inheritance thereof was secured to Henry II. To this instrument he subscribed as "Comes Cicestrie." Henry II, by a grant undated, but supposed to have been in 1155 (the year after his accession), confirms to him as "William, EARL OF ARUNDEL, the Castle of Arundel, with the whole honour of Arundel and all its appurtenances," and, by the same instrument, bestows on him the third penny of the pleas of the county of SUSSEX unde Comes est. No doubt, however, he was more generally known as "EARL OF ARUNDEL," and as such (only) he is spoken of by his son and heir (who styles himself Earl of Sussex) in a charter to the Priory of Wymondham; and as Earl of Arundel (only) he is described in the record of his death in the Annals of Waverley. He was justly held in great esteem by Henry II, and was one of the embassy to Rome in 1163/4, and to Saxony (on the espousal of the Princess to the Duke of Saxony) in 1168. He was also in command of the Royal army in August 1173, in Normandy, against the King's rebellious sons, where he distinguished himself for his "swiftness and velocity," and, on 29 September following he assisted at the defeat, near Bury St. Edmunds, of the Earl of Leicester, who, with his Flemings, had invaded Suffolk.

- He married, in 1138 (the 3rd year of her widowhood) Adeliz, QUEEN DOWAGER OF ENGLAND (widow of Henry I), 1st daughter of Godefroy à la Barbe, DUKE OF LOTHIER (i.e.

Lorraine Inférieure), COUNT OF BRABANT AND LOUVAIN, by his 1st wife, Ide, daughter of Albert III, COUNT OF NAMUR. His wife, the Queen Dowager, retired in 1150 to a nunnery at Afflighem, in South Brabant, where she died, and was buried 23 April 1151, aged about 48. He survived her 25 years, and died 12 October 1176, at Waverley Abbey, Surrey, and was buried, with his father, at Wymondham Priory, Norfolk. [Complete Peerage I:233-35, XIV:37, (transcribed by Dave Utzinger)]

- William de Albini, surnamed "William with the strong hand," from the following circumstance, as related by Dugdale:---

- " It happened that the Queen of France, being then a widow, and a very beautify woman, became much in love with a knight of that country, who was a comely person, and in the flower of his youth: and because she thought that no man excelled him in valour, she caused a tournament to be proclaimed throughout her dominions, promising to reward those who should exercise themselves therein, according to their respective demerits; and concluding that if the person whom she so well affected could act his part better than the others in those military exercises, she might marry him without any dishonour to herself. Hereupon divers gallant men, from forrain parts hastening to Paris, amongst others came this our William de Albini, bravely accoutered, and in the tournament excelled all others, overcoming many, and wounding one mortally with his lance, which being observed by the queen, she became exceedingly enamoured of him, and forthwith invited him to a costly banquet, and afterwards bestowing certain jewels upon him, offered him marriage; but, having plighted his troth to the Queen of England, then a widow, he refused her, whereat she grew so much discontented that she consulted with her maids how she might take away his life; and in pursuance of that design, inticed him into a garden, where there was a secret cave, and in it a fierce lion, unto which she descended by divers steps, under colour of shewing him the beast; and when she told him of its fierceness, he answered, that it was a womanish and not a manly quality to be afraid thereof. But having him there, by the advantage of a folding door, thrust him in to the lion; being therefore in this danger, he rolled his mantle about his arm and, putting his hand into the mouth of the beast, pulled out his tongue by the root; which done, he followed the queen to her palace and gave it to one of her maids to present her. Returning thereupon to England, with the fame of this glorious exploit, he was forthwith advanced to the Earldom of Arundel, and for his arms the lion given him."

- He subsequently obtained the hand of the Queen Adeliza, relict of King Henry I, and daughter of Godfrey, Duke of Lorraine, which Adeliza had the castle of Arundel in dowry from the deceased monarch, and thus her new lord became its feudal earl. The earl was one of those who solicited the Empress Maud to come to England, and received her and her brother, Robert, Earl of Gloucester, at the port of Arundel, in August, 1139, and in three years afterwards (1142), in the report made of King Stephen's taking William de Mandevil at St. Albans, it is stated -- "that before he could be laid hold on, he underwent a sharp skirmish with the king's party, wherein the Earl of Arundel, though a stout and expert soldier, was unhorsed in the midst of the water by Walkeline de Oxeai, and almost drowned." In 1150, his lordship wrote himself Earl of Chichester, but we find him styled again Earl of Arundel, upon a very memorable occasion -- namely, the reconciliation of Henry Duke of Normandy (afterwards Henry II) and King Stephen at the siege of Wallingford Castle in 1152. "It was scarce possible," says Rapin, "for the armies to part without fighting. Accordingly the two leaders were preparing for battle with equal ardour, when, by the prudent advice of the Earl of Arundel, who was on the king's side, they were prevented from coming to blows." A truce and peace followed this interference of the earl's, which led to the subsequent accession of Henry after Stephen's decease, in whose favour the Earl stood so high that he not only obtained for himself and his heirs the castle and honour of Arundel, but a confirmation of the Earldom of Sussex, of which county he was really earl, by a grant of the Tertium Denarium of the pleas of that shire. In 1164, we find the Earl of Arundel deputed with Gilbert Foliot, bishop of London, to remonstrate

with Lewis, King of France, upon affording an asylum to
Thomas à Becket within his dominion, and on the failure of
that mission, despatched with the archbishop of York, the
bishops of Winchester, London, Chichester, and Exeter, --
Wido Rufus, Richard de Invecestre, John de Oxford (priests) -
- Hugh de Gundevile, Bernard de St. Valery, and Henry
Fitzgerald, to lay the whole affair of Becket at the foot of the
pontifical throne. Upon levying the aid for the marriage of the
king's daughter, 12th of Henry II [1165-66], the knights' fees
of the honour of Arundel were certified to be ninety-seven,
and those in Norfolk belonging to the earl, forty-two. In 1173,
we find the Earl of Arundel commanding, in conjunction with
William, Earl of Essex, the king's army in Normandy, and
compelling the French monarch to abandon Verneuil after a
long siege, and in the next year, with Richard de Lucy, justice
of England, defeating Robert Earl of Leicester, then in
rebellion at St. Edmundsbury. This potent nobleman, after
founding and endowing several religious houses, departed this
life at Waverley, in Surrey, on the 3 October, 1176, and was
buried in the abbey of Wymondham. His lordship left by
Adeliza, his wife, widow of King Henry I, four sons and three
daughters, the eldest of whom, Alice, m. John, Earl of Ewe.
The eldest son, William de Albini, 2nd earl, had a grant from
the crow, 23rd Henry II [1177-8] of the Earldom of Sussex,
and in the 1st of Richard I [1189-90], had a confirmation from
that prince of the castle and honour of Arundel, as also of the
Tertium Denarium of the county of Sussex. [Sir Bernard
Burke, Dormant, Abeyant, Forfeited, and Extinct Peerages,
Burke's Peerage, Ltd., London, 1883, pp. 2-3, Albini, Earls of
Arundel] 593

- **Marriage Information:** William married Princess Adeliza
(Adelicia) DE LOUVAIN, daughter of Godfrey "A La Barbe"
DE LORRAINE-INFERIEUR Count of Louvain, Duke of
Brabant and Ctse Clementia DE NAMUR Duchess of Lower
Lorraine, in 1138 in London, Middlesex, England
593,3664,4054,8833. (Princess Adeliza (Adelicia) DE
LOUVAIN was born about 1103 in Brabant, Netherlands
748,925,1077,1894,3664,4051,4052,4053, died on 23 Apr
1151 in Affligem Nunnery, Brabant, Belgium (as a nun)

748,925,1077,1894,3664,4053,4054 and was buried on 23 Apr 1151 in Affligem Abbey, Brabant, Belgium.)

William D'Aubigny was born circa 1010 in St. Sauveur, Manche, Normandy, France, son of Neil de St. Sauveur III and Adela d'Ecu. He was Pincerna or "Le Botellier" of King William I, the Duke of Normandy known as "William the Conqueror". The Pincerna was the king's cupbearer and one of his most loyal confidants. He settled at Dol, in Brittany, France.

William D'Aubigny, his son, Roger D'Aubigny, and Neil de St. Sauveur III fought under William the Conqueror on 14 October 1066 in the Battle of Hastings. The Battle of Hastings was the decisive Norman victory in the Norman Conquest of England. It was fought between the Norman army of William the Conqueror, and the English army led by Harold Godwinson. The battle took place at Senlac Hill, approximately 6 miles (10 km) north-west of Hastings.

The Norman army was estimated to number as many as 8,400 and consisted of at the most 2,200 cavalry, 4,500 infantry and 1,700 archers and crossbowmen. William's strategy relied on archers to soften the enemy, followed by a general advance of the infantry, and then a cavalry charge. The Norman army was composed of nobles, mercenaries, and troops from France and Europe, including some from southern Italy. The English army is usually thought to have numbered roughly 7,500 and consisted entirely of infantry. It is most probable that all the members of the army rode to battle, but once at the appointed place they dismounted to fight on foot.

The battle was a decisive Norman victory. Harold II was killed; traditionally, it is believed he was shot through the eye with an arrow. Although there was further English resistance, this battle is seen as the point at which William gained control of England.

William married Albreda du Plessis circa 1138. Her brother was Grimoult du Plessis, the traitor of Valognes and Val-es-Dunes, who died in his dungeion in 1047.

Magna Carta

The Magna Carta was signed in June 1215 between the barons of Medieval England and King John. 'Magna Carta' is Latin and means **"Great Charter"**. The Magna Carta was one of the most important documents of Medieval England.

It was signed (by royal seal) between the feudal barons and King John at Runnymede near Windsor Castle. The document was a series of written promises between the king and his subjects that he, the king, would govern

King John signing the Magna Carta

England and deal with its people according to the customs of feudal law. Magna Carta was an attempt by the barons to stop a king - in this case John - abusing his power with the people of England suffering.

Why would a king - who was meant to be all powerful in his own country - agree to the demands of the barons who were meant to be below him in authority ?

England had for some years owned land in France. The barons had provided the king with both money and men to defend this territory. Traditionally, the king had always consulted the barons before raising taxes (as they had to collect it) and demanding more men for military service (as they had to provide the men). This was all part of the Feudal System.

So long as English kings were militarily successful abroad, relations with the barons were good. But John was not very successful in his military campaigns abroad. His constant demands for more money and men angered the barons. By 1204, John had lost his land in northern France. In response to this, John introduced high taxes without asking the barons. This was against feudal law and accepted custom.

John made mistakes in other areas as well. He angered the Roman Catholic Church. The pope, vexed by John's behaviour, banned all church services in England in 1207. Religion, and the fear of Hell, were very important to the people including the barons. The Catholic Church taught the people that they could only gain entrance to Heaven if the Catholic Church believed that they were good enough to get there. How could they show their goodness and love of God if the churches were shut ? Even worse for John was the fact that the pope excommunicated him in 1209. This meant that John could never get to Heaven until the pope withdrew the excommunication. Faced with this, John climbed down and accepted the power of the Catholic Church, giving them many privileges in 1214.

1214 was a disastrous year for John for another reason. Once again, he suffered military defeat in an attempt to get back his territory in northern France. He returned to London demanding more money from taxes. This time the barons were not willing to listen. They rebelled against his power. The barons captured London. However, they did not defeat John entirely and by the Spring of 1215, both sides were willing to discuss matters. The result was the Magna Carta.

What did the Magna Carta bring in?

All 63 clauses of the document can be found here.

The document can be divided into sections :

The first clauses concern the position of the Catholic Church in England.

Those that follow state that John will be less harsh on the barons.

Many of the clauses concern England's legal system.

Magna Carta promised laws that were good and fair. It states that everyone shall have access to courts and that costs and money should not be an issue if someone wanted to take a problem to the law courts.

It also states that no freeman (i.e. a person who was not a serf) will be imprisoned or punished without first going through the proper legal system. In future years the word "freeman" was replaced by "no one" to include everybody.

The last few sections deal with how the Magna Carta would be enforced in England. Twenty five barons were given the responsibility of making sure the king carried out what was stated in the Magna Carta - the document clearly states that they could use force if they felt it was necessary. To give the Magna Carta an impact, the royal seal of King

John was put on it to show people that it had his royal support. This is the largest red seal at the bottom of the Magna Carta above. In detail it looked like this :

King John's royal seal

Magna Carta Transcript

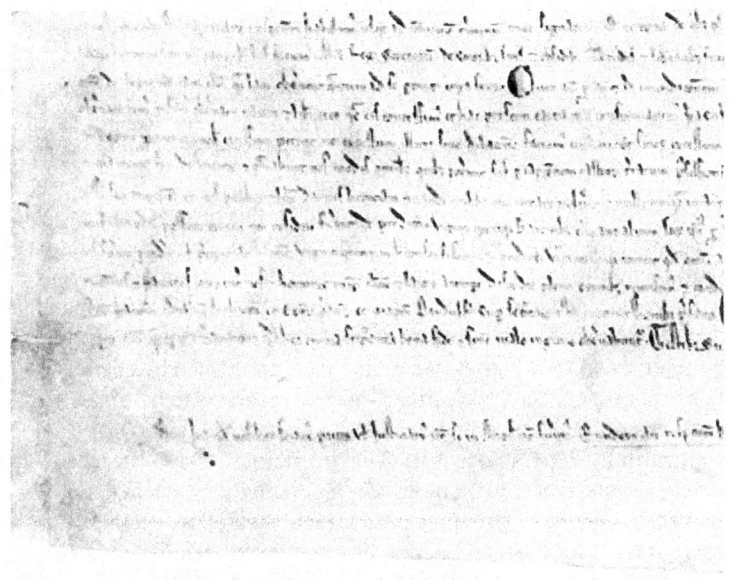

The Magna Carta (Great Charter)
Below are listed the 63 clauses of the Magna Carta (Great Charter) signed on 15th June, 1215 at Runnymeade by King John and the barons of Medieval England.

John, by the grace of God King of England, Lord of Ireland, Duke of Normandy and Aquitaine, and Count of Anjou, to his archbishops, bishops, abbots, earls, barons, justices, foresters, sheriffs, stewards, servants, and to all his officials and loyal subjects, greeting.

Know that before God, for the health of our soul and those of our ancestors and heirs, to the honour of God, the exaltation of the holy Church, and the better ordering of our kingdom, at the advice of our reverend fathers Stephen, archbishop of Canterbury, primate of all England, and cardinal of the holy Roman Church, Henry archbishop of Dublin, William bishop of London, Peter bishop of Winchester, Jocelin bishop of Bath and Glastonbury, Hugh bishop of Lincoln, Walter Bishop of Worcester, William bishop of Coventry, Benedict bishop of

Rochester, Master Pandulf subdeacon and member of the papal household, Brother Aymeric master of the Knights of the Temple in England, William Marshal, earl of Pembroke, William earl of Salisbury, William earl of Warren, William earl of Arundel, Alan de Galloway constable of Scotland, Warin Fitz Gerald, Peter Fitz Herbert, Hubert de Burgh seneschal of Poitou, Hugh de Neville, Matthew Fitz Herbert, Thomas Basset, Alan Basset, Philip Daubeny, Robert de Roppeley, John Marshal, John Fitz Hugh, and other loyal subjects:

1. First, that we have granted to God, and by this present charter have confirmed for us and our heirs in perpetuity, that the English Church shall be free, and shall have its rights undiminished, and its liberties unimpaired. That we wish this so to be observed, appears from the fact that of our own free will, before the outbreak of the present dispute between us and our barons, we granted and confirmed by charter the freedom of the Church's elections - a right reckoned to be of the greatest necessity and importance to it - and caused this to be confirmed by Pope Innocent III. This freedom we shall observe ourselves, and desire to be observed in good faith by our heirs in perpetuity. We have also granted to all free men of our realm, for us and our heirs for ever, all the liberties written out below, to have and to keep for them and their heirs, of us and our heirs:

2. If any earl, baron, or other person that holds lands directly of the Crown, for military service, shall die, and at his death his heir shall be of full age and owe a 'relief', the heir shall have his inheritance on payment of the ancient scale of 'relief'. That is to say, the heir or heirs of an earl shall pay £100 for the entire earl's barony, the heir or heirs of a knight 100 schillings at most for the entire knight's 'fee', and any man that owes less shall pay less, in accordance with the ancient usage of 'fees'

3. But if the heir of such a person is under age and a ward, when he comes of age he shall have his inheritance without 'relief' or fine.

4. The guardian of the land of an heir who is under age shall take from it only reasonable revenues, customary dues, and feudal services. He shall do this without destruction or damage to men or property. If we have given the guardianship of the land to a sheriff, or to any person answerable to us for the revenues, and he commits destruction or damage, we will exact compensation from him, and the land shall be entrusted to two worthy and prudent men of the same 'fee', who shall be

answerable to us for the revenues, or to the person to whom we have assigned them. If we have given or sold to anyone the guardianship of such land, and he causes destruction or damage, he shall lose the guardianship of it, and it shall be handed over to two worthy and prudent men of the same 'fee', who shall be similarly answerable to us.

5. For so long as a guardian has guardianship of such land, he shall maintain the houses, parks, fish preserves, ponds, mills, and everything else pertaining to it, from the revenues of the land itself. When the heir comes of age, he shall restore the whole land to him, stocked with plough teams and such implements of husbandry as the season demands and the revenues from the land can reasonably bear.

6. Heirs may be given in marriage, but not to someone of lower social standing. Before a marriage takes place, it shall be' made known to the heir's next-of-kin.

7. At her husband's death, a widow may have her marriage portion and inheritance at once and without trouble. She shall pay nothing for her dower, marriage portion, or any inheritance that she and her husband held jointly on the day of his death. She may remain in her husband's house for forty days after his death, and within this period her dower shall be assigned to her.

8. No widow shall be compelled to marry, so long as she wishes to remain without a husband. But she must give security that she will not marry without royal consent, if she holds her lands of the Crown, or without the consent of whatever other lord she may hold them of.

9. Neither we nor our officials will seize any land or rent in payment of a debt, so long as the debtor has movable goods sufficient to discharge the debt. A debtor's sureties shall not be distrained upon so long as the debtor himself can discharge his debt. If, for lack of means, the debtor is unable to discharge his debt, his sureties shall be answerable for it. If they so desire, they may have the debtor's lands and rents until they have received satisfaction for the debt that they paid for him, unless the debtor can show that he has settled his obligations to them.

10. If anyone who has borrowed a sum of money from Jews dies before the debt has been repaid, his heir shall pay no interest on the debt for so long as he remains under age, irrespective of whom he holds his lands. If such a debt falls into the hands of the Crown, it will take nothing except the principal sum specified in the bond.

11. If a man dies owing money to Jews, his wife may have her dower and pay nothing towards the debt from it. If he leaves children that are under age, their needs may also be provided for on a scale appropriate to the size of his holding of lands. The debt is to be paid out of the residue, reserving the service due to his feudal lords. Debts owed to persons other than Jews are to be dealt with similarly.

12. No 'scutage' or 'aid' may be levied in our kingdom without its general consent, unless it is for the ransom of our person, to make our eldest son a knight, and (once) to marry our eldest daughter. For these purposes ouly a reasonable 'aid' may be levied. 'Aids' from the city of London are to be treated similarly.

13. The city of London shall enjoy all its ancient liberties and free customs, both by land and by water. We also will and grant that all other cities, boroughs, towns, and ports shall enjoy all their liberties and free customs.

14. To obtain the general consent of the realm for the assessment of an 'aid' - except in the three cases specified above - or a 'scutage', we will cause the archbishops, bishops, abbots, earls, and greater barons to be summoned individually by letter. To those who hold lands directly of us we will cause a general summons to be issued, through the sheriffs and other officials, to come together on a fixed day (of which at least forty days notice shall be given) and at a fixed place. In all letters of summons, the cause of the summons will be stated. When a summons has been issued, the business appointed for the day shall go forward in accordance with the resolution of those present, even if not all those who were summoned have appeared.

15. In future we will allow no one to levy an 'aid' from his free men, except to ransom his person, to make his eldest son a knight, and (once) to marry his eldest daughter. For these purposes only a reasonable 'aid' may be levied.

16. No man shall be forced to perform more service for a knight's 'fee', or other free holding of land, than is due from it.

17. Ordinary lawsuits shall not follow the royal court around, but shall be held in a fixed place.

18. Inquests of *novel disseisin*, *mort d'ancestor*, and *darrein presentment* shall be taken only in their proper county court. We ourselves, or in our absence abroad our chief justice, will send two

justices to each county four times a year, and these justices, with four knights of the county elected by the county itself, shall hold the assizes in the county court, on the day and in the place where the court meets.

19. If any assizes cannot be taken on the day of the county court, as many knights and freeholders shall afterwards remain behind, of those who have attended the court, as will suffice for the administration of justice, having regard to the volume of business to be done.

20. For a trivial offence, a free man shall be fined only in proportion to the degree of his offence, and for a serious offence correspondingly, but not so heavily as to deprive him of his livelihood. In the same way, a merchant shall be spared his merchandise, and a husbandman the implements of his husbandry, if they fall upon the mercy of a royal court. None of these fines shall be imposed except by the assessment on oath of reputable men of the neighbourhood.

21. Earls and barons shall not be amerced save through their peers, and only according to the measure of the offence.

22. No clerk shall be amerced for his lay tenement ecept according to the manner of the other persons aforesaid; and not according to the amount of his ecclesiastical benefice.

23. Neither a town nor a man shall be forced to make bridges over the rivers, with the exception of those who, from of old and of right ought to do it.

24. No sheriff, constable, coroners, or other bailiffs of ours shall hold the pleas of our crown.

25. All counties, hundreds, wapentakes, and trithings - our demesne manors being exccepted - shall continue according to the old farms, without any increase at all.

26. If any one holding from us a lay fee shall die, and our sheriff or bailiff can show our letters patent containing our summons for the debt which the dead man owed to us, our sheriff or bailiff may be allowed to attach and enroll the chattels of the dead man to the value of that debt, through view of lawful men; in such way, however, that nothing shall be removed thence until the debt is paid which was plainly owed to us. And the residue shall be left to the executors that they may carry out the will of the dead man. And if nothing is owed to us by him, all the

chattels shall go to the use prescribed by the deceased, saving their reasonable portions to his wife and children.

27. If any freeman shall have died intestate his chattels shall be distributed through the hands of his near relatives and friends, by view of the church; saving to any one the debts which the dead man owed him.

28. No constable or other bailiff of ours shall take the corn or other chattels of any one except he straightway give money for them, or can be allowed a respite in that regard by the will of the seller.

29. No constable shall force any knight to pay money for castleward if he be willing to perform that ward in person, or - he for a reasonable cause not being able to perform it himself - through another proper man. And if we shall have led or sent him on a military expedition, he shall be quit of ward according to the amount of time during which, through us, he shall have been in military service.

30. No sheriff nor bailiff of ours, nor any one else, shall take the horses or carts of any freeman for transport, unless by the will of that freeman.

31. Neither we nor our bailiffs shall take another's wood for castles or for other private uses, unless by the will of him to whom the wood belongs.

32. We shall not hold the lands of those convicted of felony longer than a year and a day; and then the lands shall be restored to the lords of the fiefs.

33. Henceforth all the weirs in the Thames and Medway, and throughout all England, save on the sea-coast, shall be done away with entirely.

34. Henceforth the writ which is called Praecipe shall not be to served on any one for any holding so as to cause a free man to lose his court.

35. There shall be one measure of wine throughout our whole realm, and one measure of ale and one measure of corn - namely, the London quart - and one width of dyed and russet and hauberk cloths - namely, two ells below the selvage. And with weights, moreover, it shall be as with measures.

36. Henceforth nothing shall be given or taken for a writ of inquest in a matter concerning life or limb; but it shall be conceded gratis, and shall not be denied.

37. If any one hold of us in fee-farm, or in socage, or in burkage, and hold land of another by military service, we shall not, by reason of that fee-farm, or socage, or burkage, have the wardship of his heir or of his land which is held in fee from another. Nor shall we have the wardship of that fee-farm, or socage, or burkage unless that fee-farm owe military service. We shall not, by reason of some petit-serjeanty which some one holds of us through the service of giving us knives or arrows or the like, have the wardship of his heir or of the land which he holds of another by military service.

38. No bailiff, on his own simple assertion, shall henceforth any one to his law, without producing faithful witnesses in evidence.

39. No freeman shall be taken, or imprisoned, or disseized, or outlawed, or exiled, or in any way harmed - nor will we go upon or send upon him - save by the lawful judgment of his peers or by the law of the land.

40. To none will we sell, to none deny or delay, right or justice.

41. All merchants may safely and securely go out of England, and come into England, and delay and pass through England, as well by land as by water, for the purpose of buying and selling, free from all evil taxes, subject to the ancient and right customs - save in time of war, and if they are of the land at war against us. And if such be found in our land at the beginning of the war, they shall be held, without harm to their bodies and goods, until it shall be known to us or our chief justice how the merchants of our land are to be treated who shall, at that time, be found in the land at war against us. And if ours shall be safe there, the others shall be safe in our land.

42. Henceforth any person, saving fealty to us, may go out of our realm and return to it, safely and securely, by land and by water, except perhaps for a brief period in time of war, for the common good of the realm. But prisoners and outlaws are excepted according to the law of the realm; also people of a land at war against us, and the merchants, with regard to whom shall be done as we have said.

43. If a man holds lands of any 'escheat' - such as from the honour of Walingford, Nottingham, Boloin, Lancaster, or the other escheats which are in our hands and are baronies - and shall die, his heir shall not give another relief, nor shall he perform for us other service than he

would perform for a baron if that barony were in the hand of a baron; and we shall hold it in the same way in which the baron has held it.

44. Persons dwelling without the forest shall not henceforth come before the forest justices, through common summonses, unless they are impleaded or are the sponsors of some person or persons attached for matters concerning the forest.

45. We will not make men justices, constables, sheriffs, or bailiffs unless they are such as know the law of the realm, and are minded to observe it rightly.

46. All barons who have founded abbeys for which they have charters of the King of England, or ancient right of tenure, shall have, as they ought to have, their custody when vacant.

47. All forests constituted as such in our time shall straightway be annulled; and the same shall be done for river banks made into places of defence by us in our time.

48. All evil customs concerning forests and warrens, and concerning foresters and warreners, sheriffs and their servants, river banks and their guardians, shall straightway be inquired into each county, through twelve sworn knights from that county, and shall be eradicated by them, entirely, so that they shall never be renewed, within forty days after the inquest has been made; in such manner that we shall first know about them, or our justice if we be not in England.

49. We shall straightway return all hostages and charters which were delivered to us by Englishmen as a surety for peace or faithful service.

50. We shall entirey remove from their bailwicks the relatives of Gerard de Athyes, so that they shall henceforth have no bailwick in England: Engelard de Cygnes, Andrew Peter and Gyon de Chanceles, Gyon de Cygnes, Geoffrey de Martin and his brothers, Philip Mark and his brothers, and Geoffrey his nephew, and the whole following of them.

51. And straightway after peace is restored we shall remove from the realm all the foreign soldiers, crossbowmen, servants, hirelings, who may have come with horses and arms to the harm of the realm.

52. If any one shall have been disseized by us, or removed, without a legal sentence of his peers, from his lands, castles, liberties or lawful right, we shall straightway restore them to him. And if a dispute shall

arise concerning this matter it shall be settled according to the judgment of the twenty-five barons who are mentioned below as sureties for the peace. But with regard to all those things of which any one was, by King Henry our father or King Richard our brother, disseized or dispossessed without legal judgment of his peers, which we have in our hand or which others hold, and for which we ought to give a guarantee: We shall have respite until the common term for crusaders. Except with regard to those concerning which a plea was moved, or an inquest made by our order, before we took the cross. But when we return from our pilgrimage, or if, by chance, we desist from our pilgrimage, we shall straightway then show full justice regarding them.

53. We shall have the same respite, moreover, and in the same manner, in the matter of showing justice with regard to forests to be annulled and forests to remain, which Henry our father or Richard our brother constituted; and in the matter of wardships of lands which belong to the fee of another - wardships of which kind we have hitherto enjoyed by reason of the fee which some one held from us in military service - and in the matter of abbeys founded in the fee of another than ourselves - in which the lord of the fee may say that he has jurisdiction. And when we return, or if we desist from our pilgrimage, we shall straightway exhibit full justice to those complaining with regard to these matters.

54. No one shall be taken or imprisoned on account of the appeal of a woman concerning the death of another than her husband.

55. All fines imposed by us unjustly and contrary to the law of the land, and all amerciaments made unjustly and contrary to the law of the land, shall be altogether remitted, or it shall be done with regard to them according to the judgment of the twenty five barons mentioned below as sureties for the peace, or according to the judgment of the majority of them together with the aforesaid Stephen archbishop of Canterbury, if he can be present, and with others whom he may wish to associate with himself for this purpose. And if he can not be present, the affair shall nevertheless proceed without him; in such way that, if one or more of the said twenty five barons shall be concerned in a similar complaint, they shall be removed as to this particular decision, and, in their place, for this purpose alone, others shall be subtituted who shall be chosen and sworn by the remainder of those twenty five.

56. If we have disseized or dispossessed Welshmen of their lands or liberties or other things without legal judgment of their peers, in

England or in Wales, they shall straightway be restored to them. And if a dispute shall arise concerning this, then action shall be taken upon it in the March through judgment of their peers - concerning English holdings according to the law of England, concerning Welsh holdings according to the law of Wales, concerning holdings in the March according to the law of the March. The Welsh shall do likewise with regard to us and our subjects.

57. But with regard to all those things of which any one of the Welsh by King Henry our father or King Richard our brother, disseized or dispossessed without legal judgment of his peers, which we have in our hand or which others hold, and for which we ought to give a guarantee: we shall have respite until the common term for crusaders. Except with regard to those concerning which a plea was moved, or an inquest made by our order, before we took the cross. But when we return from our pilgrimage, or if, by chance, we desist from our pilgrimage, we shall straightway then show full justice regarding them, according to the laws of Wales and the aforesaid districts.

58. We shall straightway return the son of Llewelin and all the Welsh hostages, and the charters delivered to us as surety for the peace.

59. We shall act towards Alexander King of the Scots regarding the restoration of his sisters, and his hostages, and his liberties and his lawful right, as we shall act towards our other barons of England; unless it ought to be otherwise according to the charters which we hold from William, his father, the former King of the Scots. And this shall be done through judgment of his peers in our court.

60. Moreover all the subjects of our realm, clergy as well as laity, shall, as far as pertains to them, observe, with regard to their vassals, all these aforesaid customs and liberties which we have decreed shall, as far as pertains to us, be observed in our realm with regard to our own.

61. Inasmuch as, for the sake of God, and for the bettering of our realm, and for the more ready healing of the discord which has arisen between us and our barons, we have made all these aforesaid concessions, wishing them to enjoy for ever entire and firm stability, we make and grant to them the following security: that the baron, namely, may elect at their pleaure twenty five barons from the realm, who ought, with all their strength, to observe, maintain and cause to be observed, the peace and privileges which we have granted to them and confirmed by this our present charter. In such wise, namely, that if we, or our justice, or

our bailiffs, or any one of our servants shall have transgressed against any one in any respect, or shall have broken one of the articles of peace or security, and our transgression shall have been shown to four barons of the aforesaid twenty five: those four barons shall come to us, or, if we are abroad, to our justice, showing to us our error; and they shall ask us to cause that error to be amended without delay. And if we do not amend that error, or, we being abroad, if our justice do not amend it within a term of forty days from the time when it was shown to us or, we being abroad, to our justice: the aforesaid four barons shall refer the matter to the remainder of the twenty five barons, and those twenty five barons, with the whole land in common, shall distrain and oppress us in every way in their power - namely, by taking our castles, lands and possessions, and in every other way that they can, until amends shall have been made according to their judnnent. Saving the persons of ourselves, our queen and our children. And when amends shall have been made they shall be in accord with us as they had been previously. And whoever of the land wishes to do so, shall swear that in carrying out all the aforesaid measures he will obey the mandates of the aforesaid twenty five barons, and that, with them, he will oppress us to the extent of his power. And, to any one who wishes to do so, we publicly and freely give permission to swear; and we will never prevent any one from swearing. Moreover, all those in the land who shall be unwilling, themselves and of their own accord, to swear to the twenty five barons as to distraining and oppressing us with them: such ones we shall make to wear by our mandate, as has been said. And if any one of the twenty five barons shall die, or leave the country, or in any other way be prevented from carrying out the aforesaid measures,--the remainder of the aforesaid twenty five barons shall choose another in his place, according to their judgment, who shall be sworn in the same way as the others. Moreover, in all things entrusted to those twenty five barons to be carried out, if those twenty five shall be present and chance to disagree among themselves with regard to some matter, or if some of them, having been summoned, shall be unwilling or unable to be present: that which the majority of those present shall decide or decree shall be considered binding and valid, just as if all the twenty five had consented to it. And the aforesaid twenty five shall swear that they will faithfully observe all the foregoing, and will caue them be observed to the extent of their power. And we shall obtain nothing from any one, either through ourselves or through another, by which any of those concessions and liberties may be revoked or diminished. And if any such thing shall have been obtained, it shall be vain and invalid, and we shall never make use of it either through ourselves or through another.

62. And we have fully remitted to all, and pardoned, all the ill-will, anger and rancour which have arisen between us and our subjects, clergy and laity, from the time of the struggle. Moreover have fully remitted to all, clergy and laity, and - as far as pertains to us - have pardoned fully all the transgressions committed, on the occasion of that same struggle, from Easter of the sixteenth year of our reign until the re-establishment of peace. In witness of which, more-over, we have caused to be drawn up for them letters patent of lord Stephen, archbishop of Canterbury, lord Henry, archbishop of Dubland the aforesaid bishops and master Pandulf, regarding that surety and the aforesaid concessions.

63. Wherefore we will and firmly decree that the English church shall be free, and that the subjects of our realm shall have and hold all the aforesaid liberties, rights and concessions, duly and in peace, freely and quietly, fully and entirely, for themselves and their heirs from us and our heirs, in all matters and in all places, forever, as has been said. Moreover it has been sworn, on our part as well as on the part of the barons, that all these above mentioned provisions shall observed with good faith and without evil intent. The witnesses being the above mentioned and many others. Given through our hand, in the plain called Runnymede between Windsor and Stanes, on the fifteenth day of June, in the seventeenth year of our reign.

William d'Aubigny, 1st Earl of Arundel[1]
M, #102250, d. 12 October 1176

Last Edited=18 Aug 2011

William **d'Aubigny**, 1st Earl of Arundel was the son of Guillaume **d'Aubigny** and Maud le **Bigod**.[2] He married Adeliza **de Louvain**, daughter of Godefroi I **de Louvain, Duc de Basse-Lorraine** and Ida **de Namur, Comtesse de Namur**, in 1138.[3,2] He died on 12 October 1176 at Waverley Abbey, Surrey, England. He was buried at Wymondham Priory, Norfolk, England.[2]

He was created *1st Earl of Arundel [ENGLAND]* circa 1138.[2] He held the office of Lord of the Manor of Buckenham, Norfolk in 1139.[2] In

1139 he gave shelter to the Empress Maud at Arundel Castle, but ever after adhered to King Stephen.[2] In 1153 he was influential in arranging the treaty where King Stephen retained the crown for life, but with Henry II as heir.[2] In 1163/64 he was one of the embassy to Rome.[2] In 1168 he was one of the embassy to Saxony.[2] He was commander of the Royal army in Normandy, against the King's rebellious sons, where he distinguished himself with "swiftness and velocity" in August 1173.[2] He fought in the battle near Bury St. Edmunds on 29 September 1173, where he assisted in the defeat of the Earl of Leicester who had, with his Flemings, invaded Suffolk.[2] He has an extensive biographical entry in the *Dictionary of National Biography*.[4]

Children of William d'Aubigny, 1st Earl of Arundel and Adeliza de Louvain

1. Reynor **d'Aubigny**[1]
2. Henry **d'Aubigny**[1]
3. Geoffrey **d'Aubigny**[1]
4. Alice **d'Aubigny**+[1] d. 11 Sep 1188
5. Olivia **d'Aubigny**[1]
6. Agatha **d'Aubigny**[1]
7. William **d'Aubigny**, 2nd Earl of Arundel+[2] b. b 1150, d. 24 Dec 1193

Citations
1. [S106] Royal Genealogies Website (ROYAL92.GED), online ftp://ftp.cac.psu.edu/genealogy/public_html/royal/index.html. Hereinafter cited as Royal Genealogies Website.
2. [S6] G.E. Cokayne; with Vicary Gibbs, H.A. Doubleday, Geoffrey H. White, Duncan Warrand and Lord Howard de Walden, editors, *The Complete Peerage of England, Scotland, Ireland, Great Britain and the United Kingdom, Extant, Extinct or Dormant, new ed.*, 13 volumes in 14 (1910-1959; reprint in 6 volumes, Gloucester, U.K.: Alan Sutton Publishing, 2000), volume I, page 233. Hereinafter cited as *The Complete Peerage*.

3. [S11] Alison Weir, *Britain's Royal Families: The Complete Genealogy* (London, U.K.: The Bodley Head, 1999), page 48. Hereinafter cited as *Britain's Royal Families*.
4. [S18] Matthew H.C.G., editor, *Dictionary of National Biography on CD-ROM* (Oxford, U.K.: Oxford University Press, 1995). Hereinafter cited as *Dictionary of National Biography*.

Descendants of Robert Durban

Generation No. 1

1. ROBERT¹ DURBAN

Notes for ROBERT DURBAN:
Durban, Durbarn, Robert: 1495. General, England, Calendar of Wills and Administrations now preserved in the Probate Registry at Canterbury 1396-1558 (Will). Durban, Durbarn, Ivychurch C. 4 69 1495.

Child of ROBERT DURBAN is:
2.   i.   EDWARD N.² DURBIN, b. 1490.

Generation No. 2

2. EDWARD N.² DURBIN *(ROBERT¹ DURBAN)* was born 1490. He married HANNAH, daughter of RICHARD WOODWARD. She was born 1491, and died 1557.

Notes for EDWARD N. DURBIN:
Durban, Durbarn, Robert: 1495. General, England, Calendar of Wills and Administrations now preserved in the Probate Registry at Canterbury 1396-1558 (Will). Durban, Durbarn, Ivychurch C. 4 69 1495.

Aubigny, Nigel d' - From St. Martin d'Aubigny near Coutances. Eldest son took name of Mowbray, ancestor of dukes of Norfolk. Large holdings in Beds., Bucks., Leics., Warwicks.
Durham, William, Bishop of - Bishop of Durham, 1082-96. Chief justice and Domesday commissioner, driven from see by William Rufus. Abbey holdings in 9 counties from Yorks. to Beds.
Keynes, William of - Sheriff of Northamptonshire.

Doomsday Book and Little Doomsday Book: During the last years of his reign, King William (the Conqueror) had his power threatened from a number of quarters. The greatest threats came from King Canute IV of Denmark and King Olaf III of Norway. In the Eleventh Century, part of the taxes raised went into a fund called the Danegeld, which was kept to buy off marauding Danish armies. One of the most likely reasons for the record to be commissioned was for William to see how much tax he was getting from the country, and therefore how much Danegeld was available. Each record includes, for each settlement in England, its monetary value and any customary dues owed to the Crown at the time of the survey, values recorded before Domesday, and values from before 1066.

The Domesday survey is far more than just a physical record though. It is a detailed statement of lands held by the king and by his tenants and of the resources that went with those lands. It records which manors rightfully belonged to which estates, thus ending years of confusion resulting from the gradual and sometimes violent dispossession of the Anglo-Saxons by their Norman conquerors. It was moreover a 'feudal' statement, giving the identities of the tenants-in-chief (landholders) who held their lands directly from the Crown, and of their tenants and under tenants. The fact that the scheme was executed and brought to complete fruition in two years is a tribute of the political power and formidable will of William the Conqueror.

One of the most important near-contemporary accounts of the making of the Domesday survey is that of the Anglo-Saxon chronicler. He tells us that William:

"...had much though and very deep discussion about this country - how it was occupied or with what sorts of people. Then he sent his men all over England into every shire and had them find out how many hundred hides there were, or what land and cattle the king himself had, or what dues he ought to have in twelve months.

Also he had a record made of how much land his Archbishops had, and his Bishops and his Abbots and his Earls, and ... what or how much everybody had who was occupying land in England, in land or cattle, and how much money it was worth. ...there was no single hide nor a yard of land, nor indeed one ox nor one cow nor one pig which was there left out: and all these records were brought to him afterwards."

An important first-hand account of the survey was written by Robert, Bishop of Hereford, one of the ecclesiastics who William had brought to England. The king's men, he wrote,
"...made a survey of all England; of the lands in each of the counties; of the possessions of each of the magnates, their lands, their habitations, their men, both bond and free, living in huts or with their own houses or land; of ploughs, horses and other animals; of the services and payments due from each and every estate.

After these investigators came others who were sent to unfamiliar counties to check the first description and to denounce and wrong-doers to the king. And the land was troubled with many calamities arising from the gathering of the royal taxes."

Firstly, existing information about manors, people and assets was collected, including documents dating from the Anglo-Saxon period and post-1066 which listed lands and taxes in existence, and which were held both in the principal royal city of Winchester and in the shires. Also, each tenant-in-chief, whether bishop, abbot or baron, and each sheriff and other local official, was required to send in a list of manors and men.

To verify or correct this information, commissioners were assigned sections of England called circuits and travelled around the country; in every town, village and hamlet, the commissioners asked the same questions to everyone with interest in land from the barons to the villagers. As written in The Ely Inquest, a contemporary publication at the time,

"...They inquired what the manor was called; who held it at the time of King Edward; who holds it now; how many hides there are; how many ploughs in demesne (held by the lord) and how many belonging to the men; how many villagers; how many cottagers; how many slaves; how many freemen; how many sokemen; how much woodland; how much meadow; how much pasture; how many mills; how many fisheries; how much had been added to or taken away from the estate; what it used to be worth altogether; what it is worth now; and how much each freeman and sokeman had and has.

The term **soke** (/ˈsoʊk/; in Old English: *soc*, connected ultimately with *secan*, "to seek"), at the time of the Norman conquest of England generally denoted "jurisdiction", but due to vague usage probably lacks a single precise definition.

In some cases *soke* denoted the right to hold a court, and in others only the right to receive the fines and forfeitures of the men over whom it was granted when they had been condemned in a court of competent jurisdiction. Its primary meaning seems to have involved *seeking*; thus *soka faldae* was the duty of seeking the lord's court, just as *secta ad molendinum* was the duty of seeking the lord's mill. The *Leges* also speaks of pleas *in socna, id est, in quaestione sua* (pleas which are in his investigation).

Evidently, however, not long after the Norman Conquest considerable doubt prevailed about the correct meaning of the word. In some versions of the much-used tract *Interpretationes vocabulorum* soke is defined:*aver fraunc court*, and in others as *interpellacio maioris audientiae*, which glosses somewhat ambiguously as *claim ajustis et requeste*.

The word *soke* also frequently appears in association with *sak* or *sake* in the alliterative jingle *sake and soke*, but the two words lack etymological links. The word *sake* represents the Old English *sacu*, originally meaning "a matter or cause" (from *sacan* "to contend"), and later the right to have a court. The word *soke*, however, appears more commonly and appears to have had a wider range of meaning.

The term *soke*, unlike *sake*, sometimes applied to the district over which the right of jurisdiction extended (compare Soke of Peterborough).

Adolphus Ballard argued that the interpretation of the word "soke" as *jurisdiction* should be accepted only where it stands for the fuller phrase, "sake and soke", and that "soke" standing by itself denoted services.

Certainly, many passages in the Domesday Book support this contention, but in other passages "soke" seems to serve merely as a short expression for "sake and soke". The difficulties about the correct interpretation of these words will probably not unravel until historians elucidate more fully the normal functions and jurisdiction of the various local courts.

A **sokeman** belonged to a class of tenants, found chiefly in the eastern counties, occupying an intermediate position between the free tenants and the bond tenants or villeins. As a general rule they had personal freedom, but performed many of the agricultural services of the villeins. Historians generally suppose they bore the rank of "sokemen" because they belonged within a lord's *soke* or jurisdiction. Ballard, however, held that a sokeman was merely a man who rendered services, and that a **sokeland** was land from which services were rendered, and was not necessarily under the jurisdiction of a manor.

The law term, **socage**, used of this tenure, arose by adding the French suffix *-age* to *soc*.

All this was to be recorded thrice, namely as it was in the time of King Edward, as it was when King William gave it and as it is now. And it was also to be noted whether more could be taken than is now being taken."

The mass of evidence produced was written down in Latin - as was the survey as a whole - and this was then sorted several times until it could be put into counties, landholders, hundreds or wapentakes, and manors.

Little and Great Domesday

The Domesday Book was never completely finished; it was left in two volumes, one called Great Domesday and the other Little Domesday: Little Domesday - Records for Essex, Norfolk and Suffolk which were the final locations for the commissioners' work. They were probably not included in the main collection because King William died before all the records had been given to the principal scribe. The records are much longer than in Great Domesday and provide an insight into the extent of the information collected by the commissioners, and just how much had to be cut out to make the final version.

Great Domesday - A shire summary making up the main content of the Domesday volumes gathered from past records and new information gathered by the Commissioners.

Children of EDWARD DURBIN and HANNAH are:
- i. FLORENCE^3 DURBIN.
- ii. JOAN DURBIN.
- iii. JOHN DURBIN.
3.   iv. WALTER DURBIN, b. Abt. 1538, Axbridge, Somerset, England; d. February 02, 1603/04.

Generation No. 3

3. WALTER^3 DURBIN *(EDWARD N.^{2}, ROBERT^1 DURBAN)* was born Abt. 1538 in Axbridge, Somerset, England, and died February 02, 1603/04. He married (1) ALICE. She was born 1490 in England, and died September 15, 1564 in Axbridge, Somerset, England. He married (2) JOAN ADAMS.

Notes for WALTER DURBIN:
Walter Durban, cordwainer and Mayor of Axbridge (in 1560 and 1580), was born ca 1538, d. 2 Feb. 1604; bur. 6 Feb 1604 at Axbridge. His Inq. Post Mortem was held in 1604. About 1560 Christopher Kyrton (son of Richard and Elizabeth Kyrton) devised a message to Walter Durban of Axbridge (A: cities Axbridge Town Deeds). Walter was a shoemaker of Axbridge, and held land in Bedgeworth, near Wedmore.

Nov 26, 1996 The following is a transcription of notes taken by William P. Durbin and Lorraine B. Durbin in September 1977 at the Society of Genealogists, London, England. Unfortunately, time was short and expensive; thus, details on the source of information within the stacks of the Society are incomplete.

Where such sources were noted, they will be listed in this account. Also, the significance of the information many times is not clear inasmuch as the data was codified in the original text.

Card Index notes Durbin as one of 17 spellings in the Society files: Durban, Dawberne, Durburnh, Dawborn(e), Durborne, Dauburne, Durbin, Dawbarn, Durbon, Daubin, Dawbin, Durbun, Darben, Darbourn, Derbern, Dobbyn, Dabon

MARRIAGES
1652: (Newington, Kent) Marie Durban & William Humfry
1652: (Swithin) Chris Durban & Elz. Malpas
1627: (Sept 20): (Newington, Kent) Thos Durban & Dorothea Surgeon
1568: (Canterbury) Mgt Durban & Pet Veriar
1604: (Westbury-on-Tyne, Bristol) Harry Durbon & Anne Evans
1622: (Westbury-on-Tyne, Bristol) John Durbon & Mary West
1630: (Westbury-on-Tyne, Bristol) Jane Durbon & Thos Berrye

WILLS
Source: Pre-Court of Canterbury Wills 1558-1583, Vol III, British Record Society Ltd, 1898
1568: DURBANE (DURBOYNE), Thomas; Lympshawe, Somerset, 4 Sheffield
1580: DURBANE, Thomas, Axbridge, Wedmore, Somerset, 48 Arundell
1576: DURBAN, William, Clarcke, Vicar of Tickenham, Somerset, 13 Carew
Source: Administrations in the Pre Court of Canterbury: 1572 - 1580
1574: (29 August) DAROBORNE, Thomas. St. Benedict Grace Church (London) leather seller, to brother William D.

Miscellaneous Sources:
1631: DURBAN, Thomas the Elder of Cheddar, Somerset, will (20 St. John) pr. Nov 17 by relict Anne.
1618: DURBAN, Peter, Chippenham, Wilts. To Nath. Lukins, uncle of Thos D., so of Wm. D., s. dur. min. (NOTE: son during minority) of said Thos. D., 1618.

1615: DURBAN, Rd. (Richard), Easton in Gordano, Som. to Anne D., rel. 1615
1650: DURBAN, John; Portbury, Som.1658: DURBAN, Christopher; St. Mary Cole Ch, London
Source: Proc. in Chancery; In the Reign of Queen Elizabeth I

(1558 - 1603)

Plaintiff: Thomas Bulbeck
Defendant: Peter DURBAN
Suit: ...bill for discovery of frauds; Kingeston Seymour, Soms Chancery Proceedings, 1649-1714
(Estate of Richard DURBAN), defendant, widow HANNAH DURBIN and another; Uphill, Someret.
"Inhabitants of Bristol in 1696 "St. Thomas Parish, St. Thomas Street
Thomas DURBIN; 6 children: Thomas, John, Samuell, William, Alice and Mary _____, Redlife Street
Edward Durbin and Mary, wf.; 2 children: Edward and Elizabeth St. Michael Parish, in Colston's Almshouse on St. Michaels Hill
Susanah DURBINE   Elizabeth DURBIN
Grace DURBINSt. Nicholas Parish, Baldwin Street   John DURBIN, baker
Elizabeth DURBIN, wife   Children: Richard, John, George, Elizabeth
St. Mary le Port, 1632   Richard DURBAN -- Margarett Bruineford

MARRIAGES
1618: (Wedmore, Somerset) Thomas DURBAN & Hester Chalcroft
1630: (Wraxall, Somerset) Elizabeth DURBURNE & Jn. Crossman
1692: (Bristol, Somerset) John DURBAN & Elizabeth Hales
1628: (Salisbury, Somerset) Jn. DURBAN & Mgt Cook
POLL BOOK (1715)

1715: St. Thomas Parish --- Thomas DURBAN (freeholder)
        John DURBAN (soapmaker)
    St. Mary Redcliff --- Edward DURBAN (cordwainer)BONDS
1675 (June 7): marr. (Bristol) Edward DURBAN (DERBYN) (of Redcliffe) (cordwainer) and Elizabeth Powell at St. Philip

1681 (May 6): marr. (Bristol) Edward DURBAN (Redcliffe) (shoemaker), W., and Mary Tayler, St. Werburgh, aged 30 at St. Werburgh.
1668 (June 11): marr. (Bristol) John DURBAN, (Brockley, Somerset) (tailor) and Mary Willett, (Brockley) at St. Mark or St. Augustine
1692 (July 2): marr. (Bristol) John DURBAN (Bristol) (baker) and Eliz. Hales, at St. Peter.
1664 (Apr 20): marr. (Bristol) Richard DURBAN (Cheddar, Somerset) (yeoman) and Elizabeth Wrenthome, (Axbridge, Som) at St. Nicholas

MARRIAGES
1674, (22 Apr): Elizabeth DURBAN m. Thomas Somers
1699 (26 Dec): Thomas DURBAN m. Ann Jones

WILLS
1592: (Exeter) Thomas Paignton DURBORNE
1550: (Exeter, Devonshire) John Paignton DURBURN
1566: "   Robert Paignton DARBORNE
1555: "   John Paynton DURBURN, Sr.
1566: "   Robert Paynton DARBORNE
1584: "   Thomas Paington DORBREN
1697: (Surrey) (mariner) William DURBINE (Mother, Margaret)
1691: (London) Anthony DURBAN
1658: (London) Christopher DURBAN
1682: (Cheddar, Somerset) Richard DURBAND, alderman, yeoman
1560/1: (Canterbury) Margaret DURBAN
1657: (Axbridge, Som) Richard DURBAN, fuller
1613: (Almondesbury, Glouc) William DURBURNE

MARRIAGES
1681: marr. (Glouc) Edward DURBAN and Mary Tayler
1692: marr. (Glouc) John DURBAN and Elizabeth Hales

MISCELLANEOUS
1564: Listed in Somerset, Tho. DAWBORN (Congresbury)
1641: Listed in Portbury (somerset) John DURBAN

WILLS
1533, 9 Sep: will of Cecylie Bedford (Bristowe, Bristol) (St. Thomas)

cites "Alys DURBAN, my servant"
1532, 25 Jan: Jone Gurman (Yatton, Somerset) leaves " a cowe to the children of Robert DURBAN

MISCELLANEOUS

1581: Listed in Wells, Somerset, John DURBAN, a freeman
1571, 1 July: (account of Christopher Kyrton): (Cheddar) Thomas DURBAN,
draper; (Land in Axbridge belonging to Walter DURBAN); (also Thomas DURBIN); "estates granted for a term of life...to Walter and Edyth DURBAN and Richard, their son, 1 tenement in Bourough of Axbridge"
1577, 17 Jan: Thomas Leigh of Wells names his attorneys as Richard Byble and John DURBAN.
1582, 9 Mar: Richard Godwyn of Wells, in a deed, refers to "land of the Bishop of Bath and Welles on the east now in the tenure of John DURBAN"
1554, 31 Jul: In Register of Bishop (Gilbert) Bourne (of Bath and Wells) "...the like of Sir William DURBAN, clerk, to the vicarage of Tyknam, vacant by the deprivation of the last incumbent, on the presentation of Griffin Jones, of the city of Bristol"
1634/5, 23 Mar: In Assizes and General Gaol Delivery held at Taunton Castle "...that Thomas DURBAN and Richard Stayle, nowe committed gaol of this county shall be discharged...and not pay any charge to John Venn" (Apparently in 'gaol' for maliscious prosecution and summarily confined.)

WILLS

1726, 17 Oct: Bristol: Alice DURBIN, to brother Thomas ... and wife... to their children...to brother John and sister Mary, co-executors. (NOTE: unlike many wills of the period, Alice signed with a clear signature, not an X)
1613, Jan: Westbury, Henrie DURBERNE; dau. Jane

CHURCH RECORD (Westbury-on-Trym)
1606, 11 Jan: Christening, Jane, ye daughter of Henry DURBON
1607, 27 Sept: Christening, Mary, ye daughter of Henry DURBON
1611, 10 June: Burial, Mary, ye daughter of Henry DURBON

WEDDINGS IN ANCIENT PARISH OF Westbury-on-Trym (Bristol)
1565, 3 Nov: Phillip Pope & Elizabethe DURBON
1566, 15 Nov: John Willis & Joan DURBON
1574, 5 Feb: Thomas Collins & Edithe DURBON
1614, 27 Nov: John George & Annes DURBON
1620, 26 Aug: William Bowen & Joan DURBON
1622, 13 Oct: John DURBON & Marye Weste
1624, 9 Feb: Richard Halle & Agnes DURBIN
1630, 26 May: Thomas Berrye & Jane DURBON
1667, 29 Apr: William Periman & Elizabeth DURBEE

MISCELLANEOUS
1629, May: Constable Account (Manchester) ".....pd for Dyate and lodging of William DUBRIN
1684: Marriage bondsman Edward DURBAN, Bristol, cordwainer

SOMERSET WILLS from Exeter, Rawlins & Jones Frome 1952 -- abstracts of wills, mainly from the Holworthy Collection page 128: Thomas Harvey parson, Brockley, July 15, 1582/June 12, 1583, "godsons Richard and Thomas DURBAN--- 20 s(hillings)

Children of WALTER DURBIN and ALICE are:
4.   i.   RICHARD[4] DURBAN, b. 1560; d. August 24, 1618, Compton Magna.
      ii. THOMAS DURBAN, b. August 05, 1564; d. September 23, 1580; m. (1) UNKNOWN; m. (2) ELIZABETH LANDSDON, June 13, 1571.

Notes for THOMAS DURBAN:
Fuller of Axbridge and Wedmore, and Mayor of Axbridge in 1574.

Generation No. 4

4. RICHARD[4] DURBAN *(WALTER[3] DURBIN, EDWARD N.[2], ROBERT[1] DURBAN)* was born 1560, and died August 24, 1618 in Compton Magna.

Notes for RICHARD DURBAN:
His Inq. P.M. was held in 1638.

Child of RICHARD DURBAN is:
5.   i.   THOMAS[5] DURBIN, b. 1535; d. 1580.

Child of RICHARD DURBAN is:
       ii. RICHARD[5] DURBAN, b. Abt. 1615.

Generation No. 5

5. THOMAS[5] DURBIN *(RICHARD[4] DURBAN, WALTER[3] DURBIN, EDWARD N.[2], ROBERT[1] DURBAN)* was born 1535, and died 1580. He married MARY DOWNS. She died 1564.

Child of THOMAS DURBIN and MARY DOWNS is:
6.   i.   PETER[6] DURBIN, b. 1559, England; d. February 10, 1610/11, Chippenham, Wiltshire, England.

Generation No. 6

6. PETER[6] DURBIN *(THOMAS[5], RICHARD[4] DURBAN, WALTER[3] DURBIN, EDWARD N.[2], ROBERT[1] DURBAN)* was born 1559 in England, and died February 10, 1610/11 in Chippenham, Wiltshire, England.

Notes for PETER DURBIN:
In 1616 when his Inq. P.M. was held, he was styled "fuller" in Axbridge Town Deed, and elsewhere as Gentleman.

Child of PETER DURBIN is:
7.   i.   WILLIAM[7] DURBIN, b. January 18, 1589/90, Chippenham, Wiltshire, England; d. 1627, Chippenham, Wiltshire, England.

Generation No. 7

7. WILLIAM[7] DURBIN *(PETER[6], THOMAS[5], RICHARD[4] DURBAN, WALTER[3] DURBIN, EDWARD N.[2], ROBERT[1] DURBAN)* was born January 18, 1589/90 in Chippenham, Wiltshire, England, and died 1627 in Chippenham, Wiltshire, England. He married SARAH DURBIN. She was born 1600, and died 1621.

Children of WILLIAM DURBIN and SARAH DURBIN are:
          i.   MARY[8] DURBIN, m. THOMAS HOBBES.
         ii.   THOMAS DURBIN, b. 1614.
        iii. JANE DURBIN, b. 1617; d. Aft. 1657; m. MR. WILMOT.
8.   iv. WILLIAM DURBIN, b. 1620.
         v.   CHRISTOPHER THOMAS DURBIN, b. 1621, Gloucester, Cloucestershire, England; d. September 13, 1651, Baltimore, Maryland; m. MARY MARGARET BROWNE.
        vi. ANTHONY DURBIN, b. 1626.

Generation No. 8

8. WILLIAM[8] DURBIN *(WILLIAM[7], PETER[6], THOMAS[5], RICHARD[4] DURBAN, WALTER[3] DURBIN, EDWARD N.[2], ROBERT[1] DURBAN)* was born 1620.

Child of WILLIAM DURBIN is:
9.   i.   CHRISTOPHER THOMAS[9] DURBIN, b. August 31, 1621, Axebridge, Somerset, England; d. May 05, 1699, Axbridge, Somerset, England.

Generation No. 9

9. CHRISTOPHER THOMAS[9] DURBIN *(WILLIAM[8], WILLIAM[7], PETER[6], THOMAS[5], RICHARD[4] DURBAN, WALTER[3] DURBIN, EDWARD N.[2], ROBERT[1] DURBAN)* was born August 31, 1621 in Axebridge, Somerset, England, and died May 05, 1699 in Axbridge, Somerset, England. He married (1) MARY DOWNS, daughter of JOHN DOWNS and MARGARET HAMMOND. She was born 1668 in Norton, Suffolk, England, and died 1699 in Baltimore, Baltimore, MD. He married (2) ELIZABETH 1651. He married (3) MARGARET ELIZABETH BROWN 1652 in London, England, daughter of RICHARD BROWN. She was born 1621 in Westminster, London, England, and died September 13, 1652 in Westminster, London, England. He married (4) MARY DOWNS 1689 in Baltimore, Baltimore, MD, daughter of JOHN DOWNS and MARGARET HAMMOND. She was born 1668 in Norton, Suffolk, England, and died 1699 in Baltimore, Baltimore, MD.

Notes for CHRISTOPHER THOMAS DURBIN:
Baptism: 31 Aug 1651, St. Margaret's, Westminster, London. Arrived 1654, age 3, Nevis. Another source gives arrival 1662.

Thomas Durbin is listed in the taxable names taken by Selah Dorman, Constable of Potapsco Hundred, on the South Side of Back River in July Anno Dom. 1694. "Early parishes and hundreds, Baltimore County, MD, 1692, 1694, 1695." Baltimore, MD: Ida Charles Wilkins Foundation, 1954.

From the Maryland Historical Magazine:
October 13, 1676, Walter Dickerson, Planter, of Great Choptank, Talbot County, Maryland for 2,500 pounds of tobacco, conveys to Thomas Durbin of Severne, Ann Arundel County the 200 acres tract "Johnson" on the east side of Dickerson branch, on the east side of Welshmans Creek, on the north side of the Patapsco River. Sarah Dickerson releases dower.

Confirmation Deed: November 23, 1679, John Dickenson of Talbot County, brother of Walter Dickenson of same county, confirms to Thomas Durbin a sale covering the 200-acre tract "Johnston" on north side of Patapsco River, which was patented February 4, 1659-60, to John Dickenson, assigned by him December 23, 1662, to Walter Dickenson, and sold by the latter to Durbin. Witnesses: John Stroud, George Watt. Letter of attorney, November 23, 1679, John Dickenson of Talbot County appointing as attorney Michael (sic) Gibson or James Phillips to acknowledge in court a sale of 200 acres to Thomas Durbin. Witnesses: John Stroud, George Watt. Clerk Thomas Hedge certifies that on November 5 (sic) Mr. James Phillips as attorney acknowledge in court.

In April 20, 1682 there were two additional land grants for land adjacent to the "Johnson" tract, called "Thomas Addition" and "Westminster." Original records are contained in Land Office Registers, indexed starting on page vii of the introduction. Coldham, Peter Wilson, "Settlers of Maryland 1679-1783." Baltimore: Genealogical Publishing Co., Inc., 2002, page 203.

Baltimore rent rolls dated 1700-1720, Thomas Durbin, Baltimore County Hab-Nab-at-a-Venture 350 acres surveyed June 30, 1688 for Thomas Durbin, lying on North side of Patapsco River and belonging to orphants of said Durbin. This tract of land is the present site (1982) of the Druid Hill Park near John Hopkins University and the Baltimore Zoo.

Thomas Durbin witnessed the will of Jane Long on May 19, 1696. He died in the first part of 1699 or the later part of 1698 for his inventory was taken May 8, 1699, by Roger Newman, and totaled a substantial 13,158 pounds, with 60-02-8 due to the estate. Debts were paid out of the estate to John Smith, Captain Deen Cock, Roger Newman, John Thomas, Major Maxwell, and John Hall. Of particular interest is the following:

To ye funerall charges of Thomas Durbin and his wife
2 black walnutt coffins . . .

This shows that Thomas and his wife died at about the same time. It seems likely that death was sudden and unexpected, for no will was made. Perhaps it was the result of Indian problems.

Christopher Thomas Durbin Will, 23 Oct. 1709; Patapsco River, Baltimore, Maryland, British America, probate 28 Nov. 1709, death Abt 1709. Durbin, Christopher, to eldest son Thomas and younger son Christopher and hrs., dwelling plantation and land "Johnston." To son-in-law Simon Canon and dau.-in-law ___, personalty. To wife, Mary, extx., life interest in estate, and to have charge of children during their minority. Test: John Downs, Wm. Durbin, Elizabeth Holland. Part 2-12, p. 235.

"There are interesting stories and traditions handed down in every family, but one of the most interesting heard concerning the Durbin family is the connection of the City of Baltimore, Maryland, with one of the earliest Durbins. It seems a few years ago one of the Durbins' was doing research in Baltimore, and he ran across a document which indicated that a Durbin had become angry with his children and did not want any of them to have any of his estate. He leased all his lands to someone for 99 years with the stipulation that after that time the land was to return to his descendants, since all his children would have died before the 99 years had passed. In the ensuing 99 years the Durbins' moved out, and the people who had use of the and apparently forgot the deal, or simply ignored it.

The person finding the document in Baltimore contacted a lawyer with the idea of reclaiming the Durbin lands for the Durbin lands for the Durbin family, but was told that since so much time had passed, and since Baltimore was so built up, it would be impossible to get a court to issue a favorable verdict. So there the matter stands -- the City of Baltimore belongs to every Durbin living today " [Durbin-Logsdon Genealogy by Betty Jewell Durbin Carson]

Notes for MARY DOWNS:
Baptism: 20 Nov 1621, St. Olave, Bermondsey, Surrey, England.

Notes for MARGARET ELIZABETH BROWN:
The Will of George Brown:
In the name of God, Amen I, George Brown of Frederick County in the Province of Maryland being sick in health but of sound mind and memory Thanks be to God for it. .... to the c... of nature my departure draweth near, so this nineteenth day of February in the year of our Lord

seventeen hundred and sixty seven make and publish this my last will and testament in the manner and form following. That is to say Item: I will and bequeath unto my son, John Brown, all that ... tract of land called Pleasant Grove containing fifty acres lying in Baltimore County to him and his heirs forever and no more of my estate real or personal. Item: I also give and bequeath to my sons, George, Edward, and Richard, each of them the sum of one shilling sterling money to be paid unto each of them on demand at the end of one whole year after my decease and no more of my estate real or personal. Item: I also give and bequeath unto my daughters, Mary and Elizabeth each of them the sum of one shilling sterling money to be paid unto them on demand at the end of one year after my decease and no more of my estate real or personal. Item: also I give and bequeath unto my daughter Rachel, one feather bed and furniture and no more of my estate real or personal. Item: also I give and bequeath unto my four sons Viz. William, Henry, Hugh, and Joshua after the payment of my just debts all that part of the or tract of land called Brown's Plague which I shall ... of being by estimation near three hundred acres to be equally divided among them after the decease of my well beloved wife Mary Brown, to them and their heirs forever. Item also I order and desire that sale be made of such goods and chattels as is not above disposed of with all convenient speed in order to pay my debts. Otherwise some part of my land called Brown's Plague as to my ... hereafter mentioned shall sum and convenient and I also make and ordain my well beloved wife, Mary Brown and my son, Henry, executrix and executors of this my last will in trust for the ... in this my last will contained. In witness whereof I the said George Brown have to this my last will and testament set my hand and seal this day and year first above written

George Browne

Signed, sealed, and delivered by the said George Brown as and for his last will and testament presence of us Yost Runkly, John Logsdon, William Logsdon Frederick County, MD Wills, Liber A #1 f. Page. 358.

Notes for MARY DOWNS:
Baptism: 20 Nov 1621, St. Olave, Bermondsey, Surrey, England.

Children of CHRISTOPHER DURBIN and MARY DOWNS are:
10.   i.   CHRISTOPHER[10] DURBIN, b. 1682.
11.   ii.   SAMUEL CHRISTOPHER DURBIN, SR., b. Bet. 1698 - 1704, Baltimore County, Maryland; d. September 19, 1752, Frederick County, Baltimore, Maryland.

Children of CHRISTOPHER DURBIN and MARGARET BROWN are:
12.   iii. HENRY[10] DURBAN, Stepchild.
        iv. FRANCIS DURBIN, b. September 30, 1649, London, St. Margaret's Church; d. December 21, 1649, Westminster, London, England; Stepchild.
        v.   THOMAS WILLIAM DURBIN, b. August 31, 1651, Westminster, London, England; d. May 08, 1699, Baltimore, Baltimore, MD; m. MARY DOWNS; b. 1668, Norton, Suffolk, England; d. 1699, Baltimore, Baltimore, MD.

Notes for THOMAS WILLIAM DURBIN:

Thomas William DURBIN (b. August 31, 1651, d. May 08, 1699)
Thomas William DURBIN (son of Christopher Thomas DURBIN and Mary Margaret) was born August 31, 1651 in Westminster, London, England, and died May 08, 1699 in Baltimore Co., Maryland. Christened in St. Margaret's Church in London, England. He married Mary Downs.

Notes for Thomas William DURBIN:
Thomas was brought to Maryland from England with Lord Baltimore in 1638. The Durbin Family is found named in Baltimore land grants and descendants resided in what was once Baltimore County, now Harford County, and migrated to Western Md, Washington, Pa, Ohio, & points west.
Thomas bought a 200 acre tract, for 2500 lbs of tobacco, located on the north side of the Patapsco River, near

Welshman's Creek, in 1676. By 1692, Thomas was a taxable on the north side of the Patapsco Hundred in Baltimore Co., Maryland.

Thomas owned a property known as "Hab-Nab-at-a-Venture", surveyed as 350 acres on June 30,1688.The tract lying on the North side of the Patapsco River, belonged to his heirs 1700-1720, and is the present site of Druid Hill Park in Baltimore City.

Thomas witnessed the will of Jane Long of Baltimore County, Md dated May 19, 1696 proven June 3, 1696 (Will Book 7;pg 141).

According to Edwin C. Welch in "The Durbin Family of Maryland" (1961), p. 67-68; this Thomas is mentioned on 13 October 1676, when as Thomas of Severne, Anne Arundel County, he paid 2500 lbs of tobacco for the tract "Johnson", purchased from Walter Dickenson (see Maryland Historical Magazine 39: p. 274 and 30: p. 273-74). Later this same Thomas appears as a witness to a deed of Christopher Gift on 14 June 1682. Thomas appears to have been a man of some means for in a list made 15 September 1686 of the "officers for every town in the Province," he is called "Mr. Thomas Derbon" of the town of Potapsco [Archives of Maryland, 5: 502.].

Thomas Durbin witnessed the will of Jane Long on 19 May 1696 [Jane Baldwin Cottin, Maryland Calendar of Wills, 2: 100]. He died in the first part of 1699 or the latter part of 1698, for his inventory was taken 8 May 1699 by Roger Newman, and totaled a substantial 13,158 pounds, with 60.02.8 due to the estate [Accounts, Liber 18, folio 182-83]. Debts were paid out of the estate to Jno Smith, Capt. Deen Cock, Roger Newman, Jno Thomas, Majr. Maxwell, and Jno Hall. Of particular interest in the inventory is:

"To ye funerall Charges of Thomas and his wife 2 black walnutt coffins..."

Thomas Durbin and his wife likely died at about the same time. We can't help speculating that death was sudden and unexpected, for no will was made. A reference for this material is Baltimore County Families, 1659-1759 by Robert Barnes. Thomas Durbin left several children, and the Durbins who show up in the Potapsco River area from 1699-1721 can reasonably be assumed to be his children, for no other Durbins are know to exist in this area - or even the continental United States -- at this time. Further, the name Thomas is carried through several generations of his believed descendants.

The Rent Rolls affirm he left children, for: "Hab-Nab-At-A-Venture, 350 acres surveyed 6-30-1688 for Thomas Durbin, lying on North side of Potapsco River and belonging to "orphants" of said Durbin. Possession 150 acres said Durbin "orphants" 200 acres John Eggleston. [Liber 22m folio 440, Baltimore County, and Maryland Historical Maagazine 16:220 and 20: 292]
Because the record speaks in the plural, "orphants," we can be sure of more than one minor child left at Thomas Durbin's death. [Ref: the Maryland and Delaware Genealogist. Vol.18 and Family Lineage Article contributed by Kerry William Bate].
Information: Thomas Durbin was brought to Maryland from England with Lord Baltimore in 1638. The Durbin family is found named in Baltimore County land grants and descendants resided in what was once Baltimore County, now Harford County, and migrated to western Maryland, Washington County, PA, Ohio and points west.
Information: Durbin - Logsdon Genealogy by Betty Jewell Durbin Carson, Heritage Books,Bowie, MD

Durbin family of Maryland by Edwin C. Welch

R.S. Glover: "Bristol and America" pg 91 "Thomas Durbin sailed from Bristol, England (1654-1663) destination Nevis, British West Indies, pg136: William Durbin sailed on vessel "Nevis Adventure."

Notes for MARY DOWNS:
Baptism: 20 Nov 1621, St. Olave, Bermondsey, Surrey, England.

vi. CHRISTOPHER DURBIN, b. Abt. 1659; d. 1709; m. MARY ELIZABETH CANNON.

Notes for CHRISTOPHER DURBIN:
Christopher was taxed as early as 1699. His will dated 23 October, 1709, probated 28 November, 1709, leaves tract "Johnson" thus proving his right as heir of Thomas. After his death, his widow married John Downs, whose will dated 1 April, 1718, probated 3 June 1718 (MCW, 3:160, 4:161). Downs left bequests to his Durbin stepchildren.

9 Mar 1739, Christopher Durbin Shaw, planter, of Baltimore Co., Maryland to George Harryman, of same, £20, 100 acres...Middle River. Signed Christopher Durbin Shaw. Wit: Thomas Sheredine and William Bond.

Notes for MARY ELIZABETH CANNON:
9 Mar 1731, John Hammond, yeoman, of Cecil Co., Maryland to William Cannon, planter, of Baltimore Co., Maryland, 3,000 pounds of tobacco, 100 acres...Rock Run...line of John Low. Signed John Hammond. Wit: Nathaniel Ewings and Andrew Barry.

27 Oct 1731, Edward & Rachel Evans, Richard Touchstone, Thomas Cresap, William Cannon and Robert & Sophia Cannon, all of Baltimore Co., Maryland to Stephen Onion, of Cecil Co., Maryland, 30

acres...Johnsons Island in Susquehanna River. Signed Edward Evans and Robert Cannon. Wit: William Howell.

8 Aug 1734, William & Frances Cannon, planter, of Baltimore Co., Maryland to John Low, planter, of same, 1,800 pounds of tobacco, 50 acres. Signed William (x) Cannon. Wit: Roger Mathews and Joseph George.

4 Aug 1736, William & Frances Cannon, of Baltimore Co., Maryland to Stephen Onion, of same, £5, one sixth of Johnson Island in Susquehanna River. Signed William (x) Cannon and Frances (x) Cannon. Wit: Darby Lux and James Isham.

14 Aug 1738, William Wachap, of Prince William Co., Virginia to William Cannon, livestock. Signed William Wachap. Wit: Johann Heerburger, Abraham Kerslake and Sarah (x) Briant.

vii. JOHN DURBIN, b. 1680, Baltimore, Harford, MD; d. November 02, 1743, Baltimore, Harford, MD.
viii. ELIZABETH FOWLER DURBIN, b. 1685, Baltimore, Anne Arundel, Maryland; d. 1748, Baltimore, Anne Arundel, Maryland; m. (1) UNKNOWN LLOYD; m. (2) WILLIAM HOLLAND; b. Abt. 1665, Virginia?; d. Bef. October 25, 1732, Anne Arundel County, Maryland; m. (3) SAMUEL CHEW BURGESS, April 03, 1716, South River Parish, Ann Arundel, Maryland; b. November 13, 1698, All Hollow, Ann Arundel, Maryland; d. January 23, 1741/42, All Hollow, Ann Arundel, Maryland.

Notes for WILLIAM HOLLAND:
In 1721 William Holland of Baltimore County, Maryland makes bequest: To wife Elizabeth (Durbin), extx., and hrs., entire estate, real and personal, excepting legacies to follow: William Andrew (son of wife's sister Sarah (Durbin) Ann Hackman, Thomas Durbin, Elizabeth Shaw (at age 16), personalty. Test.: F. Whitehead,

William Gallaway, Samuel Durbin, Elizabeth Joy. (19,243), 16th June, 1721; probated 19th Sept. 1727.

Notes for SAMUEL CHEW BURGESS:
Named after Samuel Chew, grandfather.

 ix. SARAH DURBIN, b. 1688; m. WILLIAM ANDREW, SR..
 x. JAMES DURBIN, b. 1691, Baltimore, Baltimore, MD; d. November 1720, Parrish, Manatee, Florida.

Children of CHRISTOPHER DURBIN and MARY DOWNS are:
   xi. PHILLIP S.^{10} DURBIN, Stepchild.
13. xii. WILLIAM DURBIN, b. January 04, 1727/28, Baltimore, Baltimore, MD; d. Bet. 1753 - 1817, Harford, Baltimore, MD.

Generation No. 10

10. CHRISTOPHER^{10} DURBIN *(CHRISTOPHER THOMAS^9, WILLIAM^8, WILLIAM^7, PETER^6, THOMAS^5, RICHARD^4 DURBAN, WALTER^3 DURBIN, EDWARD N.^{2}, ROBERT^1 DURBAN)* was born 1682.

Notes for CHRISTOPHER DURBIN:
19 Feb 1733, John Brice, gentleman, of Baltimore Co., Maryland to Philip Jones, Jr., gentleman, of same, £20, 200 acres...east side of Welshmans creek...patented, 14 Feb 1659, by John Dickinson, who assigned to Walter Dickinson, who sold, 13 Oct 1676, to Thomas Durbin, who sold, 23 Nov 1679, who devised to his son, Christopher Durbin, who sold to Brice. Signed John Brice. Wit: Philip Jones Sr. and Charles Hammond.

14 Jan 1742, Luke Trotten and William Hamilton, executors of the estate of John Gardner, of Baltimore Co., Maryland to Dr. George Buchanan, of same £150, 200 acres...line of Thomas Durbin patented 6 Jun 1689, by Solomon Jones, of St. Mary's Co., Maryland, who devised

to his daughter Elinor Jones, wife of William Langley who sold, 2 Oct 1725, to said John Gardner...2nd tract ...350 acres, Jones Falls...on 2nd Run above George Watson...patented 6 May 1689, by Thomas Durbin...3rd tract, 150 acres...line of John Eaglestone, sold, 22 May 1726, by Christopher Durbin to said John. Signed Luke (x) Trotten and William Hamilton. Wit: Thomas Sheredin and Alexander Lawson.

14 Jan 1742, Luke Trotten and William Hamilton (executors of the estate of John Gardner), of Baltimore Co., Maryland to Alexander Lawson, gentleman, of same, £50, 126 acres...2nd tract, 200 acres...line of Thomas Robertson...both tracts patented by John Coale. Signed Luke (x) Trotten and William Hamilton. Wit: Thomas Sheredine and George Buchanan.

(Baltimore County, Maryland Deed Records: 1727-1757. John David Davis, 2008, pg. 306.)

Child of CHRISTOPHER DURBIN is:
14.   i.   JOHN^{11} DURBIN, b. Bef. 1686.

11. SAMUEL CHRISTOPHER^{10} DURBIN, SR. *(CHRISTOPHER THOMAS^9, WILLIAM^8, WILLIAM^7, PETER^6, THOMAS^5, RICHARD^4 DURBAN, WALTER^3 DURBIN, EDWARD N.^{2}, ROBERT^1 DURBAN)* was born Bet. 1698 - 1704 in Baltimore County, Maryland, and died September 19, 1752 in Frederick County, Baltimore, Maryland. He married (2) ANN LOGSDON July 04, 1723 in St. Paul's Episcopal Church, Baltimore, MD. She was born 1703 in Frederick County, Baltimore, Maryland, and died Aft. July 1770 in Frederick County, Baltimore, Maryland.

Notes for SAMUEL CHRISTOPHER DURBIN, SR.:
22 Sep 1730, William & Ann Logsdon of Baltimore Co., Maryland to Mathew Coulter, taylor, of same £40, 100 acres...north side of middle branch of Patapsco River...2nd tract, 200 acres...line of Ann Durbin. Signed William (x) Logsdon and Honour (x) Logsdon. Wit: William Hamilton and Richard Gist.

21 Jun 1733, Samuel Durbin, carpenter, of Baltimore Co., Maryland mortgage to John Woolly, planter, of same, £13.3, livestock. Signed: Samuel Durbin. Wit: Richard Johnson and Thomas Gist.

27 Oct 1737, Samuel & Ann Durbin, planter, of Baltimore Co., Maryland to William Mattingly, planter, of same, £16, 97.5 acres...west side of Patapsco River...surveyed for William Logsdon. Signed: Samuel Durbin. Wit: Thomas (x) Logsdon and Patrick Neal.

25 Jul 1747, Thomas & Phebe Bond, planter, of Baltimore Co., Maryland to Patrick & Elizabeth Gray, of same, £20, 100 acres...north side of Gwins Falls...line of Thomas Jonson, (William Logsdon to Samuel Durbin). Signed Thomas Bond. Wit: Richard Croxall and William Rogers.

(Baltimore County, Maryland Deed Records: 1727-1757. John David Davis, 2008, pg. 306.)
    Other Events:
    Name: Samuel DURBIN
    Death: 19 Sep 1752, Frederick, Frederick, Maryland
Notes:
Samuel Durbin was married to Ann, daughter of William Logsdon and Honor O'Flynn, at Saint Thomas Church at Owings Mills, Maryland, July 4, 1734. This marriage is also recorded at St. Paul Catholic Church in Baltimore, Maryland. Samuel Durbin is the patriarch of most, if not all, of the Durbins' of Kentucky. Samuel's will, dated September 19, 1752. It is assumed that he died soon after the September date. Ann's will dated July 8, 1770, was probated in Frederick County, Maryland, and named all thirteen of her children. Of these thirteen children, at least four were pioneer settlers of Kentucky. John came in between 1775 and 1780; Thomas, Christopher, and Edward came in circa 1788. John Durbin, according to James Virden, was the first Durbin in Kentucky, arriving with Daniel Boone in 1775, and was one of the axmen who blazed the Wilderness Trail. [Durbin-Logsdon Genealogy by Betty Jewell Durbin Carson]

Liber 28, folio 40019 Sept. 1752

DURBIN, SAMUEL, Frederick Co., planter. To son William Durbin, 100a at the lower end of Cobbs Choice in lieu of The Pleasants Green. To dau. Ann Durbin, a cow & calf. To dau. Margret Durbin, an heifer yearlin. To son John Durbin, my sorrel mares colt. My wife & extrx. [not named] is to keep all above written & the dw. plntn. if she not mar. To son Samuel Durbin, on his mother d., the dw. plntn. 50a. Witn: Edwd. Meacham, Thos. Logsdon, William Wilson. 23 Oct 1752, sworn to by all 3 witn.

Samuel Durbin, born about 1700 in colonial Maryland, is the son of Thomas and Mary Downes Durbin. It is recorded that Samuel Durbin married Ann Logsdon on 4th of July 1723 in St. Paul's Church, Baltimore, MD. Ann Logsdon was the daughter of William Logsdon and Honor O'Flynn. The children of Samuel and Ann are as follows: William, Samuel Jr., Thomas, John, Christopher, Edward, Nicholas, Benjamin, Sarah, Ann, Margaret, Mary and Honor. The last 2 girls may have been twins.

Samuel was involved in the Methodist Church of America. There are roadside signs pointing to a wonderful old home built in 1767, still standing in good condition where Samuel and Ann lived. It is likely that Samuel built the home and the nearby original log cabin where their son Christopher was born. The Durbins' became interested in Methodism and the first American ordained bishop, Francis Asbury often preached in their home as well as another famous preacher, Robert Strawbridge, recognized by many as the first Methodist preacher in America.

Samuel Durbin was married to Ann Logsdon of Frederick County, Maryland, 4 July 1723 at St. Pauls Parish, in Baltimore County, Maryland. Ann was the daughter of William Logsdon, an emigrant to Maryland in 1673 and Honor O'Flynn. Honor O'Flynn was mentioned in old records as an Irish girl of great piety, and it was through her that the Catholic element appeared in the Durbin line. The family lore handed down through the generations was of a beautiful Irish girl named Honor O'Flynn who was kidnapped from Ireland and brought to this country, and who was married to a Logsdon. These quotes were taken from some Catholic records pertaining to one Father Elisha Durbin, son of John D. Durbin and Patience Logsdon. This information

was submitted to Mrs. Ernest F. Schuchert of Chester, Illinois from Mr. Howard Steiner of Harrisburg, Pennsylvania. Some of the descendants of Durbins of this line became very staunch Catholics. However, Mr. Steiner said that the wonderful home which Samuel Durbin and his sons built in 1767 was still standing in good condition, that the homestead had been made a shrine by the Methodist Church of America. There were roadside signs pointing to its location about two miles out from Westminster, Maryland. The Durbins became interested in Methodism, and the first American ordained bishop Francis Asbury often visited with the Durbins during three generations of that family. He preached in their home as well as did Robert Strawbridge, who was recognized by many as the first Methodist preacher in America. Robert Strawbridge was a near neighbor and friend. The Durbins were active in establishing Methodism in the this country and William, a son, belonged to the First Society of Methodism. Samuel Durbinn's homestead was within two miles of Westminster, Maryland. If his children were born in the log cabin which stands near the home, then their birth place could read Carroll County, Maryland instead of Frederick County, Maryland which sounds most probable. Carroll County was once a part of Baltimore County in Maryland. This information was submitted to Mrs. Ernest F. Schuchert of Chester, Illinois from Mr. Howard Steiner of Harrisburg, Pennsylvania.
From the New Windsor District in Carroll County, Maryland came a note that not far from Pipe Creek lived William Durbin who with his wife joined the Methodist in 1768. Their son, John Durbin, was a traveling preacher.

Children of SAMUEL CHRISTOPHER DURBIN, SR. are:
    i. NICHOLAS[11] DURBIN, b. 1738, Baltimore, Baltimore, MD; d. September 21, 1811, Jefferson Co., OH; m. HONOR LOGSDON.

    Notes for HONOR LOGSDON:

    First cousin to Nicholas, her husband.

    ii. STEPHEN DURBIN, b. 1798; d. 1850.

Children of SAMUEL DURBIN and ANN LOGSDON are:

15. iii. SARAH[11] DURBIN, b. September 19, 1724, Westminster, Carroll Co., MD; d. Abt. 1795, Allegany County, Maryland.
     iv. WILLIAM DURBIN, b. January 04, 1725/26, Baltimore, Maryland; d. Abt. 1773, Maryland; m. MARY MARGARET POULSON, Abt. 1746, Baltimore, Baltimore, MD; b. Bef. 1730, Maryland; d. 1800, Maryland.

Notes for WILLIAM DURBIN:
William was the first son of Samuel Durbin & Ann Logsdon. His birth is registered in St. Paul's Church, Baltimore, Maryland, p. 57. He was a Methodist; DAR Patriot Index, Washington Co., Maryland, Corporal 8th Class, 26th Day of July 1775 Provincial Convention.

16. v. SAMUEL DURBIN, JR., b. January 29, 1726/27, Baltimore, Maryland; d. February 11, 1808, Allegany Co., Maryland.
     vi. ANN DURBIN, b. Abt. 1730.
17. vii. THOMAS DURBIN, b. July 13, 1732, Baltimore County, Maryland; d. April 13, 1810, Westminster, Carroll Co., MD.
18. viii. JOHN DURBIN, b. Abt. 1734, Westminster, Carroll Co., MD; d. 1831, Christian County, Illinois.
     ix. MARGARET DURBIN, b. July 11, 1736; d. March 20, 1795; m. EDWARD BROWN, St. Paul's Anglican Church, Baltimore, MD.
     x. MARY DURBIN, b. December 1739; m. RALPH LOGSDON.

Notes for MARY DURBIN:
First cousin to Ralph, her husband.

19. xi. CHRISTOPHER DURBIN, b. July 13, 1741, Westminster, Carroll Co., MD; d. December 1825, Madison County, Kentucky.

20. xii. EDWARD DURBIN, b. Abt. 1762, Maryland; d. August 1816, Madison County, Kentucky.
xiii. BENJAMIN DURBIN, b. March 30, 1748; d. November 20, 1813; m. SUSANNAH HAYDEN; b. 1753; d. 1837.

More About BENJAMIN DURBIN:
Burial: St. Joseph's, Westminster, Carroll County, Maryland

xiv. HONORA DURBIN, b. Abt. 1750.

Notes for HONORA DURBIN:
Crippled; never married.

12. HENRY[10] DURBAN *(CHRISTOPHER THOMAS[9] DURBIN, WILLIAM[8], WILLIAM[7], PETER[6], THOMAS[5], RICHARD[4] DURBAN, WALTER[3] DURBIN, EDWARD N.[2], ROBERT[1] DURBAN)*

Child of HENRY DURBAN is:
i. ELIZABETH[11] DURBAN, b. October 30, 1625.

Notes for ELIZABETH DURBAN:
Elizabeth Durban, baptism 30 October 1625, Ripple Kent, England. Father Henery Durban. Frank Watt Tyler. "The Tyler Collection." Canterbury, Kent, England. The Institute of Heraldic and Genealogical Studies. 1538-1874.

13. WILLIAM[10] DURBIN *(CHRISTOPHER THOMAS[9], WILLIAM[8], WILLIAM[7], PETER[6], THOMAS[5], RICHARD[4] DURBAN, WALTER[3] DURBIN, EDWARD N.[2], ROBERT[1] DURBAN)* was born January 04, 1727/28 in Baltimore, Baltimore, MD, and died Bet. 1753 - 1817 in Harford, Baltimore, MD. He married MARY POULSON Bet. 1750 - 1774. She was born Abt. 1734, and died Bet. 1752 - 1822.

Children of WILLIAM DURBIN and MARY POULSON are:
i. CHARITY[11] DURBIN.

ii. CORNELIUS DURBIN, m. MARY HARRISON, January 29, 1789, Frederick County, Maryland.
iii. MARY MARGARET DURBIN.
iv. NICHOLAS DURBIN.

Notes for NICHOLAS DURBIN:
Listed by Thomas & Williams as a settler west of Fort Cumberland in 1788, and given lots for military services. Pencil notation states married in Fayette Co., PA. Nicholas of Dunbar, Fayette Co., PA, d. 1811, Short Creek Twp., Jefferson Co., Ohio.

v. RACHEL DURBIN.
vi. REBECCA DURBIN.
vii. THOMAS W. DURBIN.
viii. WILLIAM DURBIN, b. January 15, 1748/49, Frederick County, Maryland; d. August 28, 1820, Bedford, Maryland; m. MARGARET BRUCE; b. January 02, 1748/49; d. July 05, 1808.

More About WILLIAM DURBIN:
Burial: Beard Family Farm, Bedford, Maryland

ix. ELIJAH DURBIN, b. September 12, 1772.
x. JOHN DURBIN, b. August 12, 1775; d. May 10, 1865; m. SARAH.
xi. ELIZABETH DURBIN, b. November 28, 1788.
xii. NANCY DURBIN, b. 1789.

Generation No. 11

14. JOHN^{11} DURBIN *(CHRISTOPHER^{10}, CHRISTOPHER THOMAS^{9}, WILLIAM^{8}, WILLIAM^{7}, PETER^{6}, THOMAS^{5}, RICHARD^{4} DURBAN, WALTER^{3} DURBIN, EDWARD N.^{2}, ROBERT^{1} DURBAN)* was born Bef. 1686. He married ANN WHITE August 26, 1703 in All Hallow's Parish, Anne Arundel, Maryland.

Notes for JOHN DURBIN:
At age 7, at his father's death, was bound over to Daniel Scott. John was of age and appeared in the 1702 tax list, making his birth before 1686. In June 1716, he petitioned the court to have his nephews "Thomas and Xpher" taken away from their stepfather, John Downes. (Robert W. Barnes, "Baltimore County Families 1659-1759." Baltimore: Genealogy Pub. Co., 1989)

This seems to be the only tie to Christopher Thomas, as his lands referenced are not identifiable as part of the legacy from his father. Both John Durbin, Jr. and Joshua George, on behalf of the widow, appeared 2 Nov 1743 and made election to abide by the will.

31 Jul 1746, John Darbin, (son and heir of John Darbin), of Baltimore Co., Maryland to Thomas White, merchant, of same, £26.35, 100 acres... south side of Deer creek...patented 1Feb 1725 by John Darbin Sr...2nd tract, 25 acres...east side of Rock Run. Signed John Durbin. Wit: Thomas Scarlett and Thomas Lloyd.

16 Jun 1748, John & Elizabeth Hughs, of Baltimore Co., Maryland to Thomas White, of same, £120, 204 acres total two tracts...689 acres... patented, 7 May 1687, by John Hallaway, who sold to Humphrey Jones, who sold, 20 Jan 1716, to Samuel Brown, who sold, 20 Jul1725, to Charles Whiteacre, who sold to John Durbin, who sold to Samuel Hughs, who devised to his son the said John...104 acres gave by Humphrey Jones to William & Mary Kimble, Mary Kimble later married Charles Whiteacre and then sold to Samuel Hughs. Signed John Hughs. Wit: Nicholas Ruxton Gay and Nathaniel Richardson.

7 Aug 1750, John & Mary Durbin, of Baltimore Co., Maryland to John Stump, of Cecil Co., Maryland, £90, 150 acres...Deer creek...50 acres, adjoining. Signed John Durbin. Wit: Robert Carlile and Lawrence Clark.
7 Aug 1750, John & Mary Durbin, of Baltimore Co., Maryland to William Husband, of Cecil Co., Maryland, £100, 92 acres, two tracts...line of John Stump. Signed John Durbin and Mary Durbin. Wit: Robert Carlile and Lawrence Clark.
25 Nov 1751, Daniel Durbin, planter, of Baltimore Co., Maryland to his brother Thomas Durbin, planter, of same, (the half share of 200

acres...on road from Perkins Ferry on Susquehanna River... purchased from Samuel Hughs, by John Durbin, who devised to his sons, the said Daniel and Thomas) for 25 acres. Signed Daniel Durbin. Wit: Samuel Owings and John Ridgley.

Children of JOHN DURBIN and ANN WHITE are:
21.   i.   JOHN[12] DURBIN, b. 1690.
       ii.   WILLIAM DURBIN.

           Notes for WILLIAM DURBIN:
           10 Feb 1752, William Durbin (son and heir of John Durbin), of Baltimore Co., Maryland to James Pritchard, of same, 45 lbs., 25 acres...drafts of Deer Creek ...purchased of Samuel Hughs. Signed William Durbin. Wit: William Smith and John Mathews.
           (Baltimore County, Maryland Deed Records: 1727-1757. John David Davis, 2008, pg. 306.)

       iii. JAMES DURBIN, b. Aft. 1720; m. MARGARET; d. November 1720, St. George's Parish, Baltimore (now Harford).

15. SARAH[11] DURBIN *(SAMUEL CHRISTOPHER[10], CHRISTOPHER THOMAS[9], WILLIAM[8], WILLIAM[7], PETER[6], THOMAS[5], RICHARD[4] DURBAN, WALTER[3] DURBIN, EDWARD N.[2], ROBERT[1] DURBAN)* was born September 19, 1724 in Westminster, Carroll Co., MD, and died Abt. 1795 in Allegany County, Maryland. She married WILLIAM GABRIEL MCKENZIE Abt. 1742 in St. Paul's Anglican Church, Baltimore, MD, son of JOHN MCKENZIE and KATHERINE GABRIEL.

Children of SARAH DURBIN and WILLIAM MCKENZIE are:
        i.   ANNE[12] MCKENZIE.
       ii.   MICHAEL MCKENZIE.
      iii. SAMUEL MCKENZIE, b. Abt. 1710.
22.   iv. DANIEL MCKENZIE, b. 1752, Frederick County, Baltimore, Maryland; d. 1823, Frederick County, Baltimore, Maryland.

v. JOHN MCKENZIE, b. 1765.
vi. AARON MCKENZIE, b. 1768.
vii. JOSHUA MCKENZIE, b. 1768.

16. SAMUEL[11] DURBIN, JR. *(SAMUEL CHRISTOPHER[10], CHRISTOPHER THOMAS[9], WILLIAM[8], WILLIAM[7], PETER[6], THOMAS[5], RICHARD[4] DURBAN, WALTER[3] DURBAN, EDWARD N.[2], ROBERT[1] DURBAN)* was born January 29, 1726/27 in Baltimore, Maryland, and died February 11, 1808 in Allegany Co., Maryland. He married COMFORT LOGSDON, daughter of WILLIAM LOGSDON and ANN DAVIS. She was born Abt. 1740 in Baltimore, Baltimore, MD, and died May 01, 1822 in Allegany Co., Maryland.

Notes for SAMUEL DURBIN, JR.:
His will was written 6 March 1807, where he bequeath his entire estate to his wife, Comfort, with the exception of one 2-year old heifer which he gave to his son, Isaac, who he said always claimed it. Samuel Durbin, Jr. has lost all of his land holdings which had been sold by the sheriff at auction; therefore, he did not name his other children in his will. In her will, Comfort Logsdon Durbin, dated 29 July 1817, left her entire estate to two daughters, Honor wife of Henry Mattingly and Mary wife of Aaron McKinsey (McKenzie).

Children of SAMUEL DURBIN and COMFORT LOGSDON are:
  i. ISAAC[12] DURBIN, d. Abt. 1808.
  ii. EDWARD DURBIN, b. Bef. 1755.
  iii. WILLIAM DURBIN, b. 1755.
  iv. JOHN DURBIN, b. 1762.
23. v. BENJAMIN DURBIN, b. 1772, Maryland; d. September 09, 1852, Knox Co., Mt. Vernon, OH.
  vi. NICHOLAS DURBIN, b. 1774.
  vii. MARY DURBIN, b. 1781.
  viii. HONOUR DURBIN, b. Abt. 1802.

17. THOMAS[11] DURBIN *(SAMUEL CHRISTOPHER[10], CHRISTOPHER THOMAS[9], WILLIAM[8], WILLIAM[7], PETER[6], THOMAS[5], RICHARD[4] DURBAN, WALTER[3] DURBAN, EDWARD N.[2],*

ROBERT[1] DURBAN) was born July 13, 1732 in Baltimore County, Maryland, and died April 13, 1810 in Westminster, Carroll Co., MD. He married HONOR ERBOUGH Abt. 1750, daughter of JACOB ERBOUGH and MARGARET. She was born 1730, and died 1821.

Children of THOMAS DURBIN and HONOR ERBOUGH are:
24.   i. DANN[12] DURBIN, b. 1768, Westminster, Carroll Co., MD; d. 1856, Mattingly Settlement, Zanesville, Muskingum County, Ohio.
25.   ii. NICHOLAS DURBIN, b. 1790, Westminster, Carroll Co., MD.
      iii. JOHN DURBIN, b. 1755.
      iv. MARY DURBIN, b. Abt. 1753.
      v. ANN DURBIN.
      vi. DAUGHTER DURBIN.
      vii. MARGARET DURBIN.
      viii. PHILLIP DURBIN, b. Bet. 1753 - 1759.
      ix. THOMAS BOND DURBIN, b. 1760.
      x. HONOR DURBIN.

18. JOHN[11] DURBIN *(SAMUEL CHRISTOPHER[10], CHRISTOPHER THOMAS[9], WILLIAM[8], WILLIAM[7], PETER[6], THOMAS[5], RICHARD[4] DURBAN, WALTER[3] DURBAN, EDWARD N.[2], ROBERT[1] DURBAN)* was born Abt. 1734 in Westminster, Carroll Co., MD, and died 1831 in Christian County, Illinois. He married ANN LOGSDON 1760, daughter of THOMAS LOGSDON.

Notes for JOHN DURBIN:
1732, Thomas White, of Baltimore Co., Maryland to John Durbin, 150 acres...Rock Run. Signed Thomas White. Wit: George Dreio and Edward Wakeman.

14 Oct 1732, Charles Anderson, carpenter, of Baltimore Co., Maryland to James Morgan and Elizabeth Willmer, of same, 200 acres. Signed Charles (x) Anderson. Wit: John Durbin and Francis White.

Notes for ANN LOGSDON:

First cousin to John Durbin, her husband.

Children of JOHN DURBIN and ANN LOGSDON are:
- i. DRUSILLA[12] DURBIN.
- ii. HONOR DURBIN.
- 26. iii. MARY DURBIN, b. Westminster, Carroll Co., MD.
- iv. NANCY DURBIN.
- v. SARAH DURBIN.
- vi. SUSAN DURBIN.
- vii. THOMAS DURBIN, b. Bet. 1760 - 1765.
- 27. viii. JOHN DURBIN, b. Bet. 1766 - 1831.
- ix. AUGUSTINE DURBIN, b. Bet. 1770 - 1775.

19. CHRISTOPHER[11] DURBIN *(SAMUEL CHRISTOPHER[10], CHRISTOPHER THOMAS[9], WILLIAM[8], WILLIAM[7], PETER[6], THOMAS[5], RICHARD[4] DURBAN, WALTER[3] DURBIN, EDWARD N.[2], ROBERT[1] DURBAN)* was born July 13, 1741 in Westminster, Carroll Co., MD, and died December 1825 in Madison County, Kentucky. He married MARGARET BROWN PARKINSON Bef. 1765 in Maryland.

Notes for CHRISTOPHER DURBIN:
Received land grant in 1762 and 1690 (Federick Co. Deeds, K:39).

Children of CHRISTOPHER DURBIN and MARGARET PARKINSON are:
- 28. i. AARON[12] DURBIN.
- 29. ii. EDWARD DURBIN, b. Bet. 1760 - 1768, Maryland.
- iii. JOSEPH P. DURBIN, b. 1765.
- iv. JOHN J. DURBIN, b. Bet. 1772 - 1773.
- v. CHRISTOPHER DURBIN, b. Bet. 1775 - 1777.
- vi. THOMAS DURBIN, b. Bet. 1777 - 1783.
- vii. PHILLIP S. DURBIN, b. July 12, 1781.

20. EDWARD[11] DURBIN *(SAMUEL CHRISTOPHER[10], CHRISTOPHER THOMAS[9], WILLIAM[8], WILLIAM[7], PETER[6], THOMAS[5], RICHARD[4] DURBAN, WALTER[3] DURBIN, EDWARD N.[2], ROBERT[1] DURBAN)* was born Abt. 1762 in Maryland, and died

August 1816 in Madison County, Kentucky. He married (1) ELIZABETH "BETTY" PORTER 1780 in Maryland, daughter of HENRY PORTER. He married (2) SALLY WAGERS January 26, 1813 in Estill County, Kentucky.

Notes for EDWARD DURBIN:
Named executor in parent's will.

Children of EDWARD DURBIN and ELIZABETH PORTER are:
    i. CHRISTOPHER K.^{12} DURBIN.
    ii. SAMUEL DURBIN.
    iii. SUSANNAH DURBIN, b. Abt. 1780.
    iv. AARON DURBIN, b. Abt. 1780; m. ANN LOGSDON.

Children of EDWARD DURBIN and SALLY WAGERS are:
    v. PHILLIP^{12} DURBIN.
    vi. JOSEPH H. DURBIN.
    vii. JOHN DURBIN, b. Abt. 1794.

Generation No. 12

21. JOHN^{12} DURBIN *(JOHN^{11}, CHRISTOPHER^{10}, CHRISTOPHER THOMAS^{9}, WILLIAM^{8}, WILLIAM^{7}, PETER^{6}, THOMAS^{5}, RICHARD^{4} DURBAN, WALTER^{3} DURBIN, EDWARD N.^{2}, ROBERT^{1} DURBAN)* was born 1690. He married (1) AVARILLA SCOTT. He married (2) UNKNOWN.

Children of JOHN DURBIN and AVARILLA SCOTT are:
    i. ELIZABETH^{13} DURBIN, b. October 25, 1718.
    ii. JOHN DURBIN, b. April 15, 1721.

       Notes for JOHN DURBIN:
       7 Aug 1750, John & Mary Durbin, of Baltimore Co., Maryland to John Stump, of Cecil Co., Maryland, £90., 150 acres...Deer Creek...50 acres, adjoining. Signed John Durbin. Wit: Robert Carlike and Lawrence Clark.

7 Aug 1750, John & Mary Durbin, of Baltimore Co., Maryland to William Husband, of Cecil Co., Maryland, £100, 92 acres..two tracts....line of John Stump. Signed John Durbin. Wit: Robert Carlike and Lawrence Clark. (Baltimore County, Maryland Deed Records: 1727-1757. John David Davis, 2008, pg. 306.)

30. iii. THOMAS DURBIN, b. December 18, 1723, Gunpowder Neck, Baltimore, Maryland.
  iv. DANIEL DURBIN, b. July 02, 1725, St. John's Parish, Baltimore, Maryland; m. ANN MITCHELL, August 11, 1746, St. John's Parish, Baltimore, Maryland.

  Notes for DANIEL DURBIN:
  Will dated 19 January 1774, probated 23 March 1774 (Harford Co. Wills, 2F:134-5).

  v. SARAH DURBIN, b. July 02, 1728; m. SAMUEL HOWELL, September 11, 1747.
  vi. AVARILLA DURBIN, b. August 22, 1733; m. WILLIAM PERKINS.
  vii. MARY DURBIN, b. February 22, 1734/35.

Children of JOHN DURBIN and UNKNOWN are:
  viii. HANNAH[13] DURBIN, b. October 25, 1738.
  ix. RALPH DURBIN, b. October 18, 1743, St. George's Parish.

  Notes for RALPH DURBIN:
  Went to Virginia.

22. DANIEL[12] MCKENZIE *(SARAH[11] DURBIN, SAMUEL CHRISTOPHER[10], CHRISTOPHER THOMAS[9], WILLIAM[8], WILLIAM[7], PETER[6], THOMAS[5], RICHARD[4] DURBAN, WALTER[3] DURBIN, EDWARD N.[2], ROBERT[1] DURBAN)* was born 1752 in Frederick County, Baltimore, Maryland, and died 1823 in Frederick

County, Baltimore, Maryland. He married MARY ANN CHAPMAN December 01, 1779 in Washington County, Maryland.

Child of DANIEL MCKENZIE and MARY CHAPMAN is:
31.   i.   SAMUEL[13] MCKENZIE, b. 1785.

23. BENJAMIN[12] DURBIN *(SAMUEL[11], SAMUEL CHRISTOPHER[10], CHRISTOPHER THOMAS[9], WILLIAM[8], WILLIAM[7], PETER[6], THOMAS[5], RICHARD[4] DURBAN, WALTER[3] DURBIN, EDWARD N.[2], ROBERT[1] DURBAN)* was born 1772 in Maryland, and died September 09, 1852 in Knox Co., Mt. Vernon, OH. He married ELIZABETH (LIDDY) LOGUE, daughter of SGT JAMES LOGUE and MARY LAWSON. She was born 1774 in Maryland, and died Bef. 1850 in Illinois.

Notes for Logue Family:
The Logues came from Derry (Londonderry) and Donegal Counties, Ireland. They were residents of Tukeeran and Keenaugh in Derry County and North Raphoe, East and West Inishowen in Donegal County. This area is on the northern shore of Ireland and surrounds "Lough Foyle." It is within the Primatial Sea of Armagh in Northern Ireland. Source: Nancy Mills, April 1999.

Notes for Mary Lawson/Ellison:
Died in her 99th year of age. Records at St. Patrick's Catholic Church, Cumberland, MD; she is buried in the Old Catholic cemetery. She was living with her son-in-law, Ben Durbin during 1800. Source: John H. Doty.

At the rectory of St. Patrick's, Cumberland, MD (Allegany Co.) is an entry, "Easter confessions 1824, Old Mrs. Logue," and the notation, "Grandmother Logue died Sept. 1, 1831, in her 99th year of age." In 1810-MD census, Will's Town, Allegany Co., and near Cumberland, MD, is listed a Mary Logue as head of family." Source: Mabel Logue Hopkins.

Child of BENJAMIN DURBIN and ELIZABETH LOGUE is:

32.   i.   BENJAMIN[13] DURBIN, JR., b. 1792, Knox Co., Mt. Vernon, OH.

24. DANN[12] DURBIN *(THOMAS[11], SAMUEL CHRISTOPHER[10], CHRISTOPHER THOMAS[9], WILLIAM[8], WILLIAM[7], PETER[6], THOMAS[5], RICHARD[4] DURBAN, WALTER[3] DURBIN, EDWARD N.[2], ROBERT[1] DURBAN)* was born 1768 in Westminster, Carroll Co., MD, and died 1856 in Mattingly Settlement, Zanesville, Muskingum County, Ohio. He married (1) ANN HAYDEN, daughter of WILLIAM HAYDEN and CATHERINE EMSEY. He married (2) NANCY ANN AIKENRODE. She was born 1786 in Maryland.

Children of DANN DURBIN and ANN HAYDEN are:
    i.   NICHOLAS[13] DURBIN, b. Abt. 1793; m. PLEASANT MINOR.
    ii. MARY DURBIN, b. Abt. 1796.
    iii. ANN DURBIN, b. Abt. 1797.
    iv. MARGARET DURBIN, b. Abt. 1799.
33.   v.   STEPHEN DURBIN, b. 1800.
34.   vi. HENRY DURBIN, b. 1801, Maryland; d. September 19, 1862, Adams County, Indiana.
    vii. DANIEL DURBIN, b. January 20, 1802.
35.   viii. WILLIAM DURBIN, b. October 11, 1802, Westminster, Carroll Co., MD; d. April 19, 1849, Morgan County, Ohio.
    ix. SAMUEL JAMES DURBIN, b. Abt. 1804.
    x.   HONOUR DURBIN, b. Abt. 1807.
    xi. JOSEPH DURBIN, b. Abt. 1809.
    xii. CLAYBURN DURBIN, b. 1810.
36.   xiii. BASIL DURBIN, b. June 22, 1812, Baltimore County, Maryland; d. June 28, 1883, Mercer County, Celina, Ohio.

Children of DANN DURBIN and NANCY AIKENRODE are:
37.   xiv. CATHERINE[13] DURBIN, b. Abt. 1821; d. 1896.
    xv. TERESA DURBIN, b. Abt. 1823.
    xvi. JAMES DURBIN, b. 1824.

xvii. ELEANOR APPARILA DURBIN, b. January 06, 1831.

25. NICHOLAS^{12} DURBIN *(THOMAS^{11}, SAMUEL CHRISTOPHER^{10}, CHRISTOPHER THOMAS^9, WILLIAM^8, WILLIAM^7, PETER^6, THOMAS^5, RICHARD^4 DURBAN, WALTER^3 DURBIN, EDWARD N.^{2}, ROBERT^1 DURBAN)* was born 1790 in Westminster, Carroll Co., MD. He married ANN WELLS in Brooke County, West Virginia.

Children of NICHOLAS DURBIN and ANN WELLS are:
    i. NANCY^{13} DURBIN, b. 1825.
    ii. CALEB DURBIN, b. 1826.
    iii. SAMUEL DURBIN, b. 1831.
38.   iv. WILLIAM DURBIN, b. 1834; d. 1908.
    v. BENJAMIN DURBIN, b. 1836.
    vi. NICHOLAS DURBIN, b. 1838.
    vii. AMON DURBIN, b. 1840.

26. MARY^{12} DURBIN *(JOHN^{11}, SAMUEL CHRISTOPHER^{10}, CHRISTOPHER THOMAS^9, WILLIAM^8, WILLIAM^7, PETER^6, THOMAS^5, RICHARD^4 DURBAN, WALTER^3 DURBIN, EDWARD N.^{2}, ROBERT^1 DURBAN)* was born in Westminster, Carroll Co., MD. She married RAPHAEL LOGSDON Abt. 1756, son of JOHN LOGSDON and MARGARET WOOLEY. He was born 1736, and died 1818.

Children of MARY DURBIN and RAPHAEL LOGSDON are:
    i. MARY^{13} LOGSDON.
    ii. RACHAEL LOGSDON.
    iii. NANCY ANN LOGSDON.
    iv. MARGARET LOGSDON.
    v. SARAH LOGSDON, b. September 19, 1724.
    vi. JEMIMAH LOGSDON, b. Abt. 1757.
    vii. HONORA LOGSDON, b. Abt. 1777.

27. JOHN^{12} DURBIN *(JOHN^{11}, SAMUEL CHRISTOPHER^{10}, CHRISTOPHER THOMAS^9, WILLIAM^8, WILLIAM^7, PETER^6,*

THOMAS⁵, RICHARD⁴ DURBAN, WALTER³ DURBIN, EDWARD N.², ROBERT¹ DURBAN) was born Bet. 1766 - 1831. He married SISTER LOGSDON.

Children of JOHN DURBIN and SISTER LOGSDON are:
    i. THOMAS¹³ DURBIN.
    ii. DRUSILLA DURBIN.
    iii. NANNY DURBIN.
    iv. MARY DURBIN.
    v. NANCY DURBIN.
    vi. AUGUSTINE DURBIN.
    vii. JOHN STUMPY DURBIN, b. Abt. 1767.

28. AARON¹² DURBIN *(CHRISTOPHER¹¹, SAMUEL CHRISTOPHER¹⁰, CHRISTOPHER THOMAS⁹, WILLIAM⁸, WILLIAM⁷, PETER⁶, THOMAS⁵, RICHARD⁴ DURBAN, WALTER³ DURBIN, EDWARD N.², ROBERT¹ DURBAN)* He married ELIZABETH LOGSDON Abt. 1789 in Madison County, Kentucky, daughter of ELISHA LOGSDON and REBECCA HOWARD.

Children of AARON DURBIN and ELIZABETH LOGSDON are:
    i. WILLIAM L.¹³ DURBIN.
    ii. JOSEPH P. DURBIN.

29. EDWARD¹² DURBIN *(CHRISTOPHER¹¹, SAMUEL CHRISTOPHER¹⁰, CHRISTOPHER THOMAS⁹, WILLIAM⁸, WILLIAM⁷, PETER⁶, THOMAS⁵, RICHARD⁴ DURBAN, WALTER³ DURBIN, EDWARD N.², ROBERT¹ DURBAN)* was born Bet. 1760 - 1768 in Maryland. He married PATIENCE LOGSDON April 08, 1793 in Madison County, Kentucky, daughter of ELISHA LOGSDON and REBECCA HOWARD.

Children of EDWARD DURBIN and PATIENCE LOGSDON are:
    i. JOHN J.¹³ DURBIN.
    ii. CHRISTOPHER DURBIN, b. Abt. 1794.

Generation No. 13

30. THOMAS[13] DURBIN *(JOHN[12], JOHN[11], CHRISTOPHER[10], CHRISTOPHER THOMAS[9], WILLIAM[8], WILLIAM[7], PETER[6], THOMAS[5], RICHARD[4] DURBAN, WALTER[3] DURBIN, EDWARD N.[2], ROBERT[1] DURBAN)* was born December 18, 1723 in Gunpowder Neck, Baltimore, Maryland. He married ANN CONDRY Bet. 1737 - 1738. She was born Abt. 1717.

Notes for THOMAS DURBIN:
4 Jun 1740, Lemuel & Sophia Baker, planter, of Baltimore Co., Maryland to Thomas Durbin, planter, of same, 1,500 pounds of tobacco, 50 acres...line of Charles Baker and Lemuel Hill. Signed Lemuel (x) Baker. Wit: William Bond and Thomas Franklin. (Baltimore County, Maryland Deed Records: 1727-1757. John David Davis, 2008, pg. 306.)

Children of THOMAS DURBIN and ANN CONDRY are:
    i. DRUCILLA[14] DURBIN, b. October 09, 1738.
    ii. KETURAH DURBIN, b. March 23, 1740/41.
    iii. THOMAS DURBIN, b. March 08, 1742/43.

31. SAMUEL[13] MCKENZIE *(DANIEL[12], SARAH[11] DURBIN, SAMUEL CHRISTOPHER[10], CHRISTOPHER THOMAS[9], WILLIAM[8], WILLIAM[7], PETER[6], THOMAS[5], RICHARD[4] DURBAN, WALTER[3] DURBIN, EDWARD N.[2], ROBERT[1] DURBAN)* was born 1785. He married RACHEL DURBIN May 16, 1808 in Allegany Co., Maryland, daughter of SAMUEL DURBIN and COMFORT LOGSDON. She was born 1788.

Child of SAMUEL MCKENZIE and RACHEL DURBIN is:
    i. SUSANNA[14] MCKENZIE, b. March 08, 1815.

32. BENJAMIN[13] DURBIN, JR. *(BENJAMIN[12], SAMUEL[11], SAMUEL CHRISTOPHER[10], CHRISTOPHER THOMAS[9], WILLIAM[8], WILLIAM[7], PETER[6], THOMAS[5], RICHARD[4] DURBAN, WALTER[3]*

DURBIN, EDWARD N.², ROBERT¹ DURBAN) was born 1792 in Knox Co., Mt. Vernon, OH. He married ELIZABETH REAM.

Child of BENJAMIN DURBIN and ELIZABETH REAM is:
39.   i.   LEWIS[14] DURBIN, b. March 12, 1831, Danville, OH; d. May 15, 1884, Fayette Co., IL.

33. STEPHEN[13] DURBIN *(DANN¹², THOMAS¹¹, SAMUEL CHRISTOPHER¹⁰, CHRISTOPHER THOMAS⁹, WILLIAM⁸, WILLIAM⁷, PETER⁶, THOMAS⁵, RICHARD⁴ DURBAN, WALTER³ DURBIN, EDWARD N.², ROBERT¹ DURBAN)* was born 1800. He married ELIZABETH MCCONNELL.

Children of STEPHEN DURBIN and ELIZABETH MCCONNELL are:
40.   i.   JENNIE[14] DURBIN.
41.   ii.   ENOCH DURBIN, b. 1820, Richhill Twp., Greene County, Pennsylvania.

34. HENRY[13] DURBIN *(DANN¹², THOMAS¹¹, SAMUEL CHRISTOPHER¹⁰, CHRISTOPHER THOMAS⁹, WILLIAM⁸, WILLIAM⁷, PETER⁶, THOMAS⁵, RICHARD⁴ DURBAN, WALTER³ DURBIN, EDWARD N.², ROBERT¹ DURBAN)* was born 1801 in Maryland, and died September 19, 1862 in Adams County, Indiana. He married NANCY STEPHEN Abt. 1823. She was born 1803 in Pennsylvania, and died Bef. 1850.

Children of HENRY DURBIN and NANCY STEPHEN are:
          i.   NANCY[14] DURBIN, b. 1823.
42.   ii.   JOSEPH URIAH DURBIN, b. 1828, Ohio; d. 1872.
         iii.   MARTHA ANN DURBIN, b. 1833.
         iv.   HENRY DURBIN, b. 1834.
43.   v.   JOHN DURBIN, b. March 09, 1836, Ohio; d. March 12, 1912, Adams County, Indiana.
         vi.   ELIZABETH DURBIN, b. 1838.
44.   vii.   AMBROSE DURBIN, b. 1841, Monroe Twp., Adams County, Indiana; d. 1927.

	viii.	SARAH MARY DURBIN, b. 1845, Adams County, Indiana; d. 1913.
45.		
46.	ix.	MARIAH DURBIN, b. 1848, Adams County, Indiana; d. 1930.

35. WILLIAM[13] **DURBIN** *(DANN*[12]*, THOMAS*[11]*, SAMUEL CHRISTOPHER*[10]*, CHRISTOPHER THOMAS*[9]*, WILLIAM*[8]*, WILLIAM*[7]*, PETER*[6]*, THOMAS*[5]*, RICHARD*[4] *DURBAN, WALTER*[3] *DURBIN, EDWARD N.*[2]*, ROBERT*[1] *DURBAN)* was born October 11, 1802 in Westminster, Carroll Co., MD, and died April 19, 1849 in Morgan County, Ohio. He married MARTHA NIXON, daughter of WILLIAM NIXON. She was born Abt. 1801, and died July 21, 1885 in Morgan County, Ohio.

Notes for WILLIAM DURBIN:
Honorable William Durbin was born in Frederick County, Maryland on the 11th day of October, 1802. His father's name was Dann Durbin. At the age of 12 years, he moved with his father's family to Lancaster County, PA. In about 3 years from the time they settled in Pennsylvania his mother died, and his father having a large family of children, William left home at the age of 16, without money and with but little education, to try unaided his fortune among stranger; but by his diligence and industry he learned the carpenter trade, and also attended school and acquired sufficient education to enable him to perform the duties which devolved upon him in life.

Children of WILLIAM DURBIN and MARTHA NIXON are:

	i.	BENTON NICHOLAS[14] DURBIN.
47.	ii.	SAMUEL DURBIN, b. 1826, McConnelsville, Morgan County, Ohio.
48.	iii.	WILLIAM NIXON DURBIN, b. 1829; d. 1917.
	iv.	MARTHA DURBIN, b. 1835.

36. BASIL[13] **DURBIN** *(DANN*[12]*, THOMAS*[11]*, SAMUEL CHRISTOPHER*[10]*, CHRISTOPHER THOMAS*[9]*, WILLIAM*[8]*, WILLIAM*[7]*, PETER*[6]*, THOMAS*[5]*, RICHARD*[4] *DURBAN, WALTER*[3] *DURBIN, EDWARD N.*[2]*, ROBERT*[1] *DURBAN)* was born June 22, 1812 in Baltimore County, Maryland, and died June 28, 1883 in Mercer County, Celina, Ohio. He married (1) MARY M. ROLAND September 10, 1833. He married (2) ELIZA AXE August 15, 1844 in Zanesville, Muskingum County, Ohio.

More About BASIL DURBIN:
Burial: Catholic Church Cemetery, Celina, Ohio

Children of BASIL DURBIN and MARY ROLAND are:
      i.   CELESTINE^{14} DURBIN.
49. ii. DANIEL BASIL DURBIN, b. 1836, Ohio; d. 1876.
50. iii. RUTH A. DURBIN, b. 1838, Ohio.

Children of BASIL DURBIN and ELIZA AXE are:
     iv. SUSANNA^{14} DURBIN.
51. v.   MARY CELIA DURBIN, b. 1846, Wapakakoneta, Auglaize County, Ohio; d. 1869.
52. vi. SAMUEL AUGUSTINE DURBIN, b. 1848, Xenia, Greene County, Ohio; d. 1934.
53. vii. GEORGE PATRICK PIUS DURBIN, b. March 16, 1850, St. Mary's Twp., Mercer County, Ohio; d. 1934.
54. viii. JOHN FRANCIS DURBIN, b. 1852, Zanesville, Muskingum County, Ohio.
     ix. WILLIAM J. DURBIN, b. 1854.
55. x.   MARGARET DURBIN, b. 1856, St. Mary's Twp., Auglaize County, Ohio.
56. xi. THERESA DURBIN, b. 1858.
     xii. ELIZA DURBIN, b. 1860.

37. CATHERINE^{13} DURBIN *(DANN^{12}, THOMAS^{11}, SAMUEL CHRISTOPHER^{10}, CHRISTOPHER THOMAS^{9}, WILLIAM^{8}, WILLIAM^{7}, PETER^{6}, THOMAS^{5}, RICHARD^{4} DURBAN, WALTER^{3} DURBIN, EDWARD N.^{2}, ROBERT^{1} DURBAN)* was born Abt. 1821, and died 1896. She married STEPHEN CLARK.

Child of CATHERINE DURBIN and STEPHEN CLARK is:
     i.   TERESA CATHERINE^{14} CLARK, b. 1863.

38. WILLIAM[13] DURBIN *(NICHOLAS[12], THOMAS[11], SAMUEL CHRISTOPHER[10], CHRISTOPHER THOMAS[9], WILLIAM[8], WILLIAM[7], PETER[6], THOMAS[5], RICHARD[4] DURBAN, WALTER[3] DURBIN, EDWARD N.[2], ROBERT[1] DURBAN)* was born 1834, and died 1908.

Children of WILLIAM DURBIN are:
- 57. i. EDWARD MAJOR[14] DURBIN, d. 1920.
- 58. ii. CALEB DURBIN.
- 59. iii. ORLANDO DURBIN.
- 60. iv. DANIEL DURBIN.
- 61. v. JAMES DURBIN.

Generation No. 14

39. LEWIS[14] DURBIN *(BENJAMIN[13], BENJAMIN[12], SAMUEL[11], SAMUEL CHRISTOPHER[10], CHRISTOPHER THOMAS[9], WILLIAM[8], WILLIAM[7], PETER[6], THOMAS[5], RICHARD[4] DURBAN, WALTER[3] DURBIN, EDWARD N.[2], ROBERT[1] DURBAN)* was born March 12, 1831 in Danville, OH, and died May 15, 1884 in Fayette Co., IL. He married HANNAH MARGARET MARTIN DURBIN June 10, 1856 in Vandalia, IL, daughter of JOHN DURBIN and MARY WEINBERGER. She was born 1839 in Fayette Co., IL, and died 1912 in Fayette Co., IL.

Notes for LEWIS DURBIN:
Epitah: Amiable and beloved husband farewell. Thy years were few but thy virtues many; they are recorded not on this perishing stone but on the hand of life and in the hearts of thy afflicted friends.

More About LEWIS DURBIN:
Burial: Mt. Moriah Cemetery

Notes for HANNAH MARGARET MARTIN DURBIN:
After Lewis' death, she married James Henry Stevens in 1910, who died shortly thereafter (July 30, 1910) in St. Elmo, Illinois at age 69.

More About HANNAH MARGARET MARTIN DURBIN:

She died 27 February, 1912, at age 78 years, 10 months, and 12 days from double pneumonia.
Burial: Mt. Moriah Cemetery with Lewis (no marker for her grave).

Children of LEWIS DURBIN and HANNAH DURBIN are:
62. i. EMMA SOPHONIA[15] DURBIN, b. 1860; d. October 05, 1899.
63. ii. LEWIS (LOUIS) ALVIN DURBIN, b. 1877, Effingham Co., Moccasin Twp., IL; d. 1938, Bates Co., Adrian, MO.

40. JENNIE[14] DURBIN *(STEPHEN[13], DANN[12], THOMAS[11], SAMUEL CHRISTOPHER[10], CHRISTOPHER THOMAS[9], WILLIAM[8], WILLIAM[7], PETER[6], THOMAS[5], RICHARD[4] DURBAN, WALTER[3] DURBIN, EDWARD N.[2], ROBERT[1] DURBAN)* She married A. B. BARNETT.

Children of JENNIE DURBIN and A. BARNETT are:
  i.   LENI CLARE[15] BARNETT.
  ii. NIECIE A. B. BARNETT.
  iii. BESSIE B. A. B. BARNETT.

41. ENOCH[14] DURBIN *(STEPHEN[13], DANN[12], THOMAS[11], SAMUEL CHRISTOPHER[10], CHRISTOPHER THOMAS[9], WILLIAM[8], WILLIAM[7], PETER[6], THOMAS[5], RICHARD[4] DURBAN, WALTER[3] DURBIN, EDWARD N.[2], ROBERT[1] DURBAN)* was born 1820 in Richhill Twp., Greene County, Pennsylvania. He married (1) MARY M. STAGNER. He married (2) ELIZA HOPKINS.

Children of ENOCH DURBIN and MARY STAGNER are:
  i.   PETER H.[15] DURBIN.
  ii. ELIZA J. DURBIN.
  iii. JOHN DURBIN.
64. iv. GEORGE W. DURBIN, b. 1849, Morris Twp., Greene County, Pennsylvania.

42. JOSEPH URIAH[14] DURBIN *(HENRY[13], DANN[12], THOMAS[11], SAMUEL CHRISTOPHER[10], CHRISTOPHER THOMAS[9], WILLIAM[8], WILLIAM[7], PETER[6], THOMAS[5], RICHARD[4] DURBAN, WALTER[3] DURBIN, EDWARD N.[2], ROBERT[1] DURBAN)* was born 1828 in Ohio, and died 1872. He married MARTHA SMITH. She was born 1834 in Ohio, and died 1890.

Children of JOSEPH DURBIN and MARTHA SMITH are:
  - i. MARY ANN[15] DURBIN.
  - ii. GEORGE W. DURBIN, b. 1856.
  - iii. ROBERT E. DURBIN, b. 1857.
  - iv. JOHN THOMAS DURBIN, b. 1860.
- 65. v. AMBROSE Q. DURBIN, b. 1862; d. August 10, 1928.
  - vi. MARGARET A. DURBIN, b. 1864.
  - vii. ALEXANDER MCQUELLIN DURBIN, b. 1866.
- 66. viii. JOEL ELMORE DURBIN, b. 1868; d. 1938.
  - ix. WILLIAM DURBIN, b. 1871.

43. JOHN[14] DURBIN *(HENRY[13], DANN[12], THOMAS[11], SAMUEL CHRISTOPHER[10], CHRISTOPHER THOMAS[9], WILLIAM[8], WILLIAM[7], PETER[6], THOMAS[5], RICHARD[4] DURBAN, WALTER[3] DURBIN, EDWARD N.[2], ROBERT[1] DURBAN)* was born March 09, 1836 in Ohio, and died March 12, 1912 in Adams County, Indiana. He married HANNAH JANE HEAD September 12, 1861 in Adams County, Indiana, daughter of SAMUEL HEAD and RHODA. She was born March 22, 1845 in Knox County, Ohio, and died April 16, 1928 in Monroe Twp., Adams County, Indiana.

Children of JOHN DURBIN and HANNAH HEAD are:
- 67. i. NANCY[15] DURBIN, d. 1965.
  - ii. EMMA DURBIN.
- 68. iii. DANIEL F. DURBIN, b. Bet. October 15, 1862 - 1863.
- 69. iv. SAMUEL J. DURBIN, b. 1864; d. 1931.
  - v. GEORGE W. DURBIN, b. 1866.
  - vi. JOHN C. DURBIN, b. 1868.
- 70. vii. JOSEPH D. DURBIN, b. 1870; d. 1938.
  - viii. RHODA DURBIN, b. 1872.
  - ix. SARAH E. DURBIN, b. 1874.

71. x. WILLIAM AMBROSE DURBIN, b. 1876, Monroe Twp., Adams County, Indiana; d. 1932.
72. xi. CORA E. DURBIN, b. 1880; d. 1950.
73. xii. IDA B. DURBIN, b. 1886; d. 1964.

44. AMBROSE^{14} DURBIN *(HENRY^{13}, DANN^{12}, THOMAS^{11}, SAMUEL CHRISTOPHER^{10}, CHRISTOPHER THOMAS^{9}, WILLIAM^{8}, WILLIAM^{7}, PETER^{6}, THOMAS^{5}, RICHARD^{4} DURBAN, WALTER^{3} DURBIN, EDWARD N.^{2}, ROBERT^{1} DURBAN)* was born 1841 in Monroe Twp., Adams County, Indiana, and died 1927. He married (1) ELIZABETH AHERON. He married (2) MARY ELIZABETH LUTZ. He married (3) ANGELA CAKTURY DUER. She was born 1854 in Holmes County, Ohio, and died 1933.

Child of AMBROSE DURBIN and MARY LUTZ is:
    i. JOHN F.^{15} DURBIN, b. 1866.

Children of AMBROSE DURBIN and ANGELA DUER are:
    ii. BARMAN^{15} DURBIN, b. 1875.
    iii. EFFIE V. DURBIN, b. 1876.
    iv. JAMES C. DURBIN, b. 1877.
    v. GEORGE H. DURBIN, b. 1878.
    vi. DANIEL W. DURBIN, b. 1881.
74. vii. BENTON C. DURBIN, b. 1887; d. 1996.

45. SARAH MARY^{14} DURBIN *(HENRY^{13}, DANN^{12}, THOMAS^{11}, SAMUEL CHRISTOPHER^{10}, CHRISTOPHER THOMAS^{9}, WILLIAM^{8}, WILLIAM^{7}, PETER^{6}, THOMAS^{5}, RICHARD^{4} DURBAN, WALTER^{3} DURBIN, EDWARD N.^{2}, ROBERT^{1} DURBAN)* was born 1845 in Adams County, Indiana, and died 1913. She married JOHN EVERHART. He was born 1830 in Harrison County, Ohio, and died 1901.

Children of SARAH DURBIN and JOHN EVERHART are:
    i. PHILLIP MARION^{15} EVERHART, b. 1865.
    ii. ANNA EVERHART, b. 1868.

75.   iii.   LYDIA LOUISE EVERHART, b. 1870; d. 1930.
        iv.   JOSEPH MCCELAND EVERHART, b. 1874.
        v.   CHANCE ELLIOT EVERHART, b. 1885.
        vi.   CLEO EVERHART, b. 1887.

46. MARIAH^{14} DURBIN *(HENRY^{13}, DANN^{12}, THOMAS^{11}, SAMUEL CHRISTOPHER^{10}, CHRISTOPHER THOMAS^{9}, WILLIAM^{8}, WILLIAM^{7}, PETER^{6}, THOMAS^{5}, RICHARD^{4} DURBAN, WALTER^{3} DURBIN, EDWARD N.^{2}, ROBERT^{1} DURBAN)* was born 1848 in Adams County, Indiana, and died 1930. She married JOSEPH DAYTON LHAMON. He was born 1845 in Adams County, Indiana, and died 1930.

Children of MARIAH DURBIN and JOSEPH LHAMON are:
        i.   WILLIAM FRANCIS^{15} LHAMON, b. 1869; d. 1938.
        ii.   URIE ERVIN LHAMON, b. 1872; d. 1950.
        iii.   LEVINIA JANE LHAMON, b. 1875; d. 1931.
        iv.   ALPHA R. ALLIE LHAMON, b. 1878; d. 1950.
76.   v.   CORA ELIZABETH LHAMON, b. 1883; d. 1960.
        vi.   FLORA E. LHAMON, b. 1883; d. 1944.
        vii.   ZELLA A. LHAMON, b. 1884; d. 1972.
        viii.   HARVEY C. LHAMON, b. 1888; d. 1952.

47. SAMUEL^{14} DURBIN *(WILLIAM^{13}, DANN^{12}, THOMAS^{11}, SAMUEL CHRISTOPHER^{10}, CHRISTOPHER THOMAS^{9}, WILLIAM^{8}, WILLIAM^{7}, PETER^{6}, THOMAS^{5}, RICHARD^{4} DURBAN, WALTER^{3} DURBIN, EDWARD N.^{2}, ROBERT^{1} DURBAN)* was born 1826 in McConnelsville, Morgan County, Ohio. He married NANCY E. FILLKILL.

Child of SAMUEL DURBIN and NANCY FILLKILL is:
77.   i.   WILLIAM RUBLE^{15} DURBIN, b. 1859, Ohio; d. 1934.

48. WILLIAM NIXON^{14} DURBIN *(WILLIAM^{13}, DANN^{12}, THOMAS^{11}, SAMUEL CHRISTOPHER^{10}, CHRISTOPHER THOMAS^{9}, WILLIAM^{8}, WILLIAM^{7}, PETER^{6}, THOMAS^{5}, RICHARD^{4} DURBAN,*

WALTER³ DURBIN, EDWARD N.², ROBERT¹ DURBAN) was born 1829, and died 1917. He married MARGARET ELIZABETH BORDER. She was born 1847, and died 1931.

Children of WILLIAM DURBIN and MARGARET BORDER are:
78.   i.   ALFRED¹⁵ DURBIN, b. 1875, Bloom Twp., Morgan County, Ohio; d. 1916.
       ii. SAMUEL C. DURBIN, b. 1877.
       iii. RAYMOND DURBIN, b. 1879.
79.   iv. ROBERT ALFRED DURBIN, b. 1882, Bloom Twp., Morgan County, Ohio.
       v.   VERNON DURBIN, b. 1884.
       vi. MARTHA DURBIN, b. 1889.

49. DANIEL BASIL¹⁴ DURBIN *(BASIL¹³, DANN¹², THOMAS¹¹, SAMUEL CHRISTOPHER¹⁰, CHRISTOPHER THOMAS⁹, WILLIAM⁸, WILLIAM⁷, PETER⁶, THOMAS⁵, RICHARD⁴ DURBAN, WALTER³ DURBIN, EDWARD N.², ROBERT¹ DURBAN)* was born 1836 in Ohio, and died 1876. He married MARY ANN AXE. She was born 1838 in Pennsylvania, and died 1875.

Children of DANIEL DURBIN and MARY AXE are:
80.   i.   ALBERT A.¹⁵ DURBIN, b. 1859, Ohio; d. 1939.
      ii. MARGARET A. MAGGIE DURBIN, b. 1861.
      iii. MARY E. DURBIN, b. 1864; d. 1881.
      iv. DANIEL DURBIN, b. 1868.
      v. RUTH C. DURBIN, b. 1870.
      vi. BASIL DURBIN, b. 1872.
      vii. JOSEPH DURBIN, b. 1875.

50. RUTH A.¹⁴ DURBIN *(BASIL¹³, DANN¹², THOMAS¹¹, SAMUEL CHRISTOPHER¹⁰, CHRISTOPHER THOMAS⁹, WILLIAM⁸, WILLIAM⁷, PETER⁶, THOMAS⁵, RICHARD⁴ DURBAN, WALTER³ DURBIN, EDWARD N.², ROBERT¹ DURBAN)* was born 1838 in Ohio. She married HERMANUS HALSAMAN. He was born 1827 in Germany.

Child of RUTH DURBIN and HERMANUS HALSAMAN is:
i. BASIL A.[15] HALSAMAN, b. 1873.

51. MARY CELIA[14] DURBIN *(BASIL*[13]*, DANN*[12]*, THOMAS*[11]*, SAMUEL CHRISTOPHER*[10]*, CHRISTOPHER THOMAS*[9]*, WILLIAM*[8]*, WILLIAM*[7]*, PETER*[6]*, THOMAS*[5]*, RICHARD*[4] *DURBAN, WALTER*[3] *DURBIN, EDWARD N.*[2]*, ROBERT*[1] *DURBAN)* was born 1846 in Wapakakoneta, Auglaize County, Ohio, and died 1869. She married JOHN I. MCFARLAND.

Child of MARY DURBIN and JOHN MCFARLAND is:
i. SAMUEL W.[15] MCFARLAND, b. 1868.

52. SAMUEL AUGUSTINE[14] DURBIN *(BASIL*[13]*, DANN*[12]*, THOMAS*[11]*, SAMUEL CHRISTOPHER*[10]*, CHRISTOPHER THOMAS*[9]*, WILLIAM*[8]*, WILLIAM*[7]*, PETER*[6]*, THOMAS*[5]*, RICHARD*[4] *DURBAN, WALTER*[3] *DURBIN, EDWARD N.*[2]*, ROBERT*[1] *DURBAN)* was born 1848 in Xenia, Greene County, Ohio, and died 1934. He married MARGARET THERESA EYANSON. She was born 1852 in Decatur, Adams County, Indiana, and died 1921.

Children of SAMUEL DURBIN and MARGARET EYANSON are:
- 81. i. CHARLES ARTHUR[15] DURBIN, b. 1870, St. Mary's Twp., Auglaize County, Ohio; d. 1936.
- ii. MARY ELIZABETH DURBIN, b. 1872.
- 82. iii. CLARA AGNES DURBIN, b. 1874; d. 1912.
- 83. iv. CECELIA ELLEN DURBIN, b. 1876; d. 1951.
- 84. v. WILLIAM EDWARD DURBIN, b. 1878, Decatur, Adams County, Indiana; d. 1954.
- 85. vi. JAMES CHAUNCY DURBIN, b. 1880; d. 1913.
- 86. vii. JOHN HENRY DURBIN, b. 1883; d. 1916.
- viii. FRANCES DURBIN, b. 1886.
- 87. ix. JOSEPH AUGUSTINE DURBIN, b. 1888, Adams County, Ohio; d. 1951.
- 88. x. THERESA FLORENCE DURBIN, b. 1890.
- xi. FRANCIS M. DURBIN, b. 1892.
- xii. EARL DURBIN, b. 1894.

53. GEORGE PATRICK PIUS[14] DURBIN *(BASIL[13], DANN[12], THOMAS[11], SAMUEL CHRISTOPHER[10], CHRISTOPHER THOMAS[9], WILLIAM[8], WILLIAM[7], PETER[6], THOMAS[5], RICHARD[4] DURBAN, WALTER[3] DURBIN, EDWARD N.[2], ROBERT[1] DURBAN)* was born March 16, 1850 in St. Mary's Twp., Mercer County, Ohio, and died 1934. He married BRIDGETTA ANNA MCILVOY. She was born 1854 in St. Mary's Twp., Mercer County, Ohio, and died 1934.

Notes for GEORGE PATRICK PIUS DURBIN:
Durbin, Ohio is named after George Patrick Pius Durbin. A Durbin bean bake is held every year over Labor Day at Russia, Ohio, located near Celina.

Children of GEORGE DURBIN and BRIDGETTA MCILVOY are:
89.   i.   THOMAS ANTHONY[15] DURBIN, b. 1874, Center Twp., Mercer County, Ohio; d. 1952.
      ii. WILLIAM DURBIN, b. 1878.
      iii. MARY DURBIN, b. 1882.
      iv. JAMES DURBIN, b. 1883.
90.   v.   ANGELINE DURBIN, b. 1885.
      vi. KATHRYN DURBIN, b. 1887.
      vii. J. EDGAR DURBIN, b. 1889.
      viii. ELIZABETH DURBIN, b. 1890.
      ix. THERESA DURBIN, b. 1892.
      x.   GEORGE RUSSELL DURBIN, b. 1895.
91.   xi. LEO DURBIN, b. 1899, Ohio; d. 1971.

54. JOHN FRANCIS[14] DURBIN *(BASIL[13], DANN[12], THOMAS[11], SAMUEL CHRISTOPHER[10], CHRISTOPHER THOMAS[9], WILLIAM[8], WILLIAM[7], PETER[6], THOMAS[5], RICHARD[4] DURBAN, WALTER[3] DURBIN, EDWARD N.[2], ROBERT[1] DURBAN)* was born 1852 in Zanesville, Muskingum County, Ohio. He married ELIZABETH CATHERINE BOTKIN. She was born 1854.

Children of JOHN DURBIN and ELIZABETH BOTKIN are:
      i.   FRANCIS C.[15] DURBIN, b. 1874.
92.   ii. SAMUEL BERNARD DURBIN, b. 1881, Celina, Mercer County, Ohio; d. 1958.

iii. JOSEPH C. DURBIN, b. 1883.

55. MARGARET[14] DURBIN *(BASIL[13], DANN[12], THOMAS[11], SAMUEL CHRISTOPHER[10], CHRISTOPHER THOMAS[9], WILLIAM[8], WILLIAM[7], PETER[6], THOMAS[5], RICHARD[4] DURBAN, WALTER[3] DURBIN, EDWARD N.[2], ROBERT[1] DURBAN)* was born 1856 in St. Mary's Twp., Auglaize County, Ohio. She married JAMES SCHULTZ.

Children of MARGARET DURBIN and JAMES SCHULTZ are:
    i. LILLIE[15] SCHULTZ.
    ii. JOHN SCHULTZ.
    iii. HULDA SCHULTZ.
    iv. GEORGE A. SCHULTZ, b. 1890.

56. THERESA[14] DURBIN *(BASIL[13], DANN[12], THOMAS[11], SAMUEL CHRISTOPHER[10], CHRISTOPHER THOMAS[9], WILLIAM[8], WILLIAM[7], PETER[6], THOMAS[5], RICHARD[4] DURBAN, WALTER[3] DURBIN, EDWARD N.[2], ROBERT[1] DURBAN)* was born 1858. She married HENRY DIPTHMORE. He was born 1855 in Ohio.

Children of THERESA DURBIN and HENRY DIPTHMORE are:
    i. MARY E.[15] DIPTHMORE, b. 1881.
    ii. MAGGIE DIPTHMORE, b. 1883.
    iii. NORA DIPTHMORE, b. 1889.
    iv. ARTHUR DIPTHMORE, b. 1892.

57. EDWARD MAJOR[14] DURBIN *(WILLIAM[13], NICHOLAS[12], THOMAS[11], SAMUEL CHRISTOPHER[10], CHRISTOPHER THOMAS[9], WILLIAM[8], WILLIAM[7], PETER[6], THOMAS[5], RICHARD[4] DURBAN, WALTER[3] DURBIN, EDWARD N.[2], ROBERT[1] DURBAN)* died 1920. He married METTA GERTRUDE WEBB. She was born 1864, and died 1944.

Children of EDWARD DURBIN and METTA WEBB are:
    i. LAURA ALINE[15] DURBIN, b. 1891.

93.   ii. CHARLES EDWARD DURBIN, b. 1894; d. 1960.
94.   iii. JOHN WEBB DURBIN, b. 1898; d. 1976.
95.   iv. ALICE MAY DURBIN, b. 1901; d. 1989.

58. CALEB^{14} DURBIN *(WILLIAM^{13}, NICHOLAS^{12}, THOMAS^{11}, SAMUEL CHRISTOPHER^{10}, CHRISTOPHER THOMAS^{9}, WILLIAM^{8}, WILLIAM^{7}, PETER^{6}, THOMAS^{5}, RICHARD^{4} DURBAN, WALTER^{3} DURBIN, EDWARD N.^{2}, ROBERT^{1} DURBAN)* He married CORA MEANS.

Children of CALEB DURBIN and CORA MEANS are:
    i. LENA^{15} DURBIN.
    ii. CARRIE DURBIN.
    iii. EILEEN DURBIN.

59. ORLANDO^{14} DURBIN *(WILLIAM^{13}, NICHOLAS^{12}, THOMAS^{11}, SAMUEL CHRISTOPHER^{10}, CHRISTOPHER THOMAS^{9}, WILLIAM^{8}, WILLIAM^{7}, PETER^{6}, THOMAS^{5}, RICHARD^{4} DURBAN, WALTER^{3} DURBIN, EDWARD N.^{2}, ROBERT^{1} DURBAN)* He married FANNIE TURNER.

Children of ORLANDO DURBIN and FANNIE TURNER are:
    i. FRED^{15} DURBIN.
96.   ii. GRACE DURBIN.

60. DANIEL^{14} DURBIN *(WILLIAM^{13}, NICHOLAS^{12}, THOMAS^{11}, SAMUEL CHRISTOPHER^{10}, CHRISTOPHER THOMAS^{9}, WILLIAM^{8}, WILLIAM^{7}, PETER^{6}, THOMAS^{5}, RICHARD^{4} DURBAN, WALTER^{3} DURBIN, EDWARD N.^{2}, ROBERT^{1} DURBAN)* He married VIOLET.

Children of DANIEL DURBIN and VIOLET are:
    i. WILL^{15} DURBIN.
    ii. GRACE DURBIN.
    iii. BESS DURBIN.
    iv. NELL DURBIN.
    v. CLIFFORD DURBIN, d. June 14, 1992.

61. JAMES^{14} DURBIN *(WILLIAM^{13}, NICHOLAS^{12}, THOMAS^{11}, SAMUEL CHRISTOPHER^{10}, CHRISTOPHER THOMAS^{9}, WILLIAM^{8}, WILLIAM^{7}, PETER^{6}, THOMAS^{5}, RICHARD^{4} DURBAN, WALTER^{3} DURBIN, EDWARD N.^{2}, ROBERT^{1} DURBAN)* He married LOU REDMAN.

Children of JAMES DURBIN and LOU REDMAN are:
  i. CARRIE^{15} DURBIN.
  ii. VERN DURBIN.
  iii. GEORGE DURBIN.
  iv. RUBY DURBIN.
  v. WILL DURBIN.

Generation No. 15

62. EMMA SOPHONIA^{15} DURBIN *(LEWIS^{14}, BENJAMIN^{13}, BENJAMIN^{12}, SAMUEL^{11}, SAMUEL CHRISTOPHER^{10}, CHRISTOPHER THOMAS^{9}, WILLIAM^{8}, WILLIAM^{7}, PETER^{6}, THOMAS^{5}, RICHARD^{4} DURBAN, WALTER^{3} DURBIN, EDWARD N.^{2}, ROBERT^{1} DURBAN)* was born 1860, and died October 05, 1899. She married GEORGE AUSTIN TIREY November 22, 1885.

Children of EMMA DURBIN and GEORGE TIREY are:
  i. WELBY OTTO^{16} TIREY, b. 1888; d. 1928.
  ii. FIETA BEATRICE TIREY, b. 1897; d. 1980.

63. LEWIS (LOUIS) ALVIN^{15} DURBIN *(LEWIS^{14}, BENJAMIN^{13}, BENJAMIN^{12}, SAMUEL^{11}, SAMUEL CHRISTOPHER^{10}, CHRISTOPHER THOMAS^{9}, WILLIAM^{8}, WILLIAM^{7}, PETER^{6}, THOMAS^{5}, RICHARD^{4} DURBAN, WALTER^{3} DURBIN, EDWARD N.^{2}, ROBERT^{1} DURBAN)* was born 1877 in Effingham Co., Moccasion Twp., IL, and died 1938 in Bates Co., Adrian, MO. He married LAURA ELLA EWING, daughter of HENRY EWING and CHRISTINA PHIFER. She was born September 14, 1877 in Effingham Co., Moccasion Twp., IL, and died Bet. 1953 - 1954 in Bates Co., Adrian, MO.

Children of LEWIS DURBIN and LAURA EWING are:
97. i. UFA HENRY[16] DURBIN, b. November 08, 1899, Effingham Co., Moccasion Twp., IL; d. April 03, 1958, Bates Co., Butler, MO.
  ii. EDNA CHRISTINANA DURBIN, b. June 04, 1903.
  iii. LESLIE ALVIN DURBIN, b. November 10, 1908.

64. GEORGE W.[15] DURBIN *(ENOCH[14], STEPHEN[13], DANN[12], THOMAS[11], SAMUEL CHRISTOPHER[10], CHRISTOPHER THOMAS[9], WILLIAM[8], WILLIAM[7], PETER[6], THOMAS[5], RICHARD[4] DURBAN, WALTER[3] DURBIN, EDWARD N.[2], ROBERT[1] DURBAN)* was born 1849 in Morris Twp., Greene County, Pennsylvania. He married JENNIE L. FONNER. She was born 1854.
Children of GEORGE DURBIN and JENNIE FONNER are:
  i. JAMES R.[16] DURBIN.
  ii. LIZZIE B. DURBIN.
98. iii. ALBERT F. DURBIN.
  iv. CHARLIE B. DURBIN.
  v. MAGGIE E. DURBIN.

65. AMBROSE Q.[15] DURBIN *(JOSEPH URIAH[14], HENRY[13], DANN[12], THOMAS[11], SAMUEL CHRISTOPHER[10], CHRISTOPHER THOMAS[9], WILLIAM[8], WILLIAM[7], PETER[6], THOMAS[5], RICHARD[4] DURBAN, WALTER[3] DURBIN, EDWARD N.[2], ROBERT[1] DURBAN)* was born 1862, and died August 10, 1928. He married ANNIE ELIZABETH HERRON. She was born 1868, and died June 14, 1925.

Children of AMBROSE DURBIN and ANNIE HERRON are:
99. i. ONA MAY[16] DURBIN, b. 1888.
  ii. OCO PEARL DURBIN, b. 1891.
  iii. ORA BLANCH DURBIN, b. 1893.
  iv. ORVA HENRY DURBIN, b. 1901; d. June 24, 1966.
  v. IVY GERTRUDE DURBIN, b. 1903.
  vi. OMER SYLVESTER DURBIN, b. 1908.

66. JOEL ELMORE[15] DURBIN *(JOSEPH URIAH[14], HENRY[13], DANN[12], THOMAS[11], SAMUEL CHRISTOPHER[10], CHRISTOPHER THOMAS[9], WILLIAM[8], WILLIAM[7], PETER[6], THOMAS[5], RICHARD[4] DURBAN, WALTER[3] DURBIN, EDWARD N.[2], ROBERT[1] DURBAN)* was born 1868, and died 1938. He married JENNIE MAE MULLIN. She was born 1874, and died 1938.

Children of JOEL DURBIN and JENNIE MULLIN are:
    i. FRANCIS CLEO[16] DURBIN, b. 1892.
    ii. LAWRENCE J. DURBIN, b. 1896, Adams County, Indiana; d. 1987.
100.   iii. EARL DON DURBIN, b. 1898, Adams County, Indiana; d. 1987.

67. NANCY[15] DURBIN *(JOHN[14], HENRY[13], DANN[12], THOMAS[11], SAMUEL CHRISTOPHER[10], CHRISTOPHER THOMAS[9], WILLIAM[8], WILLIAM[7], PETER[6], THOMAS[5], RICHARD[4] DURBAN, WALTER[3] DURBIN, EDWARD N.[2], ROBERT[1] DURBAN)* died 1965. She married JOHN W. COOK December 05, 1902 in Decatur, Adams County, Indiana, son of DANIEL COOK and FRANCES WALLER. He was born January 17, 1882 in Adams County, Indiana, and died Abt. 1967 in Fort Wayne, Indiana.

Child of NANCY DURBIN and JOHN COOK is:
    i. FRANCES[16] COOK.

68. DANIEL F.[15] DURBIN *(JOHN[14], HENRY[13], DANN[12], THOMAS[11], SAMUEL CHRISTOPHER[10], CHRISTOPHER THOMAS[9], WILLIAM[8], WILLIAM[7], PETER[6], THOMAS[5], RICHARD[4] DURBAN, WALTER[3] DURBIN, EDWARD N.[2], ROBERT[1] DURBAN)* was born Bet. October 15, 1862 - 1863. He married SARAH ELIZABETH HUSTON.

Children of DANIEL DURBIN and SARAH HUSTON are:
    i. GEORGE ALBERT[16] DURBIN.
    ii. JOSEPH EDWARD DURBIN.

101.   iii.   JOHN WILLIAM HENRY HARRISON DURBIN, b. September 10, 1887, Berne, Adams County, Indiana; d. December 05, 1936, Decatur, Adams County, Indiana.

69. SAMUEL J.[15] DURBIN *(JOHN*[14]*, HENRY*[13]*, DANN*[12]*, THOMAS*[11]*, SAMUEL CHRISTOPHER*[10]*, CHRISTOPHER THOMAS*[9]*, WILLIAM*[8]*, WILLIAM*[7]*, PETER*[6]*, THOMAS*[5]*, RICHARD*[4] *DURBAN, WALTER*[3] *DURBIN, EDWARD N.*[2]*, ROBERT*[1] *DURBAN)* was born 1864, and died 1931. He married LYDIA MARTZ. She was born 1869, and died 1940.

Children of SAMUEL DURBIN and LYDIA MARTZ are:
    i.   LAURA J.[16] DURBIN, b. 1888.
    ii.   HARRY C. DURBIN, b. 1895.
    iii.   BESSIE M. DURBIN, b. 1899.
    iv.   GLADYS WILMA DURBIN, b. 1903; d. May 30, 1916.

70. JOSEPH D.[15] DURBIN *(JOHN*[14]*, HENRY*[13]*, DANN*[12]*, THOMAS*[11]*, SAMUEL CHRISTOPHER*[10]*, CHRISTOPHER THOMAS*[9]*, WILLIAM*[8]*, WILLIAM*[7]*, PETER*[6]*, THOMAS*[5]*, RICHARD*[4] *DURBAN, WALTER*[3] *DURBIN, EDWARD N.*[2]*, ROBERT*[1] *DURBAN)* was born 1870, and died 1938. He married LAURA B. ASPY June 1894, daughter of LAWRENCE ASPY and MARGARET JOHNSON.

Notes for JOSEPH D. DURBIN:
Joseph Dayton Durbin died September 12,1936 after being hit by a car.

Children of JOSEPH DURBIN and LAURA ASPY are:
    i.   IRENE HOFFMAN[16] DURBIN.
    ii.   ETHEL DURBIN, b. 1904; d. April 07, 1928.

71. WILLIAM AMBROSE[15] DURBIN *(JOHN*[14]*, HENRY*[13]*, DANN*[12]*, THOMAS*[11]*, SAMUEL CHRISTOPHER*[10]*, CHRISTOPHER THOMAS*[9]*, WILLIAM*[8]*, WILLIAM*[7]*, PETER*[6]*, THOMAS*[5]*, RICHARD*[4] *DURBAN, WALTER*[3] *DURBIN, EDWARD N.*[2]*, ROBERT*[1] *DURBAN)* was born 1876 in Monroe Twp., Adams County, Indiana, and died 1932. He married OLLIE PEARL WOLFE. She was born 1885 in Adams County, Indiana, and died 1947.

Child of WILLIAM DURBIN and OLLIE WOLFE is:
102. i. LESTER V.[16] DURBIN, b. 1913, Adams County, Indiana.

72. CORA E.[15] DURBIN *(JOHN[14], HENRY[13], DANN[12], THOMAS[11], SAMUEL CHRISTOPHER[10], CHRISTOPHER THOMAS[9], WILLIAM[8], WILLIAM[7], PETER[6], THOMAS[5], RICHARD[4] DURBAN, WALTER[3] DURBIN, EDWARD N.[2], ROBERT[1] DURBAN)* was born 1880, and died 1950. She married JOHN W. REINHARD. He was born 1864, and died 1928.

Children of CORA DURBIN and JOHN REINHARD are:
 i. VIRGIL L.[16] REINHARD, b. 1912.
 ii. VIRGIL E. REINHARD, b. 1915.
 iii. DESSIE D. REINHARD, b. 1917.

73. IDA B.[15] DURBIN *(JOHN[14], HENRY[13], DANN[12], THOMAS[11], SAMUEL CHRISTOPHER[10], CHRISTOPHER THOMAS[9], WILLIAM[8], WILLIAM[7], PETER[6], THOMAS[5], RICHARD[4] DURBAN, WALTER[3] DURBIN, EDWARD N.[2], ROBERT[1] DURBAN)* was born 1886, and died 1964. She married CLYDE D. WOLFE. He was born 1881, and died 1942.

Child of IDA DURBIN and CLYDE WOLFE is:
 i. FRANKLIN DURBIN DANIEL[16] WOLFE.

74. BENTON C.[15] DURBIN *(AMBROSE[14], HENRY[13], DANN[12], THOMAS[11], SAMUEL CHRISTOPHER[10], CHRISTOPHER THOMAS[9], WILLIAM[8], WILLIAM[7], PETER[6], THOMAS[5], RICHARD[4] DURBAN, WALTER[3] DURBIN, EDWARD N.[2], ROBERT[1] DURBAN)* was born 1887, and died 1996.

Child of BENTON C. DURBIN is:
 i. BENTON[16] DURBIN, d. April 08, 1966.

75. LYDIA LOUISE[15] EVERHART *(SARAH MARY[14] DURBIN, HENRY[13], DANN[12], THOMAS[11], SAMUEL CHRISTOPHER[10],*

CHRISTOPHER THOMAS^9, WILLIAM^8, WILLIAM^7, PETER^6, THOMAS^5, RICHARD^4 DURBAN, WALTER^3 DURBAN, EDWARD N.^{2}, ROBERT^1 DURBAN) was born 1870, and died 1930. She married WILLIAM ROBERT ROSE. He was born 1868 in London, Middlesex, England, and died 1955.

Children of LYDIA EVERHART and WILLIAM ROSE are:
- i. EUGENE PHILLIP^{16} ROSE, b. 1895.
- ii. LEE WILLIAM ROSE, b. 1898.
- 103. iii. MARGARET LOU ROSE, b. 1903, Port Orchard, Washington; d. 1949.

76. CORA ELIZABETH^{15} LHAMON (MARIAH^{14} DURBIN, HENRY^{13}, DANN^{12}, THOMAS^{11}, SAMUEL CHRISTOPHER^{10}, CHRISTOPHER THOMAS^9, WILLIAM^8, WILLIAM^7, PETER^6, THOMAS^5, RICHARD^4 DURBAN, WALTER^3 DURBAN, EDWARD N.^{2}, ROBERT^1 DURBAN) was born 1883, and died 1960. She married JOHN MCQUITHY. He was born 1916 in Salt Lick, Kentucky, and died 1976.

Children of CORA LHAMON and JOHN MCQUITHY are:
- i. MARILYN^{16} MCQUITHY.
- ii. BILLIE JEAN MCQUITHY.
- iii. JOHN RICHARD MCQUITHY, b. 1946.

77. WILLIAM RUBLE^{15} DURBIN (SAMUEL^{14}, WILLIAM^{13}, DANN^{12}, THOMAS^{11}, SAMUEL CHRISTOPHER^{10}, CHRISTOPHER THOMAS^9, WILLIAM^8, WILLIAM^7, PETER^6, THOMAS^5, RICHARD^4 DURBAN, WALTER^3 DURBAN, EDWARD N.^{2}, ROBERT^1 DURBAN) was born 1859 in Ohio, and died 1934. He married MINERVA ELLEN PICKEREL. She was born 1862 in Agency, Iowa.

Child of WILLIAM DURBIN and MINERVA PICKEREL is:
- 104. i. ETHEL GERTRUDE^{16} DURBIN, b. 1895, Moline, Kansas.

78. ALFRED[15] DURBIN *(WILLIAM NIXON[14], WILLIAM[13], DANN[12], THOMAS[11], SAMUEL CHRISTOPHER[10], CHRISTOPHER THOMAS[9], WILLIAM[8], WILLIAM[7], PETER[6], THOMAS[5], RICHARD[4] DURBAN, WALTER[3] DURBIN, EDWARD N.[2], ROBERT[1] DURBAN)* was born 1875 in Bloom Twp., Morgan County, Ohio, and died 1916. He married STELLA FARRA.

Children of ALFRED DURBIN and STELLA FARRA are:
    i. MARTHA[16] DURBIN.
    ii. ROBERT A. DURBIN, b. 1902.
    iii. OLIVE MARGARET DURBIN, b. 1903.
    iv. JOHN WILLIAM DURBIN, b. 1909.

79. ROBERT ALFRED[15] DURBIN *(WILLIAM NIXON[14], WILLIAM[13], DANN[12], THOMAS[11], SAMUEL CHRISTOPHER[10], CHRISTOPHER THOMAS[9], WILLIAM[8], WILLIAM[7], PETER[6], THOMAS[5], RICHARD[4] DURBAN, WALTER[3] DURBIN, EDWARD N.[2], ROBERT[1] DURBAN)* was born 1882 in Bloom Twp., Morgan County, Ohio. He married MARTHA LENA ADRIAN.

Children of ROBERT DURBIN and MARTHA ADRIAN are:
    i. PATRICIA[16] DURBIN, b. 1924.
    ii. RICHARD ARRA DURBIN, b. 1926.

80. ALBERT A.[15] DURBIN *(DANIEL BASIL[14], BASIL[13], DANN[12], THOMAS[11], SAMUEL CHRISTOPHER[10], CHRISTOPHER THOMAS[9], WILLIAM[8], WILLIAM[7], PETER[6], THOMAS[5], RICHARD[4] DURBAN, WALTER[3] DURBIN, EDWARD N.[2], ROBERT[1] DURBAN)* was born 1859 in Ohio, and died 1939. He married (1) MARY RYLEY. He married (2) CARRIE PHILOMINA HOLTGREVEN. She was born 1875, and died 1958.

Children of ALBERT DURBIN and CARRIE HOLTGREVEN are:
105.   i. JEROME DANIEL[16] DURBIN, b. 1899; d. 1975.
      ii. MARK JOSEPH DURBIN, b. 1902.
106.   iii. MARCELLUS ALBERT DURBIN, b. 1905; d. 1992.
      iv. MARY MARGARET DURBIN, b. 1908.

81. CHARLES ARTHUR[15] DURBIN *(SAMUEL AUGUSTINE[14], BASIL[13], DANN[12], THOMAS[11], SAMUEL CHRISTOPHER[10], CHRISTOPHER THOMAS[9], WILLIAM[8], WILLIAM[7], PETER[6], THOMAS[5], RICHARD[4] DURBAN, WALTER[3] DURBAN, EDWARD N.[2], ROBERT[1] DURBAN)* was born 1870 in St. Mary's Twp., Auglaize County, Ohio, and died 1936. He married MATTIE RAINS.

Children of CHARLES DURBIN and MATTIE RAINS are:
    i. LEO[16] DURBIN.
    ii. MARGARET DURBIN.
    iii. AGNES DURBIN.
    iv. VIOLET DURBIN.
    v. CHARLES ARTHUR DURBIN, b. 1889.

82. CLARA AGNES[15] DURBIN *(SAMUEL AUGUSTINE[14], BASIL[13], DANN[12], THOMAS[11], SAMUEL CHRISTOPHER[10], CHRISTOPHER THOMAS[9], WILLIAM[8], WILLIAM[7], PETER[6], THOMAS[5], RICHARD[4] DURBAN, WALTER[3] DURBAN, EDWARD N.[2], ROBERT[1] DURBAN)* was born 1874, and died 1912. She married JOHN GOLDEN.

Children of CLARA DURBIN and JOHN GOLDEN are:
    i. CHARLES[16] GOLDEN.
    ii. JOHN GOLDEN.
    iii. MARY MARGARET GOLDEN.
    iv. FLORENCE POLLY GOLDEN.

83. CECELIA ELLEN[15] DURBIN *(SAMUEL AUGUSTINE[14], BASIL[13], DANN[12], THOMAS[11], SAMUEL CHRISTOPHER[10], CHRISTOPHER THOMAS[9], WILLIAM[8], WILLIAM[7], PETER[6], THOMAS[5], RICHARD[4] DURBAN, WALTER[3] DURBAN, EDWARD N.[2], ROBERT[1] DURBAN)* was born 1876, and died 1951. She married MICHAEL MULVIHILL.

Children of CECELIA DURBIN and MICHAEL MULVIHILL are:
    i. EDWARD[16] MULVIHILL.
    ii. VICTOR MULVIHILL.
    iii. RICHARD MULVIHILL.
    iv. NANCY THERESA MULVIHILL.

v. LLOYD MULVIHILL, b. 1905.

84. WILLIAM EDWARD[15] DURBIN *(SAMUEL AUGUSTINE[14], BASIL[13], DANN[12], THOMAS[11], SAMUEL CHRISTOPHER[10], CHRISTOPHER THOMAS[9], WILLIAM[8], WILLIAM[7], PETER[6], THOMAS[5], RICHARD[4] DURBAN, WALTER[3] DURBAN, EDWARD N.[2], ROBERT[1] DURBAN)* was born 1878 in Decatur, Adams County, Indiana, and died 1954. He married HENRIETTA JEANETTE CUMMINGS ROSS. She was born 1893 in Jersey City, New Jersey, and died 1989.

Children of WILLIAM DURBIN and HENRIETTA ROSS are:
107. i. MARGARET BERNICE[16] DURBIN, b. 1911, St. Louis, Missouri; d. 1995.
108. ii. DONALD ROSS DURBIN, b. 1912, St. Louis, Missouri; d. 1983.

85. JAMES CHAUNCY[15] DURBIN *(SAMUEL AUGUSTINE[14], BASIL[13], DANN[12], THOMAS[11], SAMUEL CHRISTOPHER[10], CHRISTOPHER THOMAS[9], WILLIAM[8], WILLIAM[7], PETER[6], THOMAS[5], RICHARD[4] DURBAN, WALTER[3] DURBAN, EDWARD N.[2], ROBERT[1] DURBAN)* was born 1880, and died 1913. He married SOPHIA BROGAN.

Children of JAMES DURBIN and SOPHIA BROGAN are:
    i. EARL[16] DURBIN.
    ii. RONALD DURBIN.
    iii. FRANCIS DURBIN.

86. JOHN HENRY[15] DURBIN *(SAMUEL AUGUSTINE[14], BASIL[13], DANN[12], THOMAS[11], SAMUEL CHRISTOPHER[10], CHRISTOPHER THOMAS[9], WILLIAM[8], WILLIAM[7], PETER[6], THOMAS[5], RICHARD[4] DURBAN, WALTER[3] DURBAN, EDWARD N.[2], ROBERT[1] DURBAN)* was born 1883, and died 1916. He married ALMA SCHINANHOLTZ.

Child of JOHN DURBIN and ALMA SCHINANHOLTZ is:

      i. MINERVA[16] DURBIN.

87. JOSEPH AUGUSTINE[15] DURBIN *(SAMUEL AUGUSTINE[14], BASIL[13], DANN[12], THOMAS[11], SAMUEL CHRISTOPHER[10], CHRISTOPHER THOMAS[9], WILLIAM[8], WILLIAM[7], PETER[6], THOMAS[5], RICHARD[4] DURBAN, WALTER[3] DURBIN, EDWARD N.[2], ROBERT[1] DURBAN)* was born 1888 in Adams County, Ohio, and died 1951. He married MARY SHEA.

Children of JOSEPH DURBIN and MARY SHEA are:
      i. WILLIAM[16] DURBIN.
     ii. ELMER DURBIN.
    iii. MILDRED DURBIN.

88. THERESA FLORENCE[15] DURBIN *(SAMUEL AUGUSTINE[14], BASIL[13], DANN[12], THOMAS[11], SAMUEL CHRISTOPHER[10], CHRISTOPHER THOMAS[9], WILLIAM[8], WILLIAM[7], PETER[6], THOMAS[5], RICHARD[4] DURBAN, WALTER[3] DURBIN, EDWARD N.[2], ROBERT[1] DURBAN)* was born 1890. She married WILLIAM LESLIE BRAND. He was born 1880 in Edina, Knox County, Missouri.

Children of THERESA DURBIN and WILLIAM BRAND are:
	i.	ROBERTSON AUGUSTINE[16] BRAND, b. 1911.
	ii.	MILLARD FRANCIS BRAND, b. 1912.
	iii.	EUGENE KENNETH BRAND, b. 1914.
	iv.	VIVIAN RUTH BRAND, b. 1917.
109.	v.	MARY RITA BRAND, b. 1919, Muncie, Delaware County, Indiana.
110.	vi.	WILLIAM FREDERICK BRAND, b. 1921, Muncie, Delaware County, Indiana.
111.	vii.	MARGARET ANN BRAND, b. 1922, Muncie, Delaware County, Indiana.
	viii.	THOMAS LESLIE BRAND, b. 1924.
	ix.	BLANCHE ELLEN BRAND, b. 1927.
	x.	JOSEPH FRANKLIN BRAND, b. 1929.
	xi.	REBECCA JEANETTE BRAND, b. 1930.
	xii.	JOAN FLORENCE BRAND, b. 1931.

xiii. JANE FRANCES BRAND, b. 1931.
xiv. EELINOR ALICE BRAND, b. 1933.
xv. CAROLYN SUZANNE BRAND, b. 1934.

89. THOMAS ANTHONY^{15} DURBIN *(GEORGE PATRICK PIUS^{14}, BASIL^{13}, DANN^{12}, THOMAS^{11}, SAMUEL CHRISTOPHER^{10}, CHRISTOPHER THOMAS^{9}, WILLIAM^{8}, WILLIAM^{7}, PETER^{6}, THOMAS^{5}, RICHARD^{4} DURBAN, WALTER^{3} DURBIN, EDWARD N.^{2}, ROBERT^{1} DURBAN)* was born 1874 in Center Twp., Mercer County, Ohio, and died 1952. He married MARY FRANCES PUTHOFF. She was born 1874 in Jefferson Twp., Mercer County, Ohio, and died 1948.

Children of THOMAS DURBIN and MARY PUTHOFF are:
112. i. ESTHER^{16} DURBIN.
ii. BERNICE DURBIN.
iii. FLORENCE DURBIN.
113. iv. MARY EVELYN DURBIN.
114. v. HENRY LEROY ROY DURBIN, b. 1902, Fort Recovery, Mercer County, Ohio; d. 1961.
115. vi. PAUL EDGAR DURBIN, b. 1911, Celina, Mercer County, Ohio; d. 1985.

90. ANGELINE^{15} DURBIN *(GEORGE PATRICK PIUS^{14}, BASIL^{13}, DANN^{12}, THOMAS^{11}, SAMUEL CHRISTOPHER^{10}, CHRISTOPHER THOMAS^{9}, WILLIAM^{8}, WILLIAM^{7}, PETER^{6}, THOMAS^{5}, RICHARD^{4} DURBAN, WALTER^{3} DURBIN, EDWARD N.^{2}, ROBERT^{1} DURBAN)* was born 1885. She married FRED WINTER.

Children of ANGELINE DURBIN and FRED WINTER are:
116. i. MARY^{16} WINTER.
117. ii. WILLIAM RUSSELL WINTER, b. 1911.
118. iii. RICHARD EDWARD WINTER, b. 1930.

91. LEO^{15} DURBIN *(GEORGE PATRICK PIUS^{14}, BASIL^{13}, DANN^{12}, THOMAS^{11}, SAMUEL CHRISTOPHER^{10}, CHRISTOPHER THOMAS^{9}, WILLIAM^{8}, WILLIAM^{7}, PETER^{6}, THOMAS^{5}, RICHARD^{4} DURBAN,*

WALTER³ DURBIN, EDWARD N.², ROBERT¹ DURBAN) was born 1899 in Ohio, and died 1971. He married MARY CAIN.

Children of LEO DURBIN and MARY CAIN are:
- 119. i. MARY LEE¹⁶ DURBIN.
- 120. ii. JOHN D. DURBIN.
- 121. iii. G. DAVID DURBIN.
- iv. RUTH LYNN DURBIN.
- 122. v. JAMES E. DURBIN, b. 1926.
- 123. vi. DONALD LEO DURBIN, b. 1927, Rush County, Indiana; d. 1997.
- vii. ROBERT C. DURBIN, b. 1931.

92. SAMUEL BERNARD¹⁵ DURBIN *(JOHN FRANCIS¹⁴, BASIL¹³, DANN¹², THOMAS¹¹, SAMUEL CHRISTOPHER¹⁰, CHRISTOPHER THOMAS⁹, WILLIAM⁸, WILLIAM⁷, PETER⁶, THOMAS⁵, RICHARD⁴ DURBAN, WALTER³ DURBIN, EDWARD N.², ROBERT¹ DURBAN)* was born 1881 in Celina, Mercer County, Ohio, and died 1958. He married MARGARET JANE BURSON. She was born 1887 in Montpelier, Blackford County, Indiana.

Children of SAMUEL DURBIN and MARGARET BURSON are:
- i. JOHN WILLIAM¹⁶ DURBIN.
- ii. DONALD BERNARD DURBIN.
- 124. iii. HAROLD BERNARD DURBIN, b. 1904, Gas City, Grant County, Indiana.
- iv. FORREST W. DURBIN, b. 1908.
- v. JAMES L. DURBIN, b. 1918.

93. CHARLES EDWARD¹⁵ DURBIN *(EDWARD MAJOR¹⁴, WILLIAM¹³, NICHOLAS¹², THOMAS¹¹, SAMUEL CHRISTOPHER¹⁰, CHRISTOPHER THOMAS⁹, WILLIAM⁸, WILLIAM⁷, PETER⁶, THOMAS⁵, RICHARD⁴ DURBAN, WALTER³ DURBIN, EDWARD N.², ROBERT¹ DURBAN)* was born 1894, and died 1960. He married RUTH MAY SHEET. She was born 1892, and died 1970.

Children of CHARLES DURBIN and RUTH SHEET are:
- 125. i. METTA ELIZABETH¹⁶ DURBIN, b. 1920.

126.   ii.   ALICE LEA DURBIN, b. 1921.
        iii. ALINE LAURA DURBIN, b. 1923.
127.   iv.   FRANK EDWARD DURBIN, b. 1924; d. 1990.
128.   v.   EMERA MAHLON DURBIN, b. 1927.

94. JOHN WEBB^{15} DURBIN *(EDWARD MAJOR^{14}, WILLIAM^{13}, NICHOLAS^{12}, THOMAS^{11}, SAMUEL CHRISTOPHER^{10}, CHRISTOPHER THOMAS^{9}, WILLIAM^{8}, WILLIAM^{7}, PETER^{6}, THOMAS^{5}, RICHARD^{4} DURBAN, WALTER^{3} DURBIN, EDWARD N.^{2}, ROBERT^{1} DURBAN)* was born 1898, and died 1976. He married EDITH OPAL LYMAN.

Children of JOHN DURBIN and EDITH LYMAN are:
129.   i.   GENE L.^{16} DURBIN.
130.   ii.   RONALD REID DURBIN.
131.   iii. JACK THADDEUS DURBIN.

95. ALICE MAY^{15} DURBIN *(EDWARD MAJOR^{14}, WILLIAM^{13}, NICHOLAS^{12}, THOMAS^{11}, SAMUEL CHRISTOPHER^{10}, CHRISTOPHER THOMAS^{9}, WILLIAM^{8}, WILLIAM^{7}, PETER^{6}, THOMAS^{5}, RICHARD^{4} DURBAN, WALTER^{3} DURBIN, EDWARD N.^{2}, ROBERT^{1} DURBAN)* was born 1901, and died 1989. She married LUTHER W. MORGAN.

Child of ALICE DURBIN and LUTHER MORGAN is:
132.   i.   JOHN DURBIN^{16} MORGAN.

96. GRACE^{15} DURBIN *(ORLANDO^{14}, WILLIAM^{13}, NICHOLAS^{12}, THOMAS^{11}, SAMUEL CHRISTOPHER^{10}, CHRISTOPHER THOMAS^{9}, WILLIAM^{8}, WILLIAM^{7}, PETER^{6}, THOMAS^{5}, RICHARD^{4} DURBAN, WALTER^{3} DURBIN, EDWARD N.^{2}, ROBERT^{1} DURBAN)* She married JACK JOHNSON.

Children of GRACE DURBIN and JACK JOHNSON are:
        i.   HELEN^{16} JOHNSON.
        ii.   AMIL JOHNSON.

Generation No. 16

97. UFA HENRY[16] DURBIN *(LEWIS (LOUIS) ALVIN[15], LEWIS[14], BENJAMIN[13], BENJAMIN[12], SAMUEL[11], SAMUEL CHRISTOPHER[10], CHRISTOPHER THOMAS[9], WILLIAM[8], WILLIAM[7], PETER[6], THOMAS[5], RICHARD[4] DURBAN, WALTER[3] DURBIN, EDWARD N.[2], ROBERT[1] DURBAN)* was born November 08, 1899 in Effingham Co., Moccasion Twp., IL, and died April 03, 1958 in Bates Co., Butler, MO. He married NELLIE BARKLEY, daughter of JOSEPH BARKLEY and MARY BARBER. She was born August 06, 1900 in Cass Co., Archie, MO, and died October 27, 1948 in Bates Co., Butler MO.

Children of UFA DURBIN and NELLIE BARKLEY are:
    i. MARVIN DARRELL[17] DURBIN, b. April 08, 1924.
    ii. JACK CALVIN DURBIN, b. September 23, 1925.
    iii. LEONARD LEROY DURBIN, b. August 20, 1927.
    iv. BETTY JEWELL DURBIN, b. February 02, 1931, Bates Co., Shawnee Twp., MO.
    v. DORIS MAY DURBIN, b. August 11, 1932.
    vi. PEGGY JOYCE DURBIN, b. July 02, 1936.
    vii. CAROL JEAN DURBIN, b. July 01, 1940.

98. ALBERT F.[16] DURBIN *(GEORGE W.[15], ENOCH[14], STEPHEN[13], DANN[12], THOMAS[11], SAMUEL CHRISTOPHER[10], CHRISTOPHER THOMAS[9], WILLIAM[8], WILLIAM[7], PETER[6], THOMAS[5], RICHARD[4] DURBAN, WALTER[3] DURBAN, EDWARD N.[2], ROBERT[1] DURBAN)* He married STELLA.

Children of ALBERT DURBIN and STELLA are:
    i. MISS[17] DURBIN.
    ii. JOHN DURBIN.
133.   iii. RAYMOND A. DURBIN, b. 1900; d. 1967, McConnelsville, Morgan County, Ohio.

99. ONA MAY[16] DURBIN *(AMBROSE Q.[15], JOSEPH URIAH[14], HENRY[13], DANN[12], THOMAS[11], SAMUEL CHRISTOPHER[10], CHRISTOPHER THOMAS[9], WILLIAM[8], WILLIAM[7], PETER[6],*

THOMAS⁵, RICHARD⁴ DURBAN, WALTER³ DURBIN, EDWARD N.², ROBERT¹ DURBAN) was born 1888. She married HENRY M. COOK.

Children of ONA DURBIN and HENRY COOK are:
    i.   GLEN E.¹⁷ COOK, b. 1910.
    ii. GALE E. COOK, b. 1913.
    iii. ESTHER COOK, b. 1916.

100. EARL DON¹⁶ DURBIN *(JOEL ELMORE¹⁵, JOSEPH URIAH¹⁴, HENRY¹³, DANN¹², THOMAS¹¹, SAMUEL CHRISTOPHER¹⁰, CHRISTOPHER THOMAS⁹, WILLIAM⁸, WILLIAM⁷, PETER⁶, THOMAS⁵, RICHARD⁴ DURBAN, WALTER³ DURBIN, EDWARD N.², ROBERT¹ DURBAN)* was born 1898 in Adams County, Indiana, and died 1987. He married LUELLA JOHANNA BECHERT. She was born 1900 in Indianapolis, Marion County, Indiana, and died 1980.

Children of EARL DURBIN and LUELLA BECHERT are:
134.   i.   JOAN GERTRUDE¹⁷ DURBIN, b. 1925.
135.   ii. MARGARET LENORE DURBIN, b. 1927.
136.   iii. PHYLLIS JEAN DURBIN, b. 1928.
137.   iv. EARL DON DURBIN, b. 1935.
138.   v. MARILYN LUELLA DURBIN, b. 1937.
139.   vi. JAMES LAWRENCE DURBIN, b. 1934.

101. JOHN WILLIAM HENRY HARRISON¹⁶ DURBIN *(DANIEL F.¹⁵, JOHN¹⁴, HENRY¹³, DANN¹², THOMAS¹¹, SAMUEL CHRISTOPHER¹⁰, CHRISTOPHER THOMAS⁹, WILLIAM⁸, WILLIAM⁷, PETER⁶, THOMAS⁵, RICHARD⁴ DURBAN, WALTER³ DURBIN, EDWARD N.², ROBERT¹ DURBAN)* was born September 10, 1887 in Berne, Adams County, Indiana, and died December 05, 1936 in Decatur, Adams County, Indiana. He married SARAH M. ROOP May 10, 1913 in Kalamazoo, Michigan, daughter of FRANK ROOP and NETTIE HART.

Notes for JOHN WILLIAM HENRY HARRISON DURBIN:
He eloped with Sarah M. Roop. John William Henry Harrison Durbin died from injuries suffered in a car, truck crash in Pleasant Mills; he

was hauling logs. The impact from the accident caused the logs to come into the cab of the truck. Died in the Adams County Hospital December 1936,

More About SARAH M. ROOP:
Burial: Decatur, Adams County, Indiana

Children of JOHN DURBIN and SARAH ROOP are:
- 140. i. DANIEL FRANKLIN[17] DURBIN, b. April 04, 1915, Wells County, Indiana; d. October 01, 1985, Decatur, Adams County, Indiana.
- 141. ii. RICHARD GEORGE DURBIN, b. September 17, 1917; d. 1937.
- 142. iii. JOHN ROBERT DURBIN, b. November 03, 1919; d. October 23, 1994, Fort Wayne, Indiana.
-   iv. WILLIAM MAX DURBIN, b. November 27, 1922.
- 143. v. KENNETH EUGENE DURBIN, b. December 05, 1930.

102. LESTER V.[16] DURBIN *(WILLIAM AMBROSE[15], JOHN[14], HENRY[13], DANN[12], THOMAS[11], SAMUEL CHRISTOPHER[10], CHRISTOPHER THOMAS[9], WILLIAM[8], WILLIAM[7], PETER[6], THOMAS[5], RICHARD[4] DURBAN, WALTER[3] DURBIN, EDWARD N.[2], ROBERT[1] DURBAN)* was born 1913 in Adams County, Indiana. He married CHARLOTTE BELLE BERRY. She was born 1912 in Adams County, Indiana, and died 1977.

Child of LESTER DURBIN and CHARLOTTE BERRY is:
- 144. i. DEANNA JUDITH[17] DURBIN, b. 1942, Fort Wayne, Indiana.

103. MARGARET LOU[16] ROSE *(LYDIA LOUISE[15] EVERHART, SARAH MARY[14] DURBIN, HENRY[13], DANN[12], THOMAS[11], SAMUEL CHRISTOPHER[10], CHRISTOPHER THOMAS[9], WILLIAM[8], WILLIAM[7], PETER[6], THOMAS[5], RICHARD[4] DURBAN, WALTER[3] DURBIN, EDWARD N.[2], ROBERT[1] DURBAN)* was born 1903 in Port Orchard, Washington, and died 1949. She married ROLLIN

WALLACE FRENCH. He was born 1902 in Baraboo, Wisconsin, and died 1963.

Children of MARGARET ROSE and ROLLIN FRENCH are:
    i. DAWN SHIRLEY^{17} FRENCH, b. 1923.
    ii. JEAN MARGARET FRENCH, b. 1925.

104. ETHEL GERTRUDE^{16} DURBIN *(WILLIAM RUBLE^{15}, SAMUEL^{14}, WILLIAM^{13}, DANN^{12}, THOMAS^{11}, SAMUEL CHRISTOPHER^{10}, CHRISTOPHER THOMAS^{9}, WILLIAM^{8}, WILLIAM^{7}, PETER^{6}, THOMAS^{5}, RICHARD^{4} DURBAN, WALTER^{3} DURBIN, EDWARD N.^{2}, ROBERT^{1} DURBAN)* was born 1895 in Moline, Kansas. She married CLYDE SLOCUM. He was born 1897.

Child of ETHEL DURBIN and CLYDE SLOCUM is:
    i. FRANKLIN RUSSELL^{17} SLOCUM, b. 1918, Osawatomie, Kansas.

105. JEROME DANIEL^{16} DURBIN *(ALBERT A.^{15}, DANIEL BASIL^{14}, BASIL^{13}, DANN^{12}, THOMAS^{11}, SAMUEL CHRISTOPHER^{10}, CHRISTOPHER THOMAS^{9}, WILLIAM^{8}, WILLIAM^{7}, PETER^{6}, THOMAS^{5}, RICHARD^{4} DURBAN, WALTER^{3} DURBIN, EDWARD N.^{2}, ROBERT^{1} DURBAN)* was born 1899, and died 1975. He married HAZEL COINES. She was born 1901, and died 1969.

Child of JEROME DURBIN and HAZEL COINES is:
    i. JAMES PHILLIP^{17} DURBIN, b. 1932.

106. MARCELLUS ALBERT^{16} DURBIN *(ALBERT A.^{15}, DANIEL BASIL^{14}, BASIL^{13}, DANN^{12}, THOMAS^{11}, SAMUEL CHRISTOPHER^{10}, CHRISTOPHER THOMAS^{9}, WILLIAM^{8}, WILLIAM^{7}, PETER^{6}, THOMAS^{5}, RICHARD^{4} DURBAN, WALTER^{3} DURBIN, EDWARD N.^{2}, ROBERT^{1} DURBAN)* was born 1905, and died 1992. He married LUCILLE G. FOSTER. She was born 1908, and died 1987.

Children of MARCELLUS DURBIN and LUCILLE FOSTER are:

145. i. DIANE[17] DURBIN.
   ii. THOMAS A. DURBIN.

107. MARGARET BERNICE[16] DURBIN *(WILLIAM EDWARD[15], SAMUEL AUGUSTINE[14], BASIL[13], DANN[12], THOMAS[11], SAMUEL CHRISTOPHER[10], CHRISTOPHER THOMAS[9], WILLIAM[8], WILLIAM[7], PETER[6], THOMAS[5], RICHARD[4] DURBAN, WALTER[3] DURBIN, EDWARD N.[2], ROBERT[1] DURBAN)* was born 1911 in St. Louis, Missouri, and died 1995. She married MARLIN VICTORY SMITH. He was born 1911 in Mendon, St. Joseph, Missouri, and died 1981.

Children of MARGARET DURBIN and MARLIN SMITH are:
   i. VICKI ANN[17] SMITH, b. 1940, Battle Creek, Calhoun County.
   ii. KATHLEEN MARY SMITH, b. 1943.
   iii. ROSS EDWARD SMITH, b. 1945, Battle Creek, Calhoun County.

108. DONALD ROSS[16] DURBIN *(WILLIAM EDWARD[15], SAMUEL AUGUSTINE[14], BASIL[13], DANN[12], THOMAS[11], SAMUEL CHRISTOPHER[10], CHRISTOPHER THOMAS[9], WILLIAM[8], WILLIAM[7], PETER[6], THOMAS[5], RICHARD[4] DURBAN, WALTER[3] DURBIN, EDWARD N.[2], ROBERT[1] DURBAN)* was born 1912 in St. Louis, Missouri, and died 1983. He married DOROTHY MAY SCHMITZER. She was born 1914 in Minneapolis, Hennepin County, Minnesota, and died 1990.

Children of DONALD DURBIN and DOROTHY SCHMITZER are:
146. i. COL. DONALD ROSS[17] DURBIN, b. 1937, Battle Creek, Calhoun County, Michigan.
147. ii. WILLIAM FRANCIS DURBIN, b. 1940, Battle Creek, Calhoun County.
148. iii. JAMES ROBERT DURBIN, b. 1942, Battle Creek, Calhoun County.

109. MARY RITA[16] BRAND *(THERESA FLORENCE[15] DURBIN, SAMUEL AUGUSTINE[14], BASIL[13], DANN[12], THOMAS[11], SAMUEL CHRISTOPHER[10], CHRISTOPHER THOMAS[9], WILLIAM[8], WILLIAM[7], PETER[6], THOMAS[5], RICHARD[4] DURBAN, WALTER[3] DURBIN, EDWARD N.[2], ROBERT[1] DURBAN)* was born 1919 in Muncie, Delaware County, Indiana. She married (1) PAUL WOOLEY. She married (2) RAY FOSTER.

Children of MARY BRAND and PAUL WOOLEY are:
    i. LINDA[17] WOOLEY.
    ii. PAUL TERRY WOOLEY.
    iii. DIXIE WOOLEY.

110. WILLIAM FREDERICK[16] BRAND *(THERESA FLORENCE[15] DURBIN, SAMUEL AUGUSTINE[14], BASIL[13], DANN[12], THOMAS[11], SAMUEL CHRISTOPHER[10], CHRISTOPHER THOMAS[9], WILLIAM[8], WILLIAM[7], PETER[6], THOMAS[5], RICHARD[4] DURBAN, WALTER[3] DURBIN, EDWARD N.[2], ROBERT[1] DURBAN)* was born 1921 in Muncie, Delaware County, Indiana. He married MARTY.

Children of WILLIAM BRAND and MARTY are:
    i. MARY CELESTE[17] BRAND, b. 1959.
    ii. FREDERICK LESLIE BRAND, b. 1960.
    iii. THERESA GAIL BRAND, b. 1961.
    iv. MARTHA JOAN BRAND, b. 1964.
    v. CLAUDETTE SUZANNE BRAND, b. 1967.

111. MARGARET ANN[16] BRAND *(THERESA FLORENCE[15] DURBIN, SAMUEL AUGUSTINE[14], BASIL[13], DANN[12], THOMAS[11], SAMUEL CHRISTOPHER[10], CHRISTOPHER THOMAS[9], WILLIAM[8], WILLIAM[7], PETER[6], THOMAS[5], RICHARD[4] DURBAN, WALTER[3] DURBIN, EDWARD N.[2], ROBERT[1] DURBAN)* was born 1922 in Muncie, Delaware County, Indiana. She married ROBERT HOOVER. He died 1986.

Child of MARGARET BRAND and ROBERT HOOVER is:
    i. ROBERT[17] HOOVER.

112. ESTHER[16] DURBIN *(THOMAS ANTHONY[15], GEORGE PATRICK PIUS[14], BASIL[13], DANN[12], THOMAS[11], SAMUEL CHRISTOPHER[10], CHRISTOPHER THOMAS[9], WILLIAM[8], WILLIAM[7], PETER[6], THOMAS[5], RICHARD[4] DURBAN, WALTER[3] DURBIN, EDWARD N.[2], ROBERT[1] DURBAN)* She married JOSEPH A. BRADLEY.

Children of ESTHER DURBIN and JOSEPH BRADLEY are:
    i. JAMES[17] BRADLEY.
    ii. MARY BRADLEY.
    iii. CHARLES BRADLEY.

113. MARY EVELYN[16] DURBIN *(THOMAS ANTHONY[15], GEORGE PATRICK PIUS[14], BASIL[13], DANN[12], THOMAS[11], SAMUEL CHRISTOPHER[10], CHRISTOPHER THOMAS[9], WILLIAM[8], WILLIAM[7], PETER[6], THOMAS[5], RICHARD[4] DURBAN, WALTER[3] DURBIN, EDWARD N.[2], ROBERT[1] DURBAN)* She married FRANK SCHULTZ.

Children of MARY DURBIN and FRANK SCHULTZ are:
    i. JANE[17] SCHULTZ.
    ii. KATHLEEN SCHULTZ.

114. HENRY LEROY ROY[16] DURBIN *(THOMAS ANTHONY[15], GEORGE PATRICK PIUS[14], BASIL[13], DANN[12], THOMAS[11], SAMUEL CHRISTOPHER[10], CHRISTOPHER THOMAS[9], WILLIAM[8], WILLIAM[7], PETER[6], THOMAS[5], RICHARD[4] DURBAN, WALTER[3] DURBIN, EDWARD N.[2], ROBERT[1] DURBAN)* was born 1902 in Fort Recovery, Mercer County, Ohio, and died 1961. He married CAROLYN LOUISE BOERGERT. She was born 1912.

Children of HENRY DURBIN and CAROLYN BOERGERT are:
149.   i. TIMOTHY E.[17] DURBIN, b. 1940.
150.   ii. JOHN HENRY DURBIN, b. 1943.
       iii. ROBERT THOMAS DURBIN, b. 1946.
151.   iv. SUSAN CAROLYN DURBIN, b. 1948.

115. PAUL EDGAR[16] DURBIN *(THOMAS ANTHONY[15], GEORGE PATRICK PIUS[14], BASIL[13], DANN[12], THOMAS[11], SAMUEL CHRISTOPHER[10], CHRISTOPHER THOMAS[9], WILLIAM[8], WILLIAM[7], PETER[6], THOMAS[5], RICHARD[4] DURBAN, WALTER[3] DURBIN, EDWARD N.[2], ROBERT[1] DURBAN)* was born 1911 in Celina, Mercer County, Ohio, and died 1985. He married MARIAN LEORA SPEACE. She was born 1914 in Owosso, Shiawassee County, Michigan, and died 1967.

Children of PAUL DURBIN and MARIAN SPEACE are:
152.   i.   THOMAS GEORGE[17] DURBIN, b. 1933, Saginaw, Michigan.
153.   ii.   CAROL ANN DURBIN, b. 1935, Saginaw, Michigan.
154.   iii.   PAUL LYLE DURBIN, b. 1941, Saginaw, Michigan.

116. MARY[16] WINTER *(ANGELINE[15] DURBIN, GEORGE PATRICK PIUS[14], BASIL[13], DANN[12], THOMAS[11], SAMUEL CHRISTOPHER[10], CHRISTOPHER THOMAS[9], WILLIAM[8], WILLIAM[7], PETER[6], THOMAS[5], RICHARD[4] DURBAN, WALTER[3] DURBIN, EDWARD N.[2], ROBERT[1] DURBAN)* She married MR. BRADLEY.

Child of MARY WINTER and MR. BRADLEY is:
    i.   MARY JANE[17] BRADLEY.

117. WILLIAM RUSSELL[16] WINTER *(ANGELINE[15] DURBIN, GEORGE PATRICK PIUS[14], BASIL[13], DANN[12], THOMAS[11], SAMUEL CHRISTOPHER[10], CHRISTOPHER THOMAS[9], WILLIAM[8], WILLIAM[7], PETER[6], THOMAS[5], RICHARD[4] DURBAN, WALTER[3] DURBIN, EDWARD N.[2], ROBERT[1] DURBAN)* was born 1911.

Children of WILLIAM RUSSELL WINTER are:
    i.   SALLY[17] WINTER.
    ii.   JANET WINTER.
    iii.   MARY LOU WINTER.

118. RICHARD EDWARD^{16} WINTER *(ANGELINE^{15} DURBIN, GEORGE PATRICK PIUS^{14}, BASIL^{13}, DANN^{12}, THOMAS^{11}, SAMUEL CHRISTOPHER^{10}, CHRISTOPHER THOMAS^{9}, WILLIAM^{8}, WILLIAM^{7}, PETER^{6}, THOMAS^{5}, RICHARD^{4} DURBAN, WALTER^{3} DURBIN, EDWARD N.^{2}, ROBERT^{1} DURBAN)* was born 1930.

Children of RICHARD EDWARD WINTER are:
    i. MISHELL^{17} WINTER.
    ii. SCOTT WINTER.

119. MARY LEE^{16} DURBIN *(LEO^{15}, GEORGE PATRICK PIUS^{14}, BASIL^{13}, DANN^{12}, THOMAS^{11}, SAMUEL CHRISTOPHER^{10}, CHRISTOPHER THOMAS^{9}, WILLIAM^{8}, WILLIAM^{7}, PETER^{6}, THOMAS^{5}, RICHARD^{4} DURBAN, WALTER^{3} DURBIN, EDWARD N.^{2}, ROBERT^{1} DURBAN)* She married RALPH BALL.

Children of MARY DURBIN and RALPH BALL are:
    i. BETTY^{17} BALL.
    ii. RICK BALL.
    iii. MARY BALL.
    iv. DONALD BALL.
    v. JAMES BALL, b. 1951.

120. JOHN D.^{16} DURBIN *(LEO^{15}, GEORGE PATRICK PIUS^{14}, BASIL^{13}, DANN^{12}, THOMAS^{11}, SAMUEL CHRISTOPHER^{10}, CHRISTOPHER THOMAS^{9}, WILLIAM^{8}, WILLIAM^{7}, PETER^{6}, THOMAS^{5}, RICHARD^{4} DURBAN, WALTER^{3} DURBAN, EDWARD N.^{2}, ROBERT^{1} DURBAN)* He married MARLENE ELLIOT.

Children of JOHN DURBIN and MARLENE ELLIOT are:
    i. JACKIE^{17} DURBIN.
    ii. JEFFREY DURBIN.

121. G. DAVID^{16} DURBIN *(LEO^{15}, GEORGE PATRICK PIUS^{14}, BASIL^{13}, DANN^{12}, THOMAS^{11}, SAMUEL CHRISTOPHER^{10}, CHRISTOPHER THOMAS^{9}, WILLIAM^{8}, WILLIAM^{7}, PETER^{6},*

THOMAS⁵, RICHARD⁴ DURBAN, WALTER³ DURBAN, EDWARD N.², ROBERT¹ DURBAN) He married JO BYRNE.

Children of G. DURBIN and JO BYRNE are:
    i. SYLVIA¹⁷ DURBIN.
    ii. KATHLEEN DURBIN.
    iii. CAROL DURBIN.
    iv. JEANNE DURBIN.
    v. JUDY DURBIN.

122. JAMES E.¹⁶ DURBIN *(LEO¹⁵, GEORGE PATRICK PIUS¹⁴, BASIL¹³, DANN¹², THOMAS¹¹, SAMUEL CHRISTOPHER¹⁰, CHRISTOPHER THOMAS⁹, WILLIAM⁸, WILLIAM⁷, PETER⁶, THOMAS⁵, RICHARD⁴ DURBAN, WALTER³ DURBAN, EDWARD N.², ROBERT¹ DURBAN)* was born 1926. He married MARY HOLMES.

Children of JAMES DURBIN and MARY HOLMES are:
    i. DANIEL¹⁷ DURBIN.
    ii. DAVID DURBIN.
    iii. BETH DURBIN.
    iv. JOHN DURBIN.
    v. THOMAS DURBIN.

123. DONALD LEO¹⁶ DURBIN *(LEO¹⁵, GEORGE PATRICK PIUS¹⁴, BASIL¹³, DANN¹², THOMAS¹¹, SAMUEL CHRISTOPHER¹⁰, CHRISTOPHER THOMAS⁹, WILLIAM⁸, WILLIAM⁷, PETER⁶, THOMAS⁵, RICHARD⁴ DURBAN, WALTER³ DURBAN, EDWARD N.², ROBERT¹ DURBAN)* was born 1927 in Rush County, Indiana, and died 1997. He married LOIS FISCHER.

Children of DONALD DURBIN and LOIS FISCHER are:
    i. STEPHEN¹⁷ DURBIN.
    ii. MARLENE DURBIN.
    iii. GREGORY DURBIN.

124. HAROLD BERNARD[16] DURBIN *(SAMUEL BERNARD[15], JOHN FRANCIS[14], BASIL[13], DANN[12], THOMAS[11], SAMUEL CHRISTOPHER[10], CHRISTOPHER THOMAS[9], WILLIAM[8], WILLIAM[7], PETER[6], THOMAS[5], RICHARD[4] DURBAN, WALTER[3] DURBIN, EDWARD N.[2], ROBERT[1] DURBAN)* was born 1904 in Gas City, Grant County, Indiana. He married GRACE VIRGINIA MANNING.

Children of HAROLD DURBIN and GRACE MANNING are:
    i. DONALD BERNARD[17] DURBIN, b. 1930.
    ii. JOHN R. DURBIN, b. 1933.

125. METTA ELIZABETH[16] DURBIN *(CHARLES EDWARD[15], EDWARD MAJOR[14], WILLIAM[13], NICHOLAS[12], THOMAS[11], SAMUEL CHRISTOPHER[10], CHRISTOPHER THOMAS[9], WILLIAM[8], WILLIAM[7], PETER[6], THOMAS[5], RICHARD[4] DURBAN, WALTER[3] DURBIN, EDWARD N.[2], ROBERT[1] DURBAN)* was born 1920. She married (1) JOSEPH FRANCIS LARKIN. He was born 1915, and died 1991. She married (2) EDDIE LEE BARNES. He was born 1925, and died 1991.

Children of METTA DURBIN and JOSEPH LARKIN are:
    i. WILLIAM JOSEPH[17] LARKIN, b. 1939.
    ii. RUTH ANN LARKIN, b. 1940.
    iii. ALICE ELIZABETH LARKIN, b. 1942.

126. ALICE LEA[16] DURBIN *(CHARLES EDWARD[15], EDWARD MAJOR[14], WILLIAM[13], NICHOLAS[12], THOMAS[11], SAMUEL CHRISTOPHER[10], CHRISTOPHER THOMAS[9], WILLIAM[8], WILLIAM[7], PETER[6], THOMAS[5], RICHARD[4] DURBAN, WALTER[3] DURBIN, EDWARD N.[2], ROBERT[1] DURBAN)* was born 1921. She married (1) ? KETCHUM. She married (2) JERRY FRAZIER.

Child of ALICE DURBIN and ? KETCHUM is:
    i. DENNIS[17] KETCHUM.

127. FRANK EDWARD[16] DURBIN *(CHARLES EDWARD[15], EDWARD MAJOR[14], WILLIAM[13], NICHOLAS[12], THOMAS[11], SAMUEL CHRISTOPHER[10], CHRISTOPHER THOMAS[9], WILLIAM[8], WILLIAM[7], PETER[6], THOMAS[5], RICHARD[4] DURBAN, WALTER[3] DURBIN, EDWARD N.[2], ROBERT[1] DURBAN)* was born 1924, and died 1990. He married VERA MARIE MEAD. She was born 1925.

Children of FRANK DURBIN and VERA MEAD are:
155.   i.   REBECCA DEE[17] DURBIN, b. 1949.
156.   ii.   KIMY LOU DURBIN, b. 1952.
157.   iii.   RANDAL LEE DURBIN, b. 1954.

128. EMERA MAHLON[16] DURBIN *(CHARLES EDWARD[15], EDWARD MAJOR[14], WILLIAM[13], NICHOLAS[12], THOMAS[11], SAMUEL CHRISTOPHER[10], CHRISTOPHER THOMAS[9], WILLIAM[8], WILLIAM[7], PETER[6], THOMAS[5], RICHARD[4] DURBAN, WALTER[3] DURBIN, EDWARD N.[2], ROBERT[1] DURBAN)* was born 1927. He married (1) BARBARA HAINLIN. She was born 1931. He married (2) BARBARA JEAN RATLIF.

Children of EMERA DURBIN and BARBARA HAINLIN are:
158.   i.   PATRICIA RUTH[17] DURBIN, b. 1950.
159.   ii.   DANIEL DEAN DURBIN, b. 1952.
            iii.   CHARLES MAHLON DURBIN, b. 1968.
            iv.   ROBERT LEE DURBIN, b. 1972.

129. GENE L.[16] DURBIN *(JOHN WEBB[15], EDWARD MAJOR[14], WILLIAM[13], NICHOLAS[12], THOMAS[11], SAMUEL CHRISTOPHER[10], CHRISTOPHER THOMAS[9], WILLIAM[8], WILLIAM[7], PETER[6], THOMAS[5], RICHARD[4] DURBAN, WALTER[3] DURBIN, EDWARD N.[2], ROBERT[1] DURBAN)* He married BONNIE BAUGHMAN.

Children of GENE DURBIN and BONNIE BAUGHMAN are:
160.   i.   RONNIE[17] DURBIN.
161.   ii.   JANICE LYNN DURBIN.
            iii.   CATHY DURBIN.

130. RONALD REID[16] DURBIN *(JOHN WEBB[15], EDWARD MAJOR[14], WILLIAM[13], NICHOLAS[12], THOMAS[11], SAMUEL CHRISTOPHER[10], CHRISTOPHER THOMAS[9], WILLIAM[8], WILLIAM[7], PETER[6], THOMAS[5], RICHARD[4] DURBAN, WALTER[3] DURBIN, EDWARD N.[2], ROBERT[1] DURBAN)* He married ELLA MAE MURPHY.

Children of RONALD DURBIN and ELLA MURPHY are:
162.   i.   SHARON[17] DURBIN.
        ii.   RONALD REID DURBIN.
        iii. DEANNA DURBIN.
163.   iv. NANCY DURBIN.

131. JACK THADDEUS[16] DURBIN *(JOHN WEBB[15], EDWARD MAJOR[14], WILLIAM[13], NICHOLAS[12], THOMAS[11], SAMUEL CHRISTOPHER[10], CHRISTOPHER THOMAS[9], WILLIAM[8], WILLIAM[7], PETER[6], THOMAS[5], RICHARD[4] DURBAN, WALTER[3] DURBIN, EDWARD N.[2], ROBERT[1] DURBAN)* He married CYNTHIA SMART.

Child of JACK DURBIN and CYNTHIA SMART is:
        i.   DANA[17] DURBIN.

132. JOHN DURBIN[16] MORGAN *(ALICE MAY[15] DURBIN, EDWARD MAJOR[14], WILLIAM[13], NICHOLAS[12], THOMAS[11], SAMUEL CHRISTOPHER[10], CHRISTOPHER THOMAS[9], WILLIAM[8], WILLIAM[7], PETER[6], THOMAS[5], RICHARD[4] DURBAN, WALTER[3] DURBIN, EDWARD N.[2], ROBERT[1] DURBAN)* He married PEGGIE ROBERTS.

Children of JOHN MORGAN and PEGGIE ROBERTS are:
        i.   DEBORAH JANE[17] MORGAN.
        ii.   SARAH LYNN MORGAN.
        iii. MICHAEL GLEN MORGAN.
        iv. MARY ELIZABETH MORGAN.

Generation No. 17

133. RAYMOND A.^{17} DURBIN *(ALBERT F.^{16}, GEORGE W.^{15}, ENOCH^{14}, STEPHEN^{13}, DANN^{12}, THOMAS^{11}, SAMUEL CHRISTOPHER^{10}, CHRISTOPHER THOMAS^{9}, WILLIAM^{8}, WILLIAM^{7}, PETER^{6}, THOMAS^{5}, RICHARD^{4} DURBAN, WALTER^{3} DURBIN, EDWARD N.^{2}, ROBERT^{1} DURBAN)* was born 1900, and died 1967 in McConnelsville, Morgan County, Ohio. He married MARGARET DOVER.

Children of RAYMOND DURBIN and MARGARET DOVER are:
    i. ?^{18} DURBIN.
    ii. LT. COL. RICHARD DURBIN.
    iii. LT. COL. ROBERT FREDERICK DURBIN.

134. JOAN GERTRUDE^{17} DURBIN *(EARL DON^{16}, JOEL ELMORE^{15}, JOSEPH URIAH^{14}, HENRY^{13}, DANN^{12}, THOMAS^{11}, SAMUEL CHRISTOPHER^{10}, CHRISTOPHER THOMAS^{9}, WILLIAM^{8}, WILLIAM^{7}, PETER^{6}, THOMAS^{5}, RICHARD^{4} DURBAN, WALTER^{3} DURBIN, EDWARD N.^{2}, ROBERT^{1} DURBAN)* was born 1925. She married DONALD WAYNE GUDGET. He was born 1926.

Children of JOAN DURBIN and DONALD GUDGET are:
    i. DENNIS LEE^{18} GUDGET, b. 1948.
    ii. DAVID EDWARD GUDGET, b. 1950.

135. MARGARET LENORE^{17} DURBIN *(EARL DON^{16}, JOEL ELMORE^{15}, JOSEPH URIAH^{14}, HENRY^{13}, DANN^{12}, THOMAS^{11}, SAMUEL CHRISTOPHER^{10}, CHRISTOPHER THOMAS^{9}, WILLIAM^{8}, WILLIAM^{7}, PETER^{6}, THOMAS^{5}, RICHARD^{4} DURBAN, WALTER^{3} DURBIN, EDWARD N.^{2}, ROBERT^{1} DURBAN)* was born 1927. She married CARLO LOUIS TOFFOLO. He was born 1926, and died 1985.

Children of MARGARET DURBIN and CARLO TOFFOLO are:
    i. RICHARD LOUIS^{18} TOFFOLO, b. 1949.
    ii. KATHLEEN MARIE TOFFOLO, b. 1951.

      iii.   CARLA LOUISE TOFFOLO, b. 1955.
      iv.   JOHN EARL TOFFOLO, b. 1957.

136. PHYLLIS JEAN^{17} DURBIN *(EARL DON^{16}, JOEL ELMORE^{15}, JOSEPH URIAH^{14}, HENRY^{13}, DANN^{12}, THOMAS^{11}, SAMUEL CHRISTOPHER^{10}, CHRISTOPHER THOMAS^{9}, WILLIAM^{8}, WILLIAM^{7}, PETER^{6}, THOMAS^{5}, RICHARD^{4} DURBAN, WALTER^{3} DURBIN, EDWARD N.^{2}, ROBERT^{1} DURBAN)* was born 1928. She married GEORGE W. SOUVINER. He was born 1924.

Children of PHYLLIS DURBIN and GEORGE SOUVINER are:
      i.   JAY ANDREW^{18} SOUVINER, b. 1951.
      ii.   JULIE ANN SOUVINER, b. 1957.
      iii.   JENNY ANNE SOUVINER, b. 1960.

137. EARL DON^{17} DURBIN *(EARL DON^{16}, JOEL ELMORE^{15}, JOSEPH URIAH^{14}, HENRY^{13}, DANN^{12}, THOMAS^{11}, SAMUEL CHRISTOPHER^{10}, CHRISTOPHER THOMAS^{9}, WILLIAM^{8}, WILLIAM^{7}, PETER^{6}, THOMAS^{5}, RICHARD^{4} DURBAN, WALTER^{3} DURBIN, EDWARD N.^{2}, ROBERT^{1} DURBAN)* was born 1935. He married JERRY LOU SMITH. She was born 1935.

Children of EARL DURBIN and JERRY SMITH are:
      i.   INFANT^{18} DURBIN, b. 1957; d. 1957.
      ii.   DONALD LEE DURBIN, b. 1958.
      iii.   STEVEN ANDREW DURBIN, b. 1959.
      iv.   TERI LYNN DURBIN, b. 1961.

138. MARILYN LUELLA^{17} DURBIN *(EARL DON^{16}, JOEL ELMORE^{15}, JOSEPH URIAH^{14}, HENRY^{13}, DANN^{12}, THOMAS^{11}, SAMUEL CHRISTOPHER^{10}, CHRISTOPHER THOMAS^{9}, WILLIAM^{8}, WILLIAM^{7}, PETER^{6}, THOMAS^{5}, RICHARD^{4} DURBAN, WALTER^{3} DURBIN, EDWARD N.^{2}, ROBERT^{1} DURBAN)* was born 1937. She married FRANCIS ARTHUR FELTMAN.

Children of MARILYN DURBIN and FRANCIS FELTMAN are:

    i. MICHELLE MARIE[18] FELTMAN, b. 1961.
    ii. CHRISTOPHER FRANCIS FELTMAN, b. 1963.
    iii. ROBERT JOSEPH FELTMAN, b. 1963.
    iv. SAMANTHA LYNN FELTMAN, b. 1970.
    v. GIGI NICOLE FELTMAN, b. 1974.

139. JAMES LAWRENCE[17] DURBIN *(EARL DON[16], JOEL ELMORE[15], JOSEPH URIAH[14], HENRY[13], DANN[12], THOMAS[11], SAMUEL CHRISTOPHER[10], CHRISTOPHER THOMAS[9], WILLIAM[8], WILLIAM[7], PETER[6], THOMAS[5], RICHARD[4] DURBAN, WALTER[3] DURBIN, EDWARD N.[2], ROBERT[1] DURBAN)* was born 1934.

Children of JAMES LAWRENCE DURBIN are:
    i. JAMES MICHAEL[18] DURBIN, b. 1964.
    ii. JOEL LAWRENCE DURBIN, b. 1966.

140. DANIEL FRANKLIN[17] DURBIN *(JOHN WILLIAM HENRY HARRISON[16], DANIEL F.[15], JOHN[14], HENRY[13], DANN[12], THOMAS[11], SAMUEL CHRISTOPHER[10], CHRISTOPHER THOMAS[9], WILLIAM[8], WILLIAM[7], PETER[6], THOMAS[5], RICHARD[4] DURBAN, WALTER[3] DURBIN, EDWARD N.[2], ROBERT[1] DURBAN)* was born April 04, 1915 in Wells County, Indiana, and died October 01, 1985 in Decatur, Adams County, Indiana. He married LOIS MAY SCROGHAM February 22, 1934 in Winchester, Indiana, daughter of LEONARD SCROGHAM and IONA PULLUM. She was born April 08, 1917 in Wells County, Indiana, and died August 28, 1989 in Decatur, Adams County, Indiana.

Children of DANIEL DURBIN and LOIS SCROGHAM are:
164.   i. ROBERT EUGENE[18] DURBIN, b. February 07, 1939, Decatur, Adams County, Indiana.
165.   ii. CAROL ANN DURBIN, b. May 02, 1943, Decatur, Adams County, Indiana.

141. RICHARD GEORGE[17] DURBIN *(JOHN WILLIAM HENRY HARRISON[16], DANIEL F.[15], JOHN[14], HENRY[13], DANN[12], THOMAS[11],*

SAMUEL CHRISTOPHER[10], CHRISTOPHER THOMAS[9], WILLIAM[8], WILLIAM[7], PETER[6], THOMAS[5], RICHARD[4] DURBAN, WALTER[3] DURBIN, EDWARD N.[2], ROBERT[1] DURBAN) was born September 17, 1917, and died 1937. He married NELLIE MAE HUNT, daughter of CHARLES HUNT and ADA. She was born February 13, 1919 in Tipton County, Indiana, and died Bef. November 20, 1972 in Wichita, Sedgewick County, Kansas.

Child of RICHARD DURBIN and NELLIE HUNT is:
166.   i.   CALVIN LEROY[18] DURBIN, b. June 27, 1937, Adams County, Indiana.

142. JOHN ROBERT[17] DURBIN *(JOHN WILLIAM HENRY HARRISON[16], DANIEL F.[15], JOHN[14], HENRY[13], DANN[12], THOMAS[11], SAMUEL CHRISTOPHER[10], CHRISTOPHER THOMAS[9], WILLIAM[8], WILLIAM[7], PETER[6], THOMAS[5], RICHARD[4] DURBAN, WALTER[3] DURBIN, EDWARD N.[2], ROBERT[1] DURBAN)* was born November 03, 1919, and died October 23, 1994 in Fort Wayne, Indiana. He married RUTH RAYHAUSER September 01, 1940. She was born May 29, 1925.

Children of JOHN DURBIN and RUTH RAYHAUSER are:
        i.   GARY[18] DURBIN.
        ii. DEBBIE DURBIN.

143. KENNETH EUGENE[17] DURBIN *(JOHN WILLIAM HENRY HARRISON[16], DANIEL F.[15], JOHN[14], HENRY[13], DANN[12], THOMAS[11], SAMUEL CHRISTOPHER[10], CHRISTOPHER THOMAS[9], WILLIAM[8], WILLIAM[7], PETER[6], THOMAS[5], RICHARD[4] DURBAN, WALTER[3] DURBIN, EDWARD N.[2], ROBERT[1] DURBAN)* was born December 05, 1930. He married ALICE J. GUNDER 1949. She was born March 29, 1932, and died March 25, 1999.

Children of KENNETH DURBIN and ALICE GUNDER are:
167.   i.   DIANA L.[18] DURBIN, b. February 13, 1950.
168.   ii. CHERYL K. DURBIN, b. September 21, 1952; d. July 20, 1985, Fort Wayne, Indiana.

169. iii. DENISE A. DURBIN, b. November 02, 1956.
iv. TIMOTHY E. DURBIN, b. April 12, 1960; d. April 12, 1960.
170. v. KAREN S. DURBIN, b. November 11, 1962.

144. DEANNA JUDITH^{17} DURBIN *(LESTER V.^{16}, WILLIAM AMBROSE^{15}, JOHN^{14}, HENRY^{13}, DANN^{12}, THOMAS^{11}, SAMUEL CHRISTOPHER^{10}, CHRISTOPHER THOMAS^{9}, WILLIAM^{8}, WILLIAM^{7}, PETER^{6}, THOMAS^{5}, RICHARD^{4} DURBAN, WALTER^{3} DURBIN, EDWARD N.^{2}, ROBERT^{1} DURBAN)* was born 1942 in Fort Wayne, Indiana. She married THOMAS NEAL GORDAN.

Children of DEANNA DURBIN and THOMAS GORDAN are:
    i. LORELL E.^{18} GORDAN.
    ii. LESLIE GORDAN.

145. DIANE^{17} DURBIN *(MARCELLUS ALBERT^{16}, ALBERT A.^{15}, DANIEL BASIL^{14}, BASIL^{13}, DANN^{12}, THOMAS^{11}, SAMUEL CHRISTOPHER^{10}, CHRISTOPHER THOMAS^{9}, WILLIAM^{8}, WILLIAM^{7}, PETER^{6}, THOMAS^{5}, RICHARD^{4} DURBAN, WALTER^{3} DURBIN, EDWARD N.^{2}, ROBERT^{1} DURBAN)* She married (1) ROBERT HAPNER. She married (2) EDWARD VINCENT.

Child of DIANE DURBIN and ROBERT HAPNER is:
    i. KRISTI^{18} HAPNER.

146. COL. DONALD ROSS^{17} DURBIN *(DONALD ROSS^{16}, WILLIAM EDWARD^{15}, SAMUEL AUGUSTINE^{14}, BASIL^{13}, DANN^{12}, THOMAS^{11}, SAMUEL CHRISTOPHER^{10}, CHRISTOPHER THOMAS^{9}, WILLIAM^{8}, WILLIAM^{7}, PETER^{6}, THOMAS^{5}, RICHARD^{4} DURBAN, WALTER^{3} DURBIN, EDWARD N.^{2}, ROBERT^{1} DURBAN)* was born 1937 in Battle Creek, Calhoun County, Michigan. He married (1) MARIE JOICE MACK. She was born 1936. He married (2) LYNN JOAN KOHL.

Children of COL. DURBIN and MARIE MACK are:

	i.	KAREN LEE[18] DURBIN, b. 1960.
171.	ii.	STEPHEN CHRISTOPHER DURBIN, b. 1964, Battle Creek, Calhoun County.

147. WILLIAM FRANCIS[17] DURBIN *(DONALD ROSS[16], WILLIAM EDWARD[15], SAMUEL AUGUSTINE[14], BASIL[13], DANN[12], THOMAS[11], SAMUEL CHRISTOPHER[10], CHRISTOPHER THOMAS[9], WILLIAM[8], WILLIAM[7], PETER[6], THOMAS[5], RICHARD[4] DURBAN, WALTER[3] DURBIN, EDWARD N.[2], ROBERT[1] DURBAN)* was born 1940 in Battle Creek, Calhoun County. He married (1) CAROLYN LORAINE SANDERS. She was born 1948, and died 1987. He married (2) LUCILLE SMITH. He married (3) CHARLENE MARIE STEVENS. She was born 1945 in Battle Creek, Calhoun County.

Child of WILLIAM DURBIN and CAROLYN SANDERS is:
172.   i.   DEBORAH LORRAINE[18] DURBIN, b. 1961.

Children of WILLIAM DURBIN and CHARLENE STEVENS are:
       ii. DEBORAH LORRAINE ANNE[18] DURBIN, b. 1961.
173.   iii. JOHN EDWARD DURBIN, b. 1963.

148. JAMES ROBERT[17] DURBIN *(DONALD ROSS[16], WILLIAM EDWARD[15], SAMUEL AUGUSTINE[14], BASIL[13], DANN[12], THOMAS[11], SAMUEL CHRISTOPHER[10], CHRISTOPHER THOMAS[9], WILLIAM[8], WILLIAM[7], PETER[6], THOMAS[5], RICHARD[4] DURBAN, WALTER[3] DURBIN, EDWARD N.[2], ROBERT[1] DURBAN)* was born 1942 in Battle Creek, Calhoun County. He married JEANNE ANN MURDOCK. She was born 1941 in Ocala, Marion County, Florida.

Children of JAMES DURBIN and JEANNE MURDOCK are:
174.   i.   CHRISTINE RENEE[18] DURBIN, b. 1971, Sao Paulo, Brazil, South America.
       ii. ROBERT JAMES DURBIN, b. 1972.

149. TIMOTHY E.[17] DURBIN *(HENRY LEROY ROY[16], THOMAS ANTHONY[15], GEORGE PATRICK PIUS[14], BASIL[13], DANN[12], THOMAS[11], SAMUEL CHRISTOPHER[10], CHRISTOPHER THOMAS[9], WILLIAM[8], WILLIAM[7], PETER[6], THOMAS[5], RICHARD[4] DURBAN, WALTER[3] DURBIN, EDWARD N.[2], ROBERT[1] DURBAN)* was born 1940. He married ?.

Children of TIMOTHY DURBIN and ? are:
    i. JEFF[18] DURBIN.
    ii. CHRIST DURBIN.
    iii. STEPHANIE DURBIN.

150. JOHN HENRY[17] DURBIN *(HENRY LEROY ROY[16], THOMAS ANTHONY[15], GEORGE PATRICK PIUS[14], BASIL[13], DANN[12], THOMAS[11], SAMUEL CHRISTOPHER[10], CHRISTOPHER THOMAS[9], WILLIAM[8], WILLIAM[7], PETER[6], THOMAS[5], RICHARD[4] DURBAN, WALTER[3] DURBIN, EDWARD N.[2], ROBERT[1] DURBAN)* was born 1943. He married JENNY.

Children of JOHN DURBIN and JENNY are:
    i. MIKE[18] DURBIN.
    ii. MARK DURBIN.

151. SUSAN CAROLYN[17] DURBIN *(HENRY LEROY ROY[16], THOMAS ANTHONY[15], GEORGE PATRICK PIUS[14], BASIL[13], DANN[12], THOMAS[11], SAMUEL CHRISTOPHER[10], CHRISTOPHER THOMAS[9], WILLIAM[8], WILLIAM[7], PETER[6], THOMAS[5], RICHARD[4] DURBAN, WALTER[3] DURBIN, EDWARD N.[2], ROBERT[1] DURBAN)* was born 1948. She married JOHN NOLING.

Child of SUSAN DURBIN and JOHN NOLING is:
    i. ZACHARY JOHN[18] NOLING, b. 1979.

152. THOMAS GEORGE[17] DURBIN *(PAUL EDGAR[16], THOMAS ANTHONY[15], GEORGE PATRICK PIUS[14], BASIL[13], DANN[12], THOMAS[11], SAMUEL CHRISTOPHER[10], CHRISTOPHER THOMAS[9],

WILLIAM⁸, WILLIAM⁷, PETER⁶, THOMAS⁵, RICHARD⁴ DURBAN, WALTER³ DURBIN, EDWARD N.², ROBERT¹ DURBAN) was born 1933 in Saginaw, Michigan. He married (1) EVELYN RICHMOND. He married (2) SANDRA BLOOM. He married (3) VERA WELCHER.

Child of THOMAS DURBIN and EVELYN RICHMOND is:
  i. DEANNA LYNN¹⁸ DURBIN, b. 1963.

Children of THOMAS DURBIN and SANDRA BLOOM are:
  ii. COLE¹⁸ DURBIN, b. 1971.
  iii. TRAVIS DURBIN, b. 1973.
  iv. PAUL DURBIN, b. 1976.

153. CAROL ANN¹⁷ DURBIN *(PAUL EDGAR¹⁶, THOMAS ANTHONY¹⁵, GEORGE PATRICK PIUS¹⁴, BASIL¹³, DANN¹², THOMAS¹¹, SAMUEL CHRISTOPHER¹⁰, CHRISTOPHER THOMAS⁹, WILLIAM⁸, WILLIAM⁷, PETER⁶, THOMAS⁵, RICHARD⁴ DURBAN, WALTER³ DURBIN, EDWARD N.², ROBERT¹ DURBAN)* was born 1935 in Saginaw, Michigan. She married DONALD LEWIS TINGLAN. He was born 1935 in Saginaw, Michigan.

Children of CAROL DURBIN and DONALD TINGLAN are:
  i. THOMAS ANTHONY¹⁸ TINGLAN, b. 1954.
  ii. MARY MARGARET TINGLAN, b. 1955.
  iii. DONALD PAUL TINGLAN, b. 1957.
  iv. JEFFREY ALAN TINGLAN, b. 1960.
  v. KAREN ELIZABETH TINGLAN, b. 1962.
  vi. LUANN TINGLAN, b. 1965.

154. PAUL LYLE¹⁷ DURBIN *(PAUL EDGAR¹⁶, THOMAS ANTHONY¹⁵, GEORGE PATRICK PIUS¹⁴, BASIL¹³, DANN¹², THOMAS¹¹, SAMUEL CHRISTOPHER¹⁰, CHRISTOPHER THOMAS⁹, WILLIAM⁸, WILLIAM⁷, PETER⁶, THOMAS⁵, RICHARD⁴ DURBAN, WALTER³ DURBIN, EDWARD N.², ROBERT¹ DURBAN)* was born 1941 in Saginaw, Michigan. He married KAREN HARPER.

Children of PAUL DURBIN and KAREN HARPER are:
    i. CATHERINE MARIE^{18} DURBIN, b. 1966.
    ii. DAVID PAUL DURBIN, b. 1968.
    iii. LYSSA DURBIN, b. 1971.

155. REBECCA DEE^{17} DURBIN *(FRANK EDWARD^{16}, CHARLES EDWARD^{15}, EDWARD MAJOR^{14}, WILLIAM^{13}, NICHOLAS^{12}, THOMAS^{11}, SAMUEL CHRISTOPHER^{10}, CHRISTOPHER THOMAS^{9}, WILLIAM^{8}, WILLIAM^{7}, PETER^{6}, THOMAS^{5}, RICHARD^{4} DURBAN, WALTER^{3} DURBIN, EDWARD N.^{2}, ROBERT^{1} DURBAN)* was born 1949. She married ROBERT EUGENE JR. DAWSON. He was born 1949.

Child of REBECCA DURBIN and ROBERT DAWSON is:
    i. KAMI^{18} DAWSON, b. 1975.

156. KIMY LOU^{17} DURBIN *(FRANK EDWARD^{16}, CHARLES EDWARD^{15}, EDWARD MAJOR^{14}, WILLIAM^{13}, NICHOLAS^{12}, THOMAS^{11}, SAMUEL CHRISTOPHER^{10}, CHRISTOPHER THOMAS^{9}, WILLIAM^{8}, WILLIAM^{7}, PETER^{6}, THOMAS^{5}, RICHARD^{4} DURBAN, WALTER^{3} DURBIN, EDWARD N.^{2}, ROBERT^{1} DURBAN)* was born 1952. She married CHARLES EDWARD CHRISTIE. He was born 1950.

Children of KIMY DURBIN and CHARLES CHRISTIE are:
    i. DANIELLE DEANN^{18} CHRISTIE, b. 1976.
    ii. LANDON EDWARD CHRISTIE, b. 1977.

157. RANDAL LEE^{17} DURBIN *(FRANK EDWARD^{16}, CHARLES EDWARD^{15}, EDWARD MAJOR^{14}, WILLIAM^{13}, NICHOLAS^{12}, THOMAS^{11}, SAMUEL CHRISTOPHER^{10}, CHRISTOPHER THOMAS^{9}, WILLIAM^{8}, WILLIAM^{7}, PETER^{6}, THOMAS^{5}, RICHARD^{4} DURBAN, WALTER^{3} DURBIN, EDWARD N.^{2}, ROBERT^{1} DURBAN)* was born 1954. He married NANCY BELLE MORTON. She was born 1952.

Children of RANDAL DURBIN and NANCY MORTON are:

    i. NATHAN EDWARD[18] DURBIN, b. 1984.
    ii. GRANT MORTON DURBIN, b. 1986.

158. PATRICIA RUTH[17] DURBIN *(EMERA MAHLON[16], CHARLES EDWARD[15], EDWARD MAJOR[14], WILLIAM[13], NICHOLAS[12], THOMAS[11], SAMUEL CHRISTOPHER[10], CHRISTOPHER THOMAS[9], WILLIAM[8], WILLIAM[7], PETER[6], THOMAS[5], RICHARD[4] DURBAN, WALTER[3] DURBIN, EDWARD N.[2], ROBERT[1] DURBAN)* was born 1950. She married (1) GAROLD JOSEPH HELLMAN. She married (2) CHARLES LAUREL HELLWIG. She married (3) DAVID WAYNE LANFORD. He was born 1955.

Child of PATRICIA DURBIN and GAROLD HELLMAN is:
    i. WILLIAM MAHLON[18] HELLMAN, b. 1972.

159. DANIEL DEAN[17] DURBIN *(EMERA MAHLON[16], CHARLES EDWARD[15], EDWARD MAJOR[14], WILLIAM[13], NICHOLAS[12], THOMAS[11], SAMUEL CHRISTOPHER[10], CHRISTOPHER THOMAS[9], WILLIAM[8], WILLIAM[7], PETER[6], THOMAS[5], RICHARD[4] DURBAN, WALTER[3] DURBIN, EDWARD N.[2], ROBERT[1] DURBAN)* was born 1952. He married VALERIE ANN SHERMAN. She was born 1954.

Children of DANIEL DURBIN and VALERIE SHERMAN are:
    i. DUSTIN DRU[18] DURBIN, b. 1979.
    ii. CASEY CONLON DURBIN, b. 1982.

160. RONNIE[17] DURBIN *(GENE L.[16], JOHN WEBB[15], EDWARD MAJOR[14], WILLIAM[13], NICHOLAS[12], THOMAS[11], SAMUEL CHRISTOPHER[10], CHRISTOPHER THOMAS[9], WILLIAM[8], WILLIAM[7], PETER[6], THOMAS[5], RICHARD[4] DURBAN, WALTER[3] DURBIN, EDWARD N.[2], ROBERT[1] DURBAN)* He married NORMA DAVENPORT.

Child of RONNIE DURBIN and NORMA DAVENPORT is:
    i. DEDRA[18] DURBIN.

161. JANICE LYNN[17] DURBIN *(GENE L.[16], JOHN WEBB[15], EDWARD MAJOR[14], WILLIAM[13], NICHOLAS[12], THOMAS[11], SAMUEL CHRISTOPHER[10], CHRISTOPHER THOMAS[9], WILLIAM[8], WILLIAM[7], PETER[6], THOMAS[5], RICHARD[4] DURBAN, WALTER[3] DURBIN, EDWARD N.[2], ROBERT[1] DURBAN)* She married NORMAN SPEARS.

Children of JANICE DURBIN and NORMAN SPEARS are:
    i. NORMAN[18] SPEARS.
    ii. SAMMY SPEARS.

162. SHARON[17] DURBIN *(RONALD REID[16], JOHN WEBB[15], EDWARD MAJOR[14], WILLIAM[13], NICHOLAS[12], THOMAS[11], SAMUEL CHRISTOPHER[10], CHRISTOPHER THOMAS[9], WILLIAM[8], WILLIAM[7], PETER[6], THOMAS[5], RICHARD[4] DURBAN, WALTER[3] DURBIN, EDWARD N.[2], ROBERT[1] DURBAN)* She married TOM PATTERSON.

Children of SHARON DURBIN and TOM PATTERSON are:
    i. CATHY[18] PATTERSON.
    ii. WADE PATTERSON.

163. NANCY[17] DURBIN *(RONALD REID[16], JOHN WEBB[15], EDWARD MAJOR[14], WILLIAM[13], NICHOLAS[12], THOMAS[11], SAMUEL CHRISTOPHER[10], CHRISTOPHER THOMAS[9], WILLIAM[8], WILLIAM[7], PETER[6], THOMAS[5], RICHARD[4] DURBAN, WALTER[3] DURBIN, EDWARD N.[2], ROBERT[1] DURBAN)* She married KENNETH LIEBAU.

Children of NANCY DURBIN and KENNETH LIEBAU are:
    i. JUDD[18] LIEBAU.
    ii. JACOB LIEBAU.

Generation No. 18

164. ROBERT EUGENE[18] DURBIN *(DANIEL FRANKLIN[17], JOHN WILLIAM HENRY HARRISON[16], DANIEL F.[15], JOHN[14], HENRY[13], DANN[12], THOMAS[11], SAMUEL CHRISTOPHER[10], CHRISTOPHER THOMAS[9], WILLIAM[8], WILLIAM[7], PETER[6], THOMAS[5], RICHARD[4] DURBAN, WALTER[3] DURBIN, EDWARD N.[2], ROBERT[1] DURBAN)* was born February 07, 1939 in Decatur, Adams County, Indiana. He married REBECCA JANE HEYERLY February 15, 1958, daughter of ELMER HEYERLY and FREDA KAEHR. She was born August 24, 1939.

Children of ROBERT DURBIN and REBECCA HEYERLY are:
        i. JENNIFER[19] DURBIN.
175.   ii. ROBERT ALAN DURBIN, b. December 06, 1962.
176.   iii. ANTHONY WAYNE DURBIN, b. December 09, 1965.

165. CAROL ANN[18] DURBIN *(DANIEL FRANKLIN[17], JOHN WILLIAM HENRY HARRISON[16], DANIEL F.[15], JOHN[14], HENRY[13], DANN[12], THOMAS[11], SAMUEL CHRISTOPHER[10], CHRISTOPHER THOMAS[9], WILLIAM[8], WILLIAM[7], PETER[6], THOMAS[5], RICHARD[4] DURBAN, WALTER[3] DURBIN, EDWARD N.[2], ROBERT[1] DURBAN)* was born May 02, 1943 in Decatur, Adams County, Indiana. She married (1) DELMAR CHARLES ORME. She married (2) JOHN MARSHALL ANDERSON. She married (3) RICHARD BAUMAN. He was born July 16, 1937, and died November 19, 1995 in Gas City, Grant County, Indiana.

Children of CAROL DURBIN and DELMAR ORME are:
    i. KIMBERLY SUE[19] ORME, b. August 01, 1959.
    ii. ANDREA ANN ORME, b. February 28, 1962.
    iii. LINDA RENEE ORME, b. September 21, 1963.
    iv. PEGGY LYNN ORME, b. October 31, 1964.

Child of CAROL DURBIN and JOHN ANDERSON is:
    v. JOHN DAVID[19] ANDERSON, b. August 27, 1970.

Child of CAROL DURBIN and RICHARD BAUMAN is:
    vi. CATINA LEANN[19] BAUMAN, b. June 17, 1972.

166. CALVIN LEROY[18] DURBIN *(RICHARD GEORGE[17], JOHN WILLIAM HENRY HARRISON[16], DANIEL F.[15], JOHN[14], HENRY[13], DANN[12], THOMAS[11], SAMUEL CHRISTOPHER[10], CHRISTOPHER THOMAS[9], WILLIAM[8], WILLIAM[7], PETER[6], THOMAS[5], RICHARD[4] DURBAN, WALTER[3] DURBIN, EDWARD N.[2], ROBERT[1] DURBAN)* was born June 27, 1937 in Adams County, Indiana. He married SHIRLEY JEAN BOSLEY February 28, 1969.

Notes for SHIRLEY JEAN BOSLEY:
Shirley had two children from a former marriage.

Child of CALVIN DURBIN and SHIRLEY BOSLEY is:
    i. STILLBORN[19] DURBIN.

167. DIANA L.[18] DURBIN *(KENNETH EUGENE[17], JOHN WILLIAM HENRY HARRISON[16], DANIEL F.[15], JOHN[14], HENRY[13], DANN[12], THOMAS[11], SAMUEL CHRISTOPHER[10], CHRISTOPHER THOMAS[9], WILLIAM[8], WILLIAM[7], PETER[6], THOMAS[5], RICHARD[4] DURBAN, WALTER[3] DURBIN, EDWARD N.[2], ROBERT[1] DURBAN)* was born February 13, 1950. She married (1) DEAN SINGLETON. He was born May 02, 1950. She married (2) DOCTOR JOHN J. MCGLONE June 12, 1993. He was born July 02, 1937.

Children of DIANA DURBIN and DEAN SINGLETON are:
    i. CRAIG A.[19] SINGLETON, b. May 31, 1971.
    ii. JULIE N. SINGLETON, b. December 31, 1973.

168. CHERYL K.[18] DURBIN *(KENNETH EUGENE[17], JOHN WILLIAM HENRY HARRISON[16], DANIEL F.[15], JOHN[14], HENRY[13], DANN[12], THOMAS[11], SAMUEL CHRISTOPHER[10], CHRISTOPHER THOMAS[9], WILLIAM[8], WILLIAM[7], PETER[6], THOMAS[5], RICHARD[4] DURBAN, WALTER[3] DURBIN, EDWARD N.[2], ROBERT[1] DURBAN)* was born September 21, 1952, and died July 20, 1985 in Fort Wayne, Indiana. She married FREDERICK W. TEEPLE.

Children of CHERYL DURBIN and FREDERICK TEEPLE are:
    i. MATTHEW J.[19] TEEPLE, b. December 29, 1973.
    ii. JEFFREY A. TEEPLE, b. November 11, 1980.

169. DENISE A.[18] DURBIN *(KENNETH EUGENE[17], JOHN WILLIAM HENRY HARRISON[16], DANIEL F.[15], JOHN[14], HENRY[13], DANN[12], THOMAS[11], SAMUEL CHRISTOPHER[10], CHRISTOPHER THOMAS[9], WILLIAM[8], WILLIAM[7], PETER[6], THOMAS[5], RICHARD[4] DURBAN, WALTER[3] DURBIN, EDWARD N.[2], ROBERT[1] DURBAN)* was born November 02, 1956. She married KENNETH STAHL.

Children of DENISE DURBIN and KENNETH STAHL are:
    i. JAIME J.[19] STAHL.
    ii. KENDRA D. STAHL.

170. KAREN S.[18] DURBIN *(KENNETH EUGENE[17], JOHN WILLIAM HENRY HARRISON[16], DANIEL F.[15], JOHN[14], HENRY[13], DANN[12], THOMAS[11], SAMUEL CHRISTOPHER[10], CHRISTOPHER THOMAS[9], WILLIAM[8], WILLIAM[7], PETER[6], THOMAS[5], RICHARD[4] DURBAN, WALTER[3] DURBIN, EDWARD N.[2], ROBERT[1] DURBAN)* was born November 11, 1962. She married DAVID KNERR September 18, 1982. He was born December 16, 1959.

Children of KAREN DURBIN and DAVID KNERR are:
    i. KRISTA M.[19] KNERR, b. October 24, 1983.
    ii. ERIC D. KNERR, b. March 31, 1986.
    iii. TRACI L. KNERR, b. May 12, 1989.

171. STEPHEN CHRISTOPHER[18] DURBIN *(COL. DONALD ROSS[17], DONALD ROSS[16], WILLIAM EDWARD[15], SAMUEL AUGUSTINE[14], BASIL[13], DANN[12], THOMAS[11], SAMUEL CHRISTOPHER[10], CHRISTOPHER THOMAS[9], WILLIAM[8], WILLIAM[7], PETER[6], THOMAS[5], RICHARD[4] DURBAN, WALTER[3]*

DURBIN, EDWARD N.^{2}, ROBERT^1 DURBAN) was born 1964 in Battle Creek, Calhoun County. He married (1) MARNIE MANZOLLI. He married (2) GAILYNN LUCILLE CAPPIELLO. She was born 1956 in Sacramento County, California.

Child of STEPHEN DURBIN and GAILYNN CAPPIELLO is:
  i. CALEB MICHAEL^{19} DURBIN, b. 1990.

172. DEBORAH LORRAINE^{18} DURBIN *(WILLIAM FRANCIS^{17}, DONALD ROSS^{16}, WILLIAM EDWARD^{15}, SAMUEL AUGUSTINE^{14}, BASIL^{13}, DANN^{12}, THOMAS^{11}, SAMUEL CHRISTOPHER^{10}, CHRISTOPHER THOMAS^9, WILLIAM^8, WILLIAM^7, PETER^6, THOMAS^5, RICHARD^4 DURBAN, WALTER^3 DURBAN, EDWARD N.^{2}, ROBERT^1 DURBAN)* was born 1961. She married (1) DONALD COSS. She married (2) JOHN COLE.

Child of DEBORAH DURBIN and DONALD COSS is:
  i. HEATHER MARIE^{19} COSS, b. 1982.

173. JOHN EDWARD^{18} DURBIN *(WILLIAM FRANCIS^{17}, DONALD ROSS^{16}, WILLIAM EDWARD^{15}, SAMUEL AUGUSTINE^{14}, BASIL^{13}, DANN^{12}, THOMAS^{11}, SAMUEL CHRISTOPHER^{10}, CHRISTOPHER THOMAS^9, WILLIAM^8, WILLIAM^7, PETER^6, THOMAS^5, RICHARD^4 DURBAN, WALTER^3 DURBAN, EDWARD N.^{2}, ROBERT^1 DURBAN)* was born 1963. He married (1) ANGIE BRESNAHAN. She was born 1966. He married (2) MARTY.

Children of JOHN DURBIN and ANGIE BRESNAHAN are:
  i. JAMES EDWARD^{19} DURBIN, b. 1981.
  ii. AMBER DURBIN, b. 1985.

Children of JOHN DURBIN and MARTY are:
  iii. KRISTEN^{19} DURBIN, b. 1990.
  iv. JOSHUA DURBIN, b. 1993.

174. CHRISTINE RENEE[18] DURBIN *(JAMES ROBERT[17], DONALD ROSS[16], WILLIAM EDWARD[15], SAMUEL AUGUSTINE[14], BASIL[13], DANN[12], THOMAS[11], SAMUEL CHRISTOPHER[10], CHRISTOPHER THOMAS[9], WILLIAM[8], WILLIAM[7], PETER[6], THOMAS[5], RICHARD[4] DURBAN, WALTER[3] DURBIN, EDWARD N.[2], ROBERT[1] DURBAN)* was born 1971 in Sao Paulo, Brazil, South America. She married (1) ?. She married (2) JEFFREY DEAN HAWPE.

Children of CHRISTINE DURBIN and ? are:
  i. SABRINA ELIZABETH MURDOCK[19] DURBIN, b. 1994.
  ii. SADIE DURBIN, b. 1996.

Generation No. 19

175. ROBERT ALAN[19] DURBIN *(ROBERT EUGENE[18], DANIEL FRANKLIN[17], JOHN WILLIAM HENRY HARRISON[16], DANIEL F.[15], JOHN[14], HENRY[13], DANN[12], THOMAS[11], SAMUEL CHRISTOPHER[10], CHRISTOPHER THOMAS[9], WILLIAM[8], WILLIAM[7], PETER[6], THOMAS[5], RICHARD[4] DURBAN, WALTER[3] DURBIN, EDWARD N.[2], ROBERT[1] DURBAN)* was born December 06, 1962. He married KATHLEEN SUE EHINGER July 07, 1987 in Decatur, Adams County, Indiana. She was born June 06, 1963 in Decatur, Adams County, Indiana.

Children of ROBERT DURBIN and KATHLEEN EHINGER are:
  i. HALEY JANE[20] DURBIN, b. January 24, 1989.
  ii. ALEXANDREA ELLEN DURBIN, b. October 22, 1990.
  iii. ERIC ROBERT DURBIN, b. May 21, 1993.

176. ANTHONY WAYNE[19] DURBIN *(ROBERT EUGENE[18], DANIEL FRANKLIN[17], JOHN WILLIAM HENRY HARRISON[16], DANIEL F.[15], JOHN[14], HENRY[13], DANN[12], THOMAS[11], SAMUEL CHRISTOPHER[10], CHRISTOPHER THOMAS[9], WILLIAM[8], WILLIAM[7], PETER[6], THOMAS[5], RICHARD[4] DURBAN, WALTER[3] DURBIN, EDWARD N.[2], ROBERT[1] DURBAN)* was born December 09,

1965. He married SHARI LEIGH NOLL. She was born January 15, 1963 in Decatur, Adams County, Indiana.

Children of ANTHONY DURBIN and SHARI NOLL are:
    i. SARAH ALYSE[20] DURBIN, b. October 22, 1983.
    ii. KYLE VINCENT DURBIN, b. January 08, 1987.

Index

A
Adams, Joan, 76
Adda
  Lenaf, 13
  Maud, 13
Adeliza of Louvain, 32
Adrian, Martha Lena, 132
Aheron, Elizabeth, 119
Aikenrode, Nancy Ann, 109
Albert III, Count Of Namur, 24
Alexander King of the Scots, 66
Anderson
  Charles, 104
  John David, 163
  John Marshall, 163
Andrew, William, 92, 93
Appleton
  Johanna, 14, 17
  Thomas, 14, 17
Asbury, Bishop Francis, 96, 97
Aspy
  Laura B., 129
  Lawrence, 129
Auginy, Nigel, 70
Axe
  Eliza, 115
  Mary Ann, 121
B
Baker
  Charles, 112
  Lemuel, 112
  Sophia, 112
Ball
  Betty, 147
  Donald, 147
  James, 147
  Mary, 147
  Ralph, 147
  Rick, 147
Ballard, Adolphus, 74
Barber, Mary, 139
Barbutus, Godfrey, 7
Barkley
  Joseph, 139
  Nellie, 139
Barnes
  Robert, 90
  Robert W., 101
Barnett
  A. B., 117
  Bessie A. B. A., 117
  Leni Clare, 117
  Niecie A., 117
Barry, Andrew, 91
Bate, Kerry William, 90
Baughman, Bonnie, 150
Bauman
  Catina Leann, 164
  Richard, 163, 164
Bechert, Luella Johanna, 140
Bedford, Cecylie, 79
Berry, Charlotte Belle, 141
Berrye
  Thomas, 81
  Thos, 77
Bigod
  Maud, 6, 15, 21, 22, 41
  Roger, 6, 41
Bishop, Robert, 1

Index

Bishop of Coutances, 5
Bloom, Sandra, 159
Boergert, Carolyn Louise, 145
Boleyn, Anne, 8
Bond
  Phebe, 95
  Thomas, 95
  William, 91, 112
Boone, Daniel, 95
Border, Margaret Elizabeth, 121
Bosley, Shirley Jean, 164
Botkin, Elizabeth Catherine, 123
Bowen, William, 81
Bradley
  Charles, 145
  James, 145
  Joseph A., 145
  Mary, 145
  Mary Jane, 146
  Mr., 146
Brand
  Blanche Ellen, 135
  Carolyn Suzanne, 136
  Claudette Suzanne, 144
  Eelinor Alice, 136
  Eugene Kenneth, 135
  Frederick Leslie, 144
  Jane Frances, 136
  Joan Florence, 135
  Joseph Franklin, 135
  Margaret Ann, 135, 144
  Martha Joan, 144
  Marty, 144
  Mary Celeste, 144
  Mary Rita, 135, 144
  Millard Francis, 135
  Rebecca Jeanette, 135
  Robertson Augustine, 135
  Theresa Gail, 144
  Thomas Leslie, 135
  Vivian Ruth, 135
  William Frederick, 135, 144
  William Leslie, 135
Bresnahan, Angie, 166
Briant, Sarah, 92
Brice, John, 93
Brogan, Sophia, 134
Brown
  Edward, 87, 98
  Elizabeth, 87
  George, 86, 87
  Henry, 87
  Hugh, 87
  John, 87
  Joshua, 87
  Margaret, 88
  Margaret Elizabeth, 84, 86
  Mary, 87
  Mary Margaret, 88
  Rachel, 87
  Richard, 84, 87
  Samuel, 101
  William, 87
Bruce, Margaret, 100
Bruineford, Magarett, 78
Brunner, Jeanne, 18
Buchanan
  Dr. George, 93

Index

George, 94
Bulbeck, Thomas, 78
Burgess, Samuel Chew, 92, 93
Burson, Margaret Jane, 137
Byble, Richard, 80
Byrne, Jo, 148

C
Cain, Mary, 137
Cannon
  Frances, 92
  Mary Elizabeth, 91
  Robert, 91, 92
  Sophia, 91
  William, 91, 92
Canon, Simon, 86
Cappiello, Gailyn Lucille, 166
Carlike, Robert, 106, 107
Carlile, Robert, 101
Carson, Betty Jewell Durbin, 90, 95
Chalcroft, Hester, 78
Chapman, Mary Ann, 108
Chew, Samuel, 93
Christie
  Charles Edward, 160
  Danielle Deann, 160
  Landon Edward, 160
Clark
  Lawrence, 101, 106, 107
  Stephen, 115
  Teresa Catherine, 115
Coale, John, 94
Cock, Captain Deen, 85, 89

Coines, Hazel, 142
Cokayne, George Edward, 18
Coldham, Peter Wilson, 85
Collins, Thomas, 81
Condry, Ann, 112
Cook
  Daniel, 128
  Esther, 140
  Gale E., 140
  Glen E., 140
  Henry M., 140
  John W., 128
  Mgt, 78
Coss
  Donald, 166
  Heather Marie, 166
Cottin, Jane Baldwin, 89
Coulter, Mathew, 94
Cresap, Thomas, 91
Crompton, Johanna, 17
Crossman, Jn., 78
Croxall, Richard, 95
Curtmantlke, Henry, 20

D
d' Albini, William, 47
Darbin, John, 101
Darborne
  Rober Paignton, 79
  Thomas, 77
  William, 77
Daubeney
  Elizabeth, 31
  Ralph, 31
  Sir Giles, 31
  Sir Ralph, 31

Index

d'Aubigny
  Adeliza, 23, 25
  Agatha, 9, 20, 22, 69
  Agnes Of Arundel, 9
  Alice, 9, 20, 22, 69
  Earl William, 15
  Earl William, 3rd Earl Of
    Arundel, 10
  Earl William IV, 10
  Earl William, Le Breton, 15
  Earl William, The
    Stronghand, 7, 15
  Geoffrey, 9, 20, 22, 69
  Guillaume (William), 3
  Henry, 9, 22, 34, 69
  Henry I, 19
  Hugh, 11
  Humphrey, 6
  Isabel, 11, 34
  Le Sire (Roger), 3
  Matilda, 11, 12
  Maud Bigod, 20
  Nele, 4
  Nichole, 12, 16
  Nicola, 11
  Nigel, 6, 29
  Oliver, 6
  Olivia, 6, 20, 22, 29, 69
  Ralph (Reyner), 9
  Reynor, 19, 22, 69
  Roger, 15, 38, 52
  Roger de, Earl of Hereford, 4
  Ruafon (Ralph), 6
  Rualoc, 29
  William, 6, 8, 9, 11, 15, 19, 20, 22, 23, 29, 32, 34, 52
  William, 1st Earl Of Sussex/Arundel, 31
  William, 2nd Earl Of Arundel, 9, 21
  William, Earl of Albermarle, 21
  William, Earl of Arundel, 2
  William, Signer Of Magna Carta, 68
  William, The Stronghand, 9
  William "The Stronghand," 6, 46

Davenport, Norma, 161

Davis
  Ann, 103
  John David, 94, 95, 102, 107, 112

Dawborn, Tho., 79

Dawson
  Kami, 160
  Robert Eugene, Jr., 160

de Albini
  Agnes, 29
  Alice, 21, 29
  Avice, 29
  Cecilia, 10, 29
  Eleanor, 31
  Elias, 31
  Hugh, 10
  Mabel, 10
  Matilda, 30
  Nele, 4
  Nicholas, 46
  Nicola, 10, 29
  Nigel, 38

Index

Owen, 31
Philip, 31
Ralph, 30
Roger, 28, 40
Sir Helie, 31
Sir Ralph, 31
William, 10, 18, 20, 25, 29, 30, 38, 39, 41, 46
William (d'Aubigny), III, 41
William, 1st Earl Of Sussex/Arundel, 20
William, 2nd Earl Of Arundel, 44
William, 3rd Earl Of Arundel And Sussex, 44
William, Earl of Lincoln, 21
William, Senior, Surety Of The Magna Charta, 45
William "Pincerna" (Butler), 5
William "The Stronghand," 49
William-Meschines, 2nd Baron Of Belvior, 45
de Aurenges, Nigel, 28
de Botreaux, Lord, 31
de Brabant, Adeliza, 7
de Camville, Gerard, 28
de Cavalcamp, Hugo, 28
de Chaucombe, Amabilia, 12
de Chiney, Ida, 7
de Ferrieres, Robert. Earl of Derby, 2
de Flandre, Matilda, 7
de Gant
  Agnes, 28
  Alice, 28, 30
  Gilbert, 28
  Walter, 30
de Gournay
  Gerard, 29
  Gerrard, 5, 38
  Gundred, 5, 29, 30, 38
de Grentmesnil, Adeliza, 6
de Gundeville, Hugh, 27
de Haya, Ralphe, 6
de Invecestre, Richard, 27
de Keveliock, Earl Hugh, 11
de la Haye
  Nichole, 28
  Ralph, 28, 29
  Richard, 28
  William, 28
de Louvain
  Adelaide, 6, 7, 15
  Adeliza, 20, 21
de Lucy, Richard, 27
de Mahaut
  Leuca, 29
  Roger, 29
de Mandevil, William, 26, 50
de Mauley, Isabel, 31
de Meschines
  Hugh "Keveliok," 10
  Mabel, 29
de Montacute
  Alice, 31
  William, 31
de Montalt, Roger, 10
de Montbrai

173

Index

Avita, 38
Avitia, 5
Nigel, 5
de Montbray
  Amicia, 40
  Amicie de Countances, 4
  Geoffrey, 5
  Roger, 5, 40
  William, 40
de Montgomery, Roger, 32, 33
de Montibus
  Ebulo, 12
  Maud, 12, 16
de Montsorel, William, 30
de Mowbray
  Amice, 28
  Robert, 28
  William, 29
de Orreby, Phillip, 29
de Oxford, John, 27
de Plessis
  Grimaldi, 28
  NN, 3, 15
de Ros, Robert, 30
de Roumare, William, 24
de Somerie, Roger, Lord Of Dudley, 10
de Somery
  Joan, 12, 16
  Mabel, 12
  Margaret (Margery), 12
  Margery, 12
  Maud, 12
  Ralph, 12
  Roger, 12, 16, 29

de Somery Baron Dudley, Roger, 12
de St. Hilaire, Maud, 29
de St. Hilary
  Aveline, 10
  James, 10
  Maud, 10, 15
de St. Liz
  Maud, 30
  Simon, 30
de St. Sauveur III, Neil, 52
de St. Saveur
  Ivo, 28
  Neil, 28
  Niel (Nigel), 28
  Roger, 28
de St. Valery, Bernard, 27
de Tateshall, Robert, 10, 29
de Thweng
  Katherine, 31
  Marmaduke, 31
de Todeni
  Agnes, 30
  Alice, 30
  Robert, 28, 30, 44
de Toesny
  Ralph, 28
  Robert, 28
de Tosny
  Robert, 47
  William, Lord Of Belvoir, 47
de Umfreville
  Margery, 30
  Nicholas, 30
  Odonel, 30

Index

Robert, 30
Sir Odinel, 30
de Walton
  Isolda (Maud), 12, 16
  John, 12
  Lord Howard, 18
de Warenne, William, Earl of Surrey, 2
de Warren
  Isabel, 10
  William (Plantagenet), 10
de Whalesborough, Isabel, 31
de Wylington
  Eleanor, 31
  Henry, 31
del'Aigle, Gilbert, 5
Derbon, Mr. Thomas, 89
d'Eu
  Adela, 52
  Jean, Count, 29
  John, 20
d'Evreux, Bertrade, 11
Dickenson
  John, 84, 85
  Walter, 84, 85, 89
Dickerson
  Sarah, 84
  Walter, 84
Dickinson
  John, 93
  Walter, 93
Dipthmore
  Arthur, 124
  Henry, 124
  Maggie, 124

Mary E., 124
Nora, 124
Doomsday Book, 71, 75
Dorbren, Thomas Paignton, 79
Dorman, Selah, 84
Dotson, Lori Ann, 18
Doty, John H., 108
Doubleday, H. A., 18
Dover, Margaret, 152
Downes
  John, 101
  Mary, 96
Downs
  John, 84, 86, 91
  Mary, 82, 84, 87, 88, 91, 93
Dreio, George, 104
du Harcourt, James, 29
du Plessis
  Albreda, 52
  Grimoult, 3, 38
  Grimoult, Traitor Of Valognes, 52
Dubrin, William, 81
Duke William, 2
  Duke of Normandy, 5
Durban
  Alice, 76
  Alys, 80
  Anthony, 79
  Chris, 77
  Christopher, 78, 79
  Edward, 78, 79, 81
  Edward N., 70
  Edyth, 80
  Elizabeth, 79, 99

Index

Henery, 99
Henry, 88, 99
  John, 78, 79, 80
  Margaret, 79
  Marie, 77
  Mgt, 77
  Peter, 77, 78
  Richard, 78, 79, 80, 81, 82, 84, 93, 94, 99
  Robert, 70, 76, 80, 82, 84, 93, 94, 99, 102
  Sir William, 80
  Thomas, 77, 78, 79, 80, 81
  Thos, 77
  Thos D., 77
  Walter, 76, 80, 102
  William, 77
Durband, Richard, 79
Durbane, Thomas, 77
Durbarn, Robert, 70
Durbee, Elizabeth, 81
Durberne
  Henrie, 80
  Jane, 80
Durbin
  Aaron, 106, 111
  Agnes, 81, 133
  Albert A., 121, 132
  Albert F., 127, 139
  Alexander McQuellin, 118
  Alexandrea Ellen, 167
  Alfred, 121, 132
  Alice, 78, 80, 81
  Alice Lea, 138, 149
  Alice May, 125, 138
  Aline Laura, 138

Amber, 166
Ambrose, 113, 119
Ambrose Q., 118, 127
Amon, 110
Angeline, 123, 136
Ann, 95, 96, 98, 104, 109
Anthony Wayne, 163, 167
Augustine, 105, 111
Avarilla, 107
Barman, 119
Basil, 109, 114, 121
Benjamin, 96, 99, 103, 108, 110
Benjamin, Jr., 109, 112
Benton, 130
Benton C., 119, 130
Benton Nicholas, 114
Bernice, 136
Bess, 125
Bessie M., 129
Beth, 148
Betty Jewell, 139
Caleb, 110, 116, 125
Caleb Michael, 166
Calvin Leroy, 155, 164
Carol, 148
Carol Ann, 146, 154, 159, 163
Carol Jean, 139
Carrie, 125, 126
Caseu Conlong, 161
Catherine, 109, 115
Catherine Marie, 160
Cathy, 150
Cecelia Ellen, 133
Cecilia Ellen, 122

Index

Celestine, 115
Charity, 99
Charles Arthur, 122, 133
Charles Edward, 125, 137
Charles Mahlon, 150
Charlie B., 127
Cheryl K., 155, 164
Christ, 158
Christine Renee, 157, 167
Christopher, 86, 88, 91, 93, 94, 95, 96, 98, 105, 111
Christopher K., 106
Christopher Thomas, 83, 84, 86, 88, 93, 94, 99, 101, 102
Clara Agnes, 122, 133
Clayburn, 109
Clifford, 125
Col. Donald Ross, 143, 156
Cole, 159
Cora E., 119, 130
Cornelius, 100
Dana, 151
Daniel, 101, 102, 107, 109, 116, 121, 125, 148
Daniel Basil, 115, 121
Daniel Dean, 150, 161
Daniel F., 118, 128
Daniel Franklin, 141
Daniel W., 119
Dann, 104, 109, 114
David, 148
David Paul, 160
Deanna, 151
Deanna Judith, 141, 156
Deanna Lynn, 159

Debbie, 155
Deborah Lorraine, 157, 166
Deborah Lorraine Anne, 157
Dedra, 161
Denise A., 156, 165
Diana L., 155, 164
Diane, 143
Donald Bernard, 137, 149
Donald Lee, 153
Donald Leo, 137, 148
Donald Ross, 134, 143
Doris May, 139
Drusilla, 105, 111, 112
Dustin Dru, 161
Earl, 122, 134
Earl Don, 128, 140, 153
Edna Christinana, 127
Edward, 76, 78, 95, 96, 99, 103, 105, 106, 111, 135
Edward Major, 116, 124
Edward N., 82, 84, 93, 94, 99, 102
Effie V., 119
Eileen, 125
Eleanor Apparila, 110
Elijah, 100
Eliza, 115
Eliza J., 117
Elizabeth, 78, 92, 100, 106, 113, 123
Elizabeth Fowler, 92
Emera Mahlon, 138, 150
Emma, 118
Emma Sophonia, 117, 126
Enoch, 113, 117

Index

Eric Robert, 167
Esther, 136, 145
Ethel, 129
Ethel Gertrude, 131
Father Elisha, 96
Florence, 76, 136
Forrest W., 137
Frances, 122
Francis, 88, 134
Francis C., 123
Francis Cleo, 128
Francis M., 122
Frank Edward, 138, 150
Fred, 125
G. David, 137, 147
Gary, 155
Gene L., 138, 150
George, 78, 126
George Albert, 128
George H., 119
George Patrick, 115
George Patrick Pius, 123
George Russell, 123
George W., 117, 118, 127
Gladys Wilma, 129
Grace, 78, 125, 138
Grant Morton, 161
Gregory, 148
Haley Jane, 167
Hannah, 76, 78, 107
Hannah Margaret, 116
Hannah Margaret Martin, 116, 117
Harold Bernard, 137, 149
Harry C., 129
Henry, 109, 113

Henry Leroy, 136
Henry Leroy Roy, 145
Honor, 96, 103, 104, 105
Honora, 99
Honorable William, 114
Honour, 103, 109
Ida B., 119, 130
Infant, 153
Irene Hoffman, 129
Isaac, 103
Iva Gertrude, 127
J. Edgar, 123
Jack Calvin, 139
Jack Thaddeus, 138, 151
Jackie, 147
James, 93, 102, 109, 116, 123, 126
James C., 119
James Chauncy, 122, 134
James E., 137, 148
James Edward, 166
James L., 137
James Lawrence, 140, 154
James Phillip, 142
James R., 127
James Robert, 143, 157
Jane, 83
Janice Lynn, 150, 162
Jeanne, 148
Jeff, 158
Jeffrey, 147
Jennie, 113, 117
Jennifer, 163
Jenny, 158
Jerome Daniel, 132, 142
Joan, 76

Index

Joan Gertrude, 140, 152
Joel Elmore, 118, 128
John, 76, 78, 80, 92, 94, 95,
　96, 97, 98, 100, 101, 102,
　103, 104, 105, 106, 107,
　110, 113, 116, 117, 118,
　139, 148
John, Jr., 101
John C., 118
John D., 96, 137, 147
John Edward, 157, 166
John F., 119
John Francis, 115, 123
John Henry, 122, 134, 145,
　158
John J., 111
John R., 149
John Robert, 141, 155
John Stumpy, 111
John Thomas, 118
John Webb, 125, 138
John William, 132, 137
John William Henry
　Harrison, 129, 140
Joseph, 109, 121
Joseph Augustine, 122, 135
Joseph D., 118, 129
Joseph Edward, 128
Joseph H., 106
Joseph P., 111
Joseph Uriah, 113, 118
Joshua, 166
Judy, 148
Karen Lee, 157
Karen S., 156, 165
Kathleen, 148
Kathryn, 123
Kenneth Eugene, 141, 155
Keturah, 112
Kimy Lou, 150, 160
Kristen
Laura Aline, 124
Laura J., 129
Lawrence J., 128
Lena, 125
Leo, 123, 133, 136
Leonard Leroy, 139
Leslie Alvin, 127
Lester V., 130, 141
Lewis, 116, 117
Lewis (Louis) Alvin, 117,
　126
Lewis W., 113
Lizzie B., 127
Lorraine B., 76
Lt. Col. Richard, 152
Lt. Col. Robert Frederick,
　152
Lyssa, 160
Maggie E., 127
Marcellus Albert, 132, 142
Margaret, 96, 98, 102, 104,
　109, 115, 124, 133
Margaret A., 118
Margaret A. Maggie, 121
Margaret Bernice, 134, 143
Margaret Lenore, 140, 152
Mariah, 114, 120
Marilyn Luella, 140, 153
Mark, 158
Mark Joseph, 132
Marlene, 148

Index

Martha, 114, 121, 132
Martha Ann, 113
Marty, 166
Marvin Darrell, 139
Mary, 78, 80, 83, 86, 96,
  98, 101, 103, 104, 105,
  106, 107, 109, 110, 111,
  123
Mary Ann, 118
Mary Celia, 115, 122
Mary E., 121
Mary Elizabeth, 122
Mary Evelyn, 136, 145
Mary Lee, 137, 147
Mary Margaret, 100, 132
Metta Elizabeth, 137, 149
Mike, 158
Mildred, 135
Minerva, 135
Miss, 139
Nancy, 100, 105, 110, 111,
  113, 118, 128, 151, 162
Nanny, 111
Nathan Edward, 161
Nell, 125
Nicholas, 96, 97, 100, 103,
  104, 109, 110
Oca Pearl, 127
Olive Margaret, 132
Omer Sylvester, 127
Ona May, 127, 139
Ora Blanch, 127
Orlando, 116, 125
Orva Henry, 127
Patricia, 132
Patricia Ruth, 150, 161

Paul, 159
Paul Edgar, 136, 146
Paul Lyle, 146, 159
Peggy Joyce, 139
Peter, 82, 83, 84, 93, 94, 99
Peter H., 117
Phillip, 104, 106
Phillip S., 93
Phyllis Jean, 140, 153
Rachel, 100, 112
Ralph, 107
Randal Lee, 150, 160
Raymond, 121
Raymond A., 139, 152
Rebecca, 100
Rebecca Dee, 150, 160
Rhoda, 118
Richard, 78, 93
Richard Arra, 132
Richard George, 141, 154
Robert A., 132
Robert Alan, 163, 167
Robert Alfred, 121, 132
Robert C., 137
Robert E., 118
Robert Eugene, 154, 163
Robert James, 157
Robert Lee, 150
Robert Thomas, 145
Ronald, 134
Ronald Reid, 138, 151
Ronnie, 150, 161
Ruby, 126
Ruth A., 115, 121, 122
Ruth C., 121
Ruth Lynn, 137

Index

Sabrina Elizabeth Murdock, 167
Sadie, 167
Samuel, 93, 95, 96, 97, 98, 106, 110, 112, 114, 120
Samuel, Jr., 96, 98, 103
Samuel Augustine, 115, 122
Samuel Bernard, 123, 137
Samuel C., 121
Samuel Christopher, 102
Samuel Christopher, Sr., 88, 94, 97
Samuel J., 118, 129
Samuel James, 109
Samuell, 78
Sarah, 83, 92, 93, 96, 98, 102, 105, 107
Sarah Alyse, 168
Sarah E., 118
Sarah Mary, 114, 119
Sharon, 151, 162
Stella, 139
Stephanie, 158
Stephen, 97, 109, 113, 148
Stephen Christopher, 157, 165
Steven Andrew, 153
Stillborn, 164
Susan, 105
Susan Carolyn, 145, 158
Susanna, 115
Susannah, 106
Sylvia, 148
Teresa, 109
Teri Lynn, 153
Theresa, 115, 123, 124
Theresa Florence, 122, 135
Thomas, 78, 80, 82, 83, 84, 85, 86, 89, 90, 91, 92, 93, 94, 95, 96, 98, 99, 101, 102, 103, 105, 107, 111, 112, 148
Thomas A., 143
Thomas Anthony, 123, 136
Thomas Bond, 104
Thomas George, 146, 158
Thomas W., 100
Thomas William, 88
Timothy E., 145, 156, 158
Travis, 159
Ufa Henry, 127, 139
Vern, 126
Vernon, 121
Violet, 125, 133
Walter, 76, 81, 82, 84, 93, 94, 99
Will, 125, 126
William, 78, 81, 83, 84, 91, 93, 94, 96, 97, 98, 99, 100, 102, 103, 109, 110, 114, 116, 118, 123, 135
William Ambrose, 119, 129
William Edward, 122, 134
William Francis, 143, 157
William J., 115
William L., 111
William Max, 141
William Nixon, 114, 120
William P., 76
William Ruble, 120, 131
Wm., 86

Index

Xpher, 101
Durbine
  Margaret, 79
  Susanah, 78
  William, 79
Durbon
  Annes, 81
  Edithe, 81
  Elizabeth, 81
  Harry, 77
  Henry, 80
  Jane, 77, 80, 81
  Joan, 81
  Mary, 80
Durborne, Thomas Paignton, 79
Durburn
  John Payton, Sr., 79
  Thomas Paignton, 79
Durburne
  Elizabeth, 78
  William, 79
Durham, William, Bishop of Durham, 70

E
Eaglestone, John, 94
Eggleston, John, 90
Ehinger, Kathleen Sue, 167
Elliot, Marlene, 147
Empress Matilda, 34
Empress Maud, 8, 20, 23, 69
Emsey, Catherine, 109
Erbough
  Honor, 104
  Jacob, 104

Margaret, 104
Etienne I, Count of Trequier, 30
Evans
  Anne, 77
  Edward, 91, 92
  Rachel, 91
Everhart
  Anna, 119
  Chance Elliot, 120
  Cleo, 120
  John, 119
  Joseph McCeland, 120
  Lydia Louise, 120, 130
  Phillip Marion, 119
Ewing
  Henry, 126
  Laura Ella, 126
Ewings, Nathaniel, 91
Eyanson
  Margaret Theresa, 122
  Samuel Augustine, 122

F
Falls, Jones, 94
Farra, Stella, 132
Feltman
  Christopher Francis, 154
  Francis Arthur, 153
  Gigi Nicole, 154
  Michelle Marie, 154
  Robert Joseph, 154
  Samantha Lynn, 154
Fillkill, Nancy E., 120
Fischer, Lois, 148
FitzAlan

Index

John, 29, 34
John, Lord Of Oswestry, 10
Mary, 35
Richard, 35
Fitzgerald, Henry, 27
FitzJohn, Eustace, 28
FitzOsbern, Guillaume II,
   Duke of Normandy, 2
Foliot, Gilbert, Bishop Of
   London, 50
Fonner, Jennie L., 127
Foster, Lucille G., 142
Franklin, Thomas, 112
Frazier, Jerry, 149
French
   Dawn Shirley, 142
   Ethel Gertrude, 142
   Jean Margaret, 142
   Rollin Wallace, 142
Fychan
   Gruffudd O'R, 13, 16
   Lowri Ferch Gruffyd, 13, 14
   Tudor (Twdr) Gruffudd, 13

G

Gabriel, Katherine, 102
Gallaway, William, 93
Gardner, John, 93, 94
Gay, Nicholas Ruxton, 101
George
   John, 81
   Joseph, 92
   Joshua, 101
Gibbs, Vicary, 18
Gibson, Michael, 85

Giffard, William, Bishop Of
   Winchester, 31
Gift, Christopher, 89
Gildersleeve
   Elizabeth, 15, 17
   Richard, 14, 15, 17
Gist
   Richard, 94
   Thomas, 95
Glendower, Owen, 13
Glover, R. S., 91
Glumra
   Eystein, 28
   Haldrich, 28
   Richard, 28
Goch, Eleanor, 13
Godwinson, Harold, 52
Godwyn, Richard, 80
Golden
   Charles, 133
   Florence Polly, 133
   John, 133
   Mary Margaret, 133
Gordan
   Diane, 156
   Leslie, 156
   Lorell E., 156
   Thomas Neal, 156
Gray
   Elizabeth, 95
   Patrick, 95
Great Domesday Book, 75, 76
Gudget
   David Edward, 152
   Dennis Lee, 152

Index

Donald Wayne, 152
Guillaume II, Duke of Normandy, 1, 2
Gunder, Alice J., 155
Gurman, Jone, 80

H

Hackman, Ann, 92
Haget
  Bertram, 30
  Roger, 30
Hainlin, Barbara, 150
Hales
  Eliz., 79
  Elizabeth, 78, 79
Hall
  Jno., 89
  John, 85
Hallaway, John, 101
Halle, Richard, 81
Halsaman
  Basil, 122
  Hermanus, 121, 122
Hamilton, William, 93, 94
Hammond
  Charles, 93
  John, 91
  Margaret, 84
Hapner
  Kristi, 156
  Robert, 156
Harper, Karen, 159
Harrison, Mary, 100
Harryman, George, 91
Hart, Nettie, 140
Harvey, Thomas, 81

Hause
  Augustus, 17
  Carleton Marchant, Jr., 18
  Carleton Marchant, Sr., 18
  Carlisle, 18
  Eric, 18
  Frank, 18
  Jeff, 18
  John, 17
  Kathy, 18
  Laban, 17
  Michele, 18
  William, 17
Hawpe, Jeffrey Dean, 167
Hayden
  Ann, 109
  Susannah, 99
  William, 109
Head
  Hannah Jane, 118
  Rhoda, 118
  Samuel, 118
Hedge, Thomas, 85
Heerburger, Johann, 92
Hellman
  Garold Joseph, 161
  William Mahlon, 161
Hellwig, Charles Laurel, 161
Henry I, 4
Henry II, 19
Henry V, 13
Herron, Annie Elizabeth, 127
Heyerly
  Elmer, 163
  Rebecca Jane, 163
Hill, Lemuel, 112

Index

Hobbes, Thomas, 83
Holland
  Elizabeth, 86
  William, 92
Holmes, Mary, 148
Holtgreven, Carrie
  Philomina, 132
Hoover, Robert, 144
Hopkins
  Eliza, 117
  Mabel Logue, 108
Houston, John Scott, 18
Howard
  Catherine, 8
  Charles, 11th Duke Of Norfolk, 35
  Henry Charles, 36
  Rebecca, 111
  Thomas, 4th Duke Of Norfolk, 35
Howard-Gibbon
  Duke, Mayor Of Arundel, 36
  Edward, Duke, Mayor Of Arundel, 36
Howell
  Samuel, 107
  William, 92
Hughs
  Elizabeth, 101
  John, 101
  Samuel, 101, 102
Humfry, William, 77
Hunt, Nellie Mae, 155
Husband, William, 101, 107
Hussey, Reginald, 31

Huston, Sarah Elizabeth, 128

I
Isaac
  Edward, 14, 17
  Mary, 14, 17
Isham, James, 92

J
Jarvis, Eunice, 17
Johnson
  Amil, 138
  Helen, 138
  Jack, 138
  Margaret, 129
  Richard, 95
Jones
  Ann, 79
  Elinor, 94
  Griffin, 80
  Humphrey, 101
  Jane, 17
  Philip, Jr., 93
  Philip, Sr., 93
  Solomon, 93
Jonson, Thomas, 95
Joy, Elizabeth, 93

K
Kaehr, Freda, 163
Katherine of France, 13
Kerslake, Abraham, 92
Ketcham, Esther, 17
Ketchum
  Dennis, 149
  Mr., 149

Index

Keynes, William, Sheriff Of Northamptonshire, 70
Kimble
  Mary, 101
  William, 101
King Canute IV, Of Denmark, 71
King Charles III, 1
King Edward, 73
King Edward I, 34
King Edward III, 35
King Henry I, 7, 8, 23, 29, 33, 39, 48
King Henry II, 9, 24, 34, 45, 50, 69
King Henry III, 32, 46
King John, 32, 45, 46
  Magna Carta, 57
  Magna Carta Seal, 56
  Signing The Magna Carta, 53
King Olaf III, Of Norway, 71
King Richard II, 35
King Stephen, 8, 9, 20, 22, 24, 50, 69
King William, 75
  The Conqueror, 71
Knerr
  David, 165
  Eric D., 165
  Krista M., 165
  Traci L., 165
Kohl, Lynn Joan, 156
Kyrton
  Christopher, 76, 80
  Elizabeth, 76

  Richard, 76

L

Landsdon, Elizabeth, 81
Langford, David Wayne, 161
Langley, William, 94
Larkin
  Alice Elizabeth, 149
  Joseph Francis, 149
  Ruth Ann, 149
  William Joseph, 149
Larsen, Hal, 18
Lawson
  Alexander, 94
  Mary, 108
le Bigod
  Maud, 29, 39, 47
  Robert, 28
  Roger, 5, 47
le Meschines, Matilda (Mabel), 10, 15
le Strange
  Elizabeth, 12, 16
  John, 12, 16
  John, Jr., 12
Leigh, Thomas, 80
Lhamon
  Alpha R. Allie, 120
  Cora Elizabeth, 120, 131
  Flora E., 120
  Harvey C., 120
  Joseph Dayton, 120
  Levinia Jane, 120
  Urie Ervin, 120
  William Francis, 120
  Zella A., 120

Index

Liebau
  Jacob, 162
  Judd, 162
  Kenneth, 162
Little Doomsday Book, 71, 75
Llewellyn, Thomas, 13
Lloyd, Thomas, 101
Logsdon
  Ann, 94, 96, 98, 104, 105, 106
  Comfort, 103, 112
  Elisha, 111
  Elizabeth, 111
  Honor, 97
  Honora, 110
  Honour, 94
  Jemimah, 110
  John, 87, 110
  Margaret, 110
  Mary, 110
  Nancy Ann, 110
  Patience, 96, 111
  Rachael, 110
  Ralph, 98, 110
  Sarah, 110
  Sister, 111
  Thomas, 95, 104
  Thos., 96
  William, 87, 94, 95, 96, 103
Logue
  Elizabeth (Liddy), 108
  Grandmother, 108
  Mary, 108
  Old Mrs., 108
  Sgt. James, 108
Long, Jane, 85, 89
Lord Baltimore, 88, 90
Low, John, 91, 92
Loyd, Lewis W., 19
Lutz, Angela Caktury, 119
Lux, Darby, 92
Lyman, Edith Opal, 138

M
Mack, Marie Joice, 156
Malpas, Elz., 77
Manning, Grace Virginia, 149
Manzolli, Marnie, 166
Marchant, Majorie, 18
Marshal, Margaret, 12
Martz, Lydia, 129
Mathews
  John, 102
  Roger, 92
Mattingly
  Henry, 103
  Honor, 103
  William, 95
Maxwell, Major, 85, 89
McConnell, Elizabeth, 113
McFarland
  John L., 122
  Samuel, 122
McGlone, Dr. John J., 164
McIlvoy, Bridget Anna, 123
McKenzie
  Aaron, 102, 103
  Anne, 102
  Daniel, 102, 107, 108

Index

John, 102
Joshua, 102
Michael, 102
Samuel, 102, 108, 112
Susanna, 112
William Gabriel, 102
McQuithy
  Billie Jean, 131
  John, 131
  John Richard, 131
  Marilyn, 131
Meacham, Edwd., 96
Mead, Vera Marie, 150
Means, Cora, 125
Minor, Pleasant, 109
Mitchell, Ann, 107
Montgommery, Roger de, Earl of Hereford, 2
Moonsammy, Mary, 18
Morgan
  Deborah Jane, 151
  James, 104
  John Durbin, 138, 151
  Luther W., 138
  Mary Elizabeth, 151
  Michael Glen, 151
  Sarah Lynn, 151
Morton, Nancy Belle, 160
Mosley, Charles, 19
Mowbray
  Amice, 4
  Roger, 5
Mullin, Jennie Mae, 128
Mulvihill
  Edward, 133
  Michael, 133

  Nancy Theresa, 133
  Richard, 133
  Victor, 133
Murdock, Jeanne Ann, 157
Murphy, Ella Mae, 151
Muston, Elizabeth, 14, 16

N
Neal, Patrick, 95
Newman, Roger, 85, 89
Nixon
  Martha, 114
  William, 114
Noling
  John, 158
  Zachary John, 158
Noll, Shari Leigh, 168

O
O'Flynn, Honor, 95, 96
Onion, Stephen, 91, 92
Orme
  Andrea Ann, 163
  Delmar Charles, 163
  Kimberly Sue, 163
  Linda Renee, 163
  Peggy Lynn, 163
Owings, Samuel, 102

P
Parkinson
  Aaron, 105
  Christopher, 105
  Edward, 105
  John J., 105
  Joseph P., 105

Index

Margaret, 105
Phillip S., 105
Thomas, 105
Patterson
   Cathy, 162
   Tom, 162
   Wade, 162
Periman, William, 81
Perkins, William, 107
Phifer, Christina, 126
Phillips, James, 85
Pickerel, Minerva Ellen, 131
Planche, J. R., 18
Plantagenet
   Henry, 20, 22
   Stephen, 20, 22
Pope, Phillip, 81
Porter
   Elizabeth "Betty," 106
   Henry, 106
Poulson
   Mary, 99
   Mary Margaret, 98
Powell, Elizabeth, 78
Prince Albert, 36
Pritchard, James, 102
Puleston
   Angarahad, 14, 16
   Robert, 13, 14, 16
Pullum, Iona, 154
Puthoff, Mary Frances, 136

Q
Queen Consort Adeliza, 7
Queen Dowager of England,
   Adeliz, 48

Queen Elizabeth, 78
Queen Mary I, 35
Queen of France, 25, 49
Queen Victoria, 36

R
Rains, Mattie, 133
Ratlif, Barbara Jean, 150
Rayhauser, Ruth, 155
Raymond, Fladella, 18
Ream, Elizabeth, 113
Redman, Lou, 126
Reinhard
   Dessie D., 130
   John W., 130
   Virgil E., 130
   Virgil L., 130
Remfry, P.M., 23
Richard, Abbot of St.
   Alband, 5
Richard I, Duke of
   Normandy, 1
Richard II, Duke of
   Normandy, 1
Richardson
   Douglas, 21
   Nathaniel, 101
Richmond, Evelyn, 159
Ridgley, John, 102
Robert, Bishop of Hereford, 73
Robertson
   Peggie, 151
   Thomas, 94
Rogers, William, 95
Roland, Mary M., 115

Index

Rolf the Ganger, 28
Roop
  Frank, 140
  Sarah M., 140
Rose
  Eugene Phillip, 131
  Lee William, 131
  Margaret Lou, 131, 141
  William Robert, 131
Ross, Henrietta Jeanette Cummings, 134
Rufus
  Wido, 27
  William, 70
Runkly, Yost, 87
Ryley, May, 132

S
Sanders, Carolyn Loraine, 157
Sanderson, Melissa, 17
Scarlett, Thomas, 101
Schinanholtz, Alma, 134
Schmitzer, Dorothy May, 143
Schuchert, Mrs. Earnest F., 97
Schultz
  Frank, 145
  George A., 124
  Hulda, 124
  James, 124
  Jane, 145
  John, 124
  Katherine, 145
  Lillie, 124
Schwennicke, Delev, 22

Scott
  Avarilla, 106
  Daniel, 101
Scrogham
  Leonard, 154
  Lois May, 154
Shaw
  Christopher Durbin, 91
  Elizabeth, 92
Shea, Mary, 135
Sheet, Ruth May, 137
Sheredine, Thomas, 91, 94
Sherman, Valerie Ann, 161
Signing The Magna Carta,
  Members And Rules, 58, 59, 60, 61, 62, 63, 64, 65, 66, 68
Singleton
  Craig A., 164
  Dean, 164
  Julie N., 164
Slocum
  Clyde, 142
  Franklin Russell, 142
Smart, Cynthia, 151
Smith
  Jerry Lou, 153
  Jno., 89
  John, 85
  Kathleen Mary, 143
  Lucille, 157
  Marlin Victory, 143
  Martha, 118
  Ross Edward, 143
  Vicki Ann, 143
  William, 102
Somers, Thomas, 79

Index

Souviner
  George W., 153
  Jay Andrew, 153
  Jenny Anne, 153
  Julie Ann, 153
Speace, Marian Leora, 146
Spears
  Norman, 162
  Sammy, 162
Stagner, Mary M., 117
Stahl
  Jaime J., 165
  Kendra D., 165
  Kenneth, 165
Stayle, Richard, 80
Steiner, Howard, 97
Stephen, Nancy, 113
Stevens
  Charlene Marie, 157
  James Henry, 116
Strawbridge, Robert, 96
Stroud, John, 85
Stuart, Sir John, 31
Stump, John, 101, 106, 107
Surgeon, Dorothea, 77

T
Tayler, Mary, 79
Teeple
  Frederick W., 165
  Jeffrey A., 165
  Matthew J., 165
Thomas
  Elen French, 13, 16
  Jno., 89
  John, 85

Tinglan
  Donald Lewis, 159
  Donald Paul, 159
  Jeffrey Alan, 159
  Karen Elizabeth, 159
  Luann, 159
  Mary Margaret, 159
  Thomas Anthony, 159
Tirey
  Fieta Beatrice, 126
  George Austin, 126
  Welby Otto, 126
Toffolo
  Carla Louise, 153
  Carlos Louis, 152
  John Earl, 153
  Kathleen Marie, 152
  Richard Louis, 152
Touchstone, Richard, 91
Trevor
  Edwart (Iorwerth), 14, 16
  Rose, 14, 16
Trotten, Luke, 93, 94
Turner, Fannie, 125
Tyler, Frank Watt, 99

U
Utzinger, Dave, 25

V
Venn, John, 80
Veriar, Pet, 77
Vernon, Maud, 28
Vincent, Edward, 156
Virden, James, 95

Index

W
Wachap, William, 92
Wagers, Sally, 106
Wakeman, Edward, 104
Waller, Frances, 128
Walter, John, 76
Warrand, Duncan, 18
Watson, George, 94
Watt, George, 85
Webb, Metta Gertrude, 124
Weinberger, Mary, 116
Weis, Frederick Lewis, 23
Welch, Edwin C., 89, 90
Welcher, Vera, 159
Wells, Ann, 110
Wenk, Martha, 18
Weste, Marye, 81
Whetehill
   Adrian, 14, 16
   Margery, 14, 17
   Sir Richard, 14, 16
White
   Ann, 100, 102
   Francis, 104
   Geoffrey H., 18
   Thomas, 101, 104
Whiteacre, Charles, 101
Whitehead, F., 92
Willett, Mary, 79
William II, Rufus, 4
William the Conqueror, 32, 33
Willis, John, 81
Willmer, Elizabeth, 104
Wilmot, Mr., 83
Wilson, William, 96

Winter
   Fred, 136
   Janet, 146
   Mary, 136, 146
   Mary Lou, 146
   Mishell, 147
   Richard Edward, 136, 147
   Sally, 146
   Scott, 147
   William Russell, 136, 146
Wolfe
   Clyde D., 130
   Franklin Durbin Daniel, 130
   Ollie Pearl, 129
Wood
   Jeremiah, 15, 17
   Jonathan, 17
   Joseph, 17
   Margriet (Margaret), 17
   Martha, 17
Woodward
   Hannah, 70
   Richard., 17
   , 70
Wooley
   Dixie, 144
   Linda, 144
   Margaret, 110
   Paul, 144
   Paul Terry, 144
Woolly, John, 95
Worsley
   Margaret, 14, 16
   Sir Otewell, 14, 16
Wrenthome, Elizabeth, 79

Heritage Books by Betty Jewell Durbin Carson:

*Barber/Barbour Genealogy:
Thomas Barber, The Emigrant, 1614–1662, Book 2*

*Barber/Barbour Genealogy:
Samuel Barber, 1655–1704, Book 3*

*The Brice Family Who Settled in Fairfield County, South Carolina,
about 1785 and Related Families*

*From D'Aubigny of Normandy, France to Robert Durbin of England
and Thomas Christoper Durbin of Baltimore, Maryland*

*Descendants of Thomas Mattingly (Born 1623, Omny, Sussex, England;
Death 24 July 1664, Newton, Charles, Maryland)*

Durbin and Logsdon Genealogy with Related Families, 1626–1991

*The Durbin and Logsdon Genealogy with Related Families, 1626–1991,
Volume 2*

Durbin and Logsdon Genealogy with Related Families, 1626–1994

Durbin and Logsdon Genealogy with Related Families, 1626–1998

*Durbin-Logsdon Genealogy and Related Families from Maryland to Kentucky,
Volumes 1–2*

*CD: The Durbin and Logsdon Genealogy with Related Families, 1626–2000,
3rd Revised Edition*

*History of the Barclay/Barkley Clan; Roger de Berchelai, Scotland
Barber/Barbour Genealogy: Book 1*

History of Curtis Land, 1635–1683; with Excerpt on Francis Land

Jean (John) Gaston of France

Our Ewing Heritage, with Related Families, Part One and Two, Revised Edition
Betty Jewell Durbin Carson and Doris M. Durbin Wooley

CD: Our Ewing Heritage, with Related Families, Revised Edition
Betty Jewell Durbin Carson and Doris M. Durbin Wooley

Patterson Family History

www.ingramcontent.com/pod-product-compliance
Lightning Source LLC
Chambersburg PA
CBHW071420160426
43195CB00013B/1761